Macy's, Gimbels, and Me

HOW TO EARN $90,000 A YEAR IN RETAIL ADVERTISING

Bernice Fitz-Gibbon

SIMON AND SCHUSTER
NEW YORK

The author wishes to thank the following sources for permission to reprint material:

Coats & Clark, Inc., for permission to use advertisements written by the author.

Conde Nast Publications, Inc., for permission to use "How to Make Yourself Unforgettable" and "Getting There Is All the Fun," which originally appeared in *Glamour* Magazine.

Haire Publications for permission to use the author's articles that appeared in *Profit Parade.*

Hearst Corporation for permission to use "Fitz and Starts," which originally appeared in *Good Housekeeping;* and for permission to use "Wanted: More Bounce to the Ounce," which originally appeared in *Harper's Bazaar.*

McCall Corporation for permission to use "Where Have New York's Go-Getters Gone," which originally appeared in *McCall's* Magazine.

Newsweek for permission to use "The Root of the Republican Disaster," copyright © 1964 by Newsweek, Inc.

The New York Times Company for permission to use material which originally appeared in *The New York Times.*

World Publishing Company for permission to use material from *And the Price Is Right* by Margaret Case Harriman. Copyright © 1958 by Margaret Case Harriman.

First printing

Library of Congress Catalog Card Number: 67–12922
Designed by Betty Crumley
Manufactured in the United States of America
by H. Wolff, New York

To my six grandchildren

Gretchen

Lisa

Betsy

Stephen

Geoffrey

and Victoria

Contents

Poor me

I was poor as Job's turkey when I landed in New York in the middle twenties. How poor was that? *This poor*. Sandwiched in between finishing a convent prep school and starting the University of Wisconsin, I taught in a one-room district school for a year. Why? For the money. How much? $38 a month. The university tuition fees had risen from $10 a semester to $15 a semester. A $5 increase ($10 a year) was a lot of money back in 1915 . . . a lot of money for a Wisconsin farmer. So every day I rode seven miles on horseback (heigh-ho that crick in my back) to and from Springfield Corners (a bend in the road too minuscule to appear on any map). That was fourteen miles, round trip, for $38 a month! Like most Middle West farmers of that era, we had no cash. True— country-poor is not seedy-poor like city-poor. We had acre after acre, farm after farm, but no disposable dollars. I made $304 a year salary. How do I get $304? Eight times $38. The chintzy school board in Springfield Corners thought it extravagant to pay a teacher for nine months, so I taught an eight-month school year. By 1941, my annual income was $90,000.

I survived the crick in the back, entered the University, got my degree in three years by attending summer school, taught high-school English for two years, and then started via Rockford, Illinois, and Chicago for the gold fields of New York. I landed in New York with $200.

I struck it rich and had a fine time doing it.

Since I was such an unlikely person to succeed in advertising I think I should tell you *how* I did it, and *where* and *when*. So, although this is no autobiography, there will have to be an autobiographical thread running through.

Chronologically, this is what I have been doing for the past four decades: one year at Marshall Field's in Chicago, one summer at Wanamaker's in New York, twelve years at Macy's, back to Wanamaker's again for three years, fourteen years at Gimbels, New York, twelve years in my own business—a small advertising agency—in New York.

That brings me up to the present. I shall go into the details of the *how* and *when* later.

Was I remarkable? Not at all. It was retail advertising that *was* and *is* remarkable. Anybody, but anybody, can do it.

Do you want to strike it rich? If this book can help place you in the golden field of retail advertising, you may beat my record all hollow in both achievement and income in the near by-and-by. Advancement in advertising is swift. If you are going to go up, you go up fast. I am recommending retail advertising, not an agency job in national advertising. I don't say "stay in retail." Just start in retail. It's easier that way.

You are probably saying: All this sounds too rosy. Isn't there some catch in it? Sure, there is a very big and a very bad catch: It is practically impossible to break into any kind of advertising—retail or national. Let's hope this book makes the impossible possible.

There is no such thing as a self-made man or woman. The encouragement of others, the interested criticism of friends, the "hand up" of associates, employers, and employees are all rocket boosters in one's venture into the outer space of achievement. A reminder of some forgotten anecdote, the recall of an occurrence that would lend interest to a narrative, the stimulation of one's mind to redoubled effort or just plain encouragement of any kind— all these are things success is made of. I must with gratitude spell out the names of those who have brought such inspiration to me as I soared to success in my field and say thanks to everyone who has helped me put this book together as well as those who helped me remember what retailing and retail advertising were like in the thirties, forties and fifties. What retailing was then is pretty much what it is today. Thanks especially to Jeanne O'Neill without whose free-lance help my own business would have sagged badly, and to Eleanor Appleton. Also to Rufus Bastian, Sou Chan, Phyllis Condon, Mark Dall, Margaret Fishback, Leslie Forester, Adele Garrett, Lyn Groh, Ruth Hausman, Alice Hughes, Harry Kirshbaum, Alan Koehler, James Osborne, Phil Parkes, Bea Rosenberg, Charlotte Seitlin (my editor at Simon and Schuster), Roger Wensley, Laura White, Murray Whitsett, Faith Willcox, and to my aunt, Win Bowles, the best copywriter in the Middle West.

I

A sixpence isn't enough

As the models in the TV pattern commercials say, "If *I* can sew, *you* can sew." To paraphrase them, "If *I* can be a success in advertising, *you* can be a success in advertising."

It takes no special mixture of red and white corpuscles or a particular arrangement of brain cells to produce advertising copy. It only takes a soul with a yen to sell A to B (A being a product and B the public, naturally) and a few special tools. More of these tools later. Remember, everything about advertising is *learnable*.

For years I've been puzzled by the fact that comparatively few young people, or any age people, aim for that pleasantest of all ways to make a living and a life—the rich field of advertising. (And it is vastly rich with its more than fifteen billion dollars' worth of billing.) And think what that advertising figure will be when our economy is supposed to reach a trillion—about 1975!

I have written this book (really a how-to-er) to show you how pleasant and profitable an advertising career can be. Advertising is a gold mine. You make a lot of money. You make it fast. And you have fun while you make it.

Advertising pays a woman more than anything else she can do —with the possible exception of designing or merchandise management. And advertising probably pays a man *as much as* anything he can do—with the possible exception of presidencies of store chains, great industries, or vast economic empires.

One of America's leading merchants in Carson, Pirie, Scott & Co. said, "If someone goes into retailing today—and if he is right for retailing—in five years he will be making more money than he could in any other occupation."

Hilaire Belloc said:

> *I'm tired of Love: I'm even tired of Rhyme.*
> *But Money gives me pleasure all the time.*

What's more, despite its many maligners, advertising is the noblest pursuit of all. Sure it is. Our free-enterprise system hangs on the creation of wants, and on satisfying these wants. Advertising keeps the wheels of industry turning.

When you can *do good* for the nation's economy and at the same time *do well* for yourself, that's the perfect life work.

For whom have I written this book? Anybody, but anybody. Of course, if you're a Big Brain aiming at a career in space or dreaming of pushing back the frontiers in medical research or becoming the world's finest surgeon, I wouldn't dream of deflecting you.

But if you're just a bright, quick, charming, go-getting young liberal arts major (or a bright, quick, charming, go-getting anything), for heaven's sake don't bury yourself in something dull like banking or business management. Go into advertising, full steam ahead.

I'm writing for all young people, male and female. And that definitely includes housewives—those millions of young women who yearn for some fulfillment besides being wife and mother, who have already been the target for so much advice.

I stand halfway between Betty Friedan (*The Feminine Mystique*) and Phyllis McGinley (*A Sixpence in Her Shoe*). I agree with Friedan that the housewife should have a career. I agree with McGinley that the most important job a woman can do is to create and raise a happy family. But you can't do one without the other. (By the way, I have two children and six grandchildren.)

You *can* have your cake and eat it too. Phyllis McGinley does. She's a fine one to say that housewifery alone is enough! Being loved and feted all over the world for one enchanting best-seller after another is a far cry from being known only as "Mary Alice's mother." What does McGinley know of the claustrophobic walls of a too little ranch house, a too tight budget, and no built-in appliances for letting off creative steam?

As for Betty Friedan—I've always liked this poke that Gilbert K. Chesterton took at career women:

> *I remember my mother, that day that we met,*
> *A thing I shall never entirely forget:*
> *And I toy with the fancy that, young as I am,*
> *I should know her again if we met in a tram.*
> *But mother is happy in turning a crank*
> *That increases the balance at somebody's bank;*
> *And I feel satisfaction that mother is free*
> *From the sinister task of attending to me.*

Of course there's nothing demeaning or sinister about changing diapers or scrubbing floors. Probably both are good for an advertising copywriter.

One would think that the old argument about woman's place (in the home or in the office or in both) had been worn threadbare over the decades. But it bobs up more often now than ever before in books, magazine articles, in radio and TV interviews. Its sister subject is also being worried about:

Should education for women stress the intellectual or homemaking subjects? Latin? or Tattin'?

Bel Kaufman, in an article "Reach for Happiness" in *This Week* magazine, hit the nub of the problem with these words of wisdom:

A woman who is truly satisfied and fulfilled in her marriage and family life will almost always find the energy and ingenuity to tackle things outside it. The woman who is tired, regretful, bitter, who cries, "If only I weren't . . . If only I could have . . ." is, I think, usually suffering from a basic frustration in her marriage. She is unhappy with her husband or dissatisfied with their social life; she wishes they had more money or lived someplace else. But it is too threatening to her to admit the real issues so, instead of facing them and doing something about them, she blames her unhappiness on what she *isn't* doing—her unused talents, her lost career.

So widen your world with an advertising career. Even just the *preparation* for an advertising career can widen your world. Learning to observe is good for the long haul. It will make you more interesting to yourself as well as to other people.

All this is over and above the large amount of money you will be able to earn. Maybe I have overstressed the money. Because you will not get much on your first job. So forget the money. Take anything that will enable you to squeeze into this fascinating field. Fifty dollars a week in a retail advertising department is better than $100 a week in some other field.

Learn early that it's smart to defer gratification. Indeed, deferring gratification is a good definition of being civilized. So here's your slogan: "It's civilized to defer gratification." Take less at first in order to get much more later.

I used to tell my just-beginning cubs, when they murmured about their coolie wages, that I had hundreds of applicants who would scrub floors for the chance to learn at my feet. In fact, one zealous letter of application actually said, "I will do anything. I will scrub floors with a stiff upper lip."

See how lucky you are? All *you* have to do is to sit there and flip these pages. Not really all. You'll have to get to work and polish your tools. The tools are words. You'll probably have to improve enormously your present vocabulary. You'll have to learn to select your words with professional precision. You must not be like the poor cook who grabs a frying pan for all his culinary efforts—braising, broiling, sautéing, simmering, stewing—and then wonders why everything tastes the same.

I had a cub once who called me the Manhasset Mauler (not to my face, but I'd have loved it). He'd bring in a dull bit of copy. I'd rip into him and it. He'd improve it—slightly. I'd give him a few more verbal jabs, knowing he still hadn't done his best. Finally, after about four rounds of sparring, he would come up with a gem like this one that doubled the sale of Wanamaker's salad dressing. The headline went: WHERE EVERY ASPIC PLEASES AND ONLY MAN IS VILE. (P.S. His name was Mark Dall, and he is now a topflight advertising man.)

Is it possible to teach people how to write? It depends on what you mean by "write." You *can* teach people to write advertising copy, at least *I* can. Advertising requires a different (all right, a *lesser*) kind of ability than does sustained writing. I wouldn't undertake to teach anyone how to write a novel or a biography or a play or a profile for *The New Yorker*. But I have taught over a thousand non-geniuses how to write excellent advertising. Advertising *is* learnable. You do not have to be born with a gold pun in your mouth.

When I arrived in New York in the twenties, I was just about the unlikeliest person you can imagine to get to the top in that posh, glossy business—advertising. I was even the wrong sex. In those days, advertising pretty much belonged to the men. In agencies only an occasional very chic female (a fashion plate who wore her hat all day) was hired—mainly for window dressing or to impress clients with the fact that the agency was up on the "woman's viewpoint."

I am not chic, never was, and probably never will be. While not fat when I got to New York (not yet), I was certainly fattish. All the originals at Hattie Carnegie and all the cosmetics at Elizabeth Arden couldn't have turned me into a femme skeletale.

I was a hick from the sticks. I'd grown up on an old-fashioned farm in southern Wisconsin. I'd learned my letters and numbers around the dinner table on the farm and in a quiet, dreamy convent. I'd been a musty, fusty, schoolmarm . . . of English, of course.

And I was green. My experience consisted of a dazzling career selling bank-vault equipment and office safes. That's right—bank-vault equipment. Plus a brief stint on Marshall Field's furniture floor.

In the 1940's, I was the redoubtable Bernice Fitz-Gibbon— "highest paid woman in advertising in the country," or so *The Saturday Evening Post* unblushingly put it.

How did I do it? Well, that's what this book is all about. I am going to tell you just what I did and how it all turned out.

If you're content with a crust, stay where you are; but if you want butter on your croissant and a bit of wild strawberry jam, you'll read every word. Certainly if *I* made the grade, *you* can.

II

I was a dropout

Put any two adult Americans into a room and before you can figure out the square root of 3,987 in base 5 they'll be discussing education. *Everybody* knows about education these days. Is Dr. Conant right? I wouldn't know. You see, I'm a dropout . . . a dropout from the teaching field *circa* 1915.

Back in 1915 a gal who wanted to be a teacher didn't have to have a master's degree or an ermine-lined hood to teach second grade—or even high school. All you needed was a high school diploma sprinkled with an A or two, and you were "in" with your local school board. You didn't even have to be awfully grown up. I was sweet seventeen. At that time I not only had no B.A. or M.A. or Ph.D.—I don't think I even had an I.Q. Somebody snuck in that bit of school-duggery after I matriculated.

My first teaching job was in a country school. The schoolhouse was red. It had a big bell. It had a potbellied stove, which I fed in the winter. It had a big pail and a big dipper with which I doled out fresh cold water on warm spring days. In the winter we hung wet mittens and socks around the stove, and the room smelled damp

and snug and cozy at the same time. In the spring we had trouble
with our primers and arithmetic; because the outdoors smelled and
sounded so good, what with the bees droning and the cows lowing
as they nibbled in the fragrant new grass.

What did I teach? Everything. From *Lady of the Lake* and
Silas Marner and *Hiawatha* right down to "A" is for "apple" and
$2 + 2 = 4$. Yes, in my day $2 + 2$ was 4. Now they tell me $2 + 2$
does not equal 4. I'd rather not even contemplate such heresy.

If any fault could be found with me as a teacher, it was that I
was a bit absentminded. Who wouldn't be? I had several chores
to do and a lunch pail to pack at 6:30 every morning. I had papers
to correct. I had a seven-mile ride on horseback to get to school and
another seven-mile ride back. What if I did forget the key to the
school every now and then? Nobody ever suffered. When we
couldn't get inside the schoolhouse because I had forgotten the key,
I just moved the whole school (me and the kids) up into the
branches of a maple tree that shaded the south side of the school's
front door.

One fine morning I set off down the lane that led from our farm,
checking as I went . . . the corrected papers, essays, tickets for
the school bazaar, note for Frieda Endres' mother about Frieda's
lunch pail. My own lunch pail was filled with goodies. Two
luscious thick ham sandwiches made with bread that had been in
Mother's oven the morning before; deviled eggs done with homemade boiled dressing; four gorgeous golden-brown drop cookies
filled with tender juicy raisins. Incidentally, while we're on the
subject of education, have you recently looked in a child's lunch
box? Like as not, its main attraction is a chocolate *thing* called a
snooky or a *winky* or some such, filled with a white squishy mess
like shaving cream.

I had gotten to Tommy O'Malley's corner before I went on
with my checking: *school key*. Darn. I'd forgotten it again. We
wouldn't be able to get inside the school. Well . . . never mind.
It was a fine day. The sky was blue. The sun was bright. We'd take

to the maple tree. I always put the older kids in the lower branches —they (the branches) seemed sturdier. The little tykes scooted up into the limbs that spread in a big heavily leafed circle over most of the playground. We sounded like a bunch of magpies chattering away up there. The third-graders had just gotten to the middle of the six-times table when *clomp, clomp*—through my thicket of leaves I spied a carriage coming in the direction of the school. Eleven A.M. was an odd hour for a carriage to come along. Maybe a parent in an emergency. Maybe the book salesman with the globe he had promised. The figure in the approaching carriage was large, majestic; she sat the way Victoria must have sat in her middle years. I parted the maple leaves tickling my face and looked again in horror. Bearing down on us—so help me—was the county educational supervisor come to see what kind of teacher Bernice Fitz-Gibbon might be.

I couldn't advance—I couldn't retreat. I needed time. Even a split second would help. "Sing," I said to my nestlings. "Sing 'The Cuckoo Clock.'" They loved it. Up in the tree singing, "Cuckoo, cuckoo, cuckoo." The supervisor got out of the carriage and headed for the tree. Down I climbed—I had to. I hugged the maple as long as I could, then turned and faced the supervisor. She had one of those big official-looking sheets with her—the kind a supervisor fills out. The form consisted of questions like this:

"Does the teacher motivate the class well?" "Is the teacher always in command of the classroom situation?" "Is the teacher always neat and appropriately dressed?" I was covered with bark and had a leaf or two in my hair.

"Miss Fitz-Gibbon," said the supervisor, "what an interesting place to rehearse."

"I am not rehearsing," I said. "I forgot my keys and we're holding class in the tree." That really shook her.

"I can't come back," she said, eyeing the maple tree. "If I don't turn in my report, you won't get your rating for the year."

I looked her over. The tree would just about hold her, *if* we could

get her up. "Helmut Messerschmidt," I called. "Will you come
down here." Helmut dropped down out of the tree at our feet.
"Miss A. would like to visit our school today. She's come a long way
to see me teach."

He looked her over as carefully as I had done; then he looked
at the tree and nodded. He made a step with his hands outstretched
to lift. I stood ready to push. We got her up, holding and pushing,
from coccyx to curple . . . don't ask me how. The county supervisor observed me in complete command of classes from first
through eighth grade—and if I say so myself, no teacher was ever
more in command. The kids were wonderful—never giggled, never
jiggled, never bounced on a branch.

Miss A. stayed till she could fill in the blanks on that form.
Then we had to get her down. We managed. Somehow she didn't
lose her dignity. She looked the county supervisor to the end.

Yes, those were the good old district-school days. The good old
days when I didn't have to rate the kids on group adjustment. And
Miss A. didn't have to rate *me* on adjustment to the *group*. I just
had to teach the kids, and they jolly well had to learn.

I saw the report Miss A. turned in some time later. I really
wondered if I would get any kind of rating. Her only remark was
"Miss Fitz-Gibbon is a remarkably resourceful person." Thank you,
Miss A., wherever you are.

How good a teacher did I prove to be? There's an old saying,
"The older a man gets, the farther he ran as a boy." So I'll try to
be objective . . . and not brag.

I must have been a remarkable teacher. The youngest pupil was
Frieda. Her family had recently come from Germany. None of
them could speak a word of English. Frieda must have been very
young—probably under six.

This was a German Catholic area; and every child was put in
the Catholic parochial school at the age of six. I was teaching in
the rural public school. Frieda's parents thought that Frieda could

pick up a little English before she was regularly enrolled in the parochial school. Pick up a little English? Frieda was reading fluently before the end of the school year! And remember the school year was only eight months!

What reading method did I teach? It certainly was not the "look-say" method. I didn't know there was more than one method. I chose the phonetic method. I believe it is now called phonics. I wouldn't have known *that* if I hadn't recalled how my father taught his children to read. He thought it shocking if a child couldn't read by four. There was an old family joke about how disgusted he was when one of us four-year-olds repeated the sounds of cat—*hard C short A and tuh T*—and then bellowed "barn."

Yes, I taught Frieda a lot quickly. And Frieda taught me a lot. She taught me that being dull on paper was the unforgivable sin— that even a six-year-old resents being bored with needless repetition.

I could see how her interest flagged when the reading matter was banal and repetitive:

Will Nellie roll her hoop?
Yes, Nellie will roll her hoop.
Will Ned help Nellie roll her hoop?

It was obvious that Frieda didn't give a whoop. Small children were always named Nellie and Ned in those Baldwin Reader days!

I was forced to dig up more interesting material for Frieda, because I noticed that when she was keenly interested she bounced ahead by leaps and bounds. When she was bored, she barely inched forward.

I even wrote a couple of bloodcurdling thrillers which she loved —all about the night that thieves tried to steal the new twin calves out of the pen between the cow barn and the horse stable.

Learning how to be interesting is the basic requirement for successful advertising writing. Learning to be interesting on paper is not too hard. Like the rest of advertising, it is learnable.

All you have to do is practice putting yourself in the reader's boots.

Ask yourself, What would interest *me* if *I* were a woman expecting a baby in six weeks? Or a suburban matron about to carpet her downstairs? Or a teen-ager about to buy her first high heels and nylon stockings? What would interest me if I were a Yale graduate with my foot on the first rung of the ladder?

Anyone in any advertising or entertainment medium should know what interests people, but it is surprising how few do. Here is an illustration of how an important and costly TV show can fail completely:

I squirmed in anguish one day while a panel of highly paid experts delved into the fishing situation in Florida waters. I was told and shown a lot of things I hadn't the faintest interest in knowing or seeing. "How many holes in the average fishing net?" asked the moderator of a fisherman. "There are 80,427," answered the fisherman. The whole group went into a frenetic ecstasy of excited disbelief. "Not 80,427 holes in a fishing net?" they chorused. Then the moderator went on to get more information than I or he (I'll wager) cared to have about the length of leg of the horseshoe crab.

Yes, you can learn what interests people. Gossip is almost always interesting to everybody. Boswell's *Life of Johnson* is so fascinating you hate to put it down. Go to your local library and read the collected letters of George Bernard Shaw. They are as interesting as *My Fair Lady*. Borrow the letters of Lady Mary Wortley Montagu. Lady Montagu lived more than a hundred years ago, but every word she put down back in 1820 fascinates practically everybody today. Good letters and good diaries have the easy intimacy of style that good retail copy requires.

New York had become bored with Wanamaker and Gimbel advertising

Before I went to Wanamaker's in the middle thirties it seemed to many of us that the public had become bored with the store. The advertising was pompous, dignified, and dreary. How could it be otherwise when a "Saying of the Founder" was always spread across the top of every page?

Before I went to Gimbels in 1940 it seemed to me that the public had also become bored with that store, but for different reasons. The Gimbel headlines were never pompous and dignified. They were worse—violent, black-type, hard-sell, dreary, and uninteresting.

In both places, our different kind of writing caught on quickly. We aimed to be interesting. We *were* interesting.

Not only was our copy interesting, but we had a policy of writing an interesting answer to every letter we received. Then we published the whole correspondence, brickbats as well as bouquets.

At both Wanamaker's and Gimbels many a trainee or secretary was precipitated into a copy job after he or she had demonstrated the ability to write interesting friendly letters. Good letters can help *you* up the ladder swiftly.

The best of all letter writers was twenty-year-old Alan Koehler, who melted everybody from Fred Allen to Hildegarde. Alan was a Phi Beta Kappa whom we hired right out of Columbia and put in charge of our publicity department—a rash thing to do. But Alan was a work grabber who not only pushed Gimbels into the newspapers and magazines harder than it had ever been pushed before but also did everything else around the place that he could lay his hands on. (Be careful; if you're lazy—somebody else is always eager to do your job and his own too.) One of the first things Alan used his brains on was the letter writing, but it wasn't long before he was mixed up in the advertising too. He developed so fast—thanks, I'm convinced, to his start with those fresh little letters—that a few years later he became the mainstay of my own business.

Today Alan is high up in the creativity department of the world's fifth largest advertising agency.

If you're a bore, you'll have to take a back seat

The best of my education took place around the dinner table on our Wisconsin dairy farm. (The family is big. The August 1965 family picnic brought out well over a hundred, ranging in age from nearly nought up to nearly ninety. In my immediate family there were my parents, an older sister, and two brothers.) If you were not interesting, you took a back seat . . . and you stayed there.

If you were interesting, you had a front seat; and the thrill of galvanizing the whole group—ten or twenty or thirty—was simply intoxicating.

My father explained that the way to be interesting was to learn how to look at a thing with a fresh eye and how to listen with an attentive ear.

Although I was a dropout from the teaching field I'm really a teacher at heart. I've been teaching people how to write advertising for the past thirty-five years. And since *all* my pupils have been successful, it occurred to me that either I am a genius at detecting and training talent or the field of advertising itself must be failure-proof. The latter, rather than the former, is likely to be true.

Is learning advertising easy? Well, it's not quite so easy as a

TV commercial on organs makes organ playing. A prospective purchaser is seated at the organ and is asked three questions:

"Can you play any musical instrument?" He says, "No."

"Have you ever had any musical training?" He says, "No."

"Can you point your finger?" He says, "Yes."

Right away he begins to play fluently. No, advertising writing isn't quite that easy. You have to learn to point your eye, your ear, your mind. But the important thing is—advertising writing is learnable. Anyone can learn, and have a stimulating career filled with more fun and more money than any other career I know of.

When I first came to New York in the middle 1920's, my dearest wish was to be invited to lunch—even once—at the Algonquin Round Table to meet some of my idols: Robert Benchley, Dorothy Parker, Alexander Woollcott, Heywood Broun, for example. I longed to watch them play their word games with F.P.A. and the other columnists from the page-opposite-editorials of the morning *World*, which we all admired and devoured daily. One of these games required using the word "horticulture" in a sentence. All of us Middle West farm girls were convulsed with mirth at Dorothy Parker's "You can lead a horticulture, but you cannot make her think"—which coup was duly reported in the New York morning *World*.

When I heard that the Algonquin crowd was going to Bucks County, I rented a car and spent weekends looking for a farm to buy. I figured that if I lived around there, I'd be bound to get to know some of them.

Besides, I like to buy, look for, or contemplate buying, land. Like Scarlett O'Hara's father, I have a passion for owning land, but when I compared the poor thin soil of Bucks County with the devil's-food-black richness of our Wisconsin acres, I decided to heck with land in the East. I'd work hard, make a lot of money, and spend a lot of time out in Wisconsin on rich black loam.

Our only land problem in Wisconsin has been how to *derichen* the soil—if there is such a word. How do we derichen the land? By planting a few acres of corn and tobacco, both of which are hard on land.

Years later I did get to know one of the Algonquin crowd: Frank Case's daughter, Margaret Case Harriman. She wrote a fine book on Macy's, *And the Price Is Right,* in which she devoted several pages to the Macy copywriters of that golden era. Her words give the flavor of the twenties and the feel of writing advertising in what was to become the world's largest store. Her book should be read in its entirety by anyone eager to get into retail advertising. I quote from her chapter, "The Girls":

It was not until almost the mid-twenties that humor and exceptionally good writing came into department store ads. In this long step forward, Macy's, under the fierce guidance of Jesse Straus, can truthfully be called a pioneer.

Mr. Straus had engaged Kenneth Collins, a young Harvard teacher of English, as copy chief in the advertising department because, as he said, "We need somebody to write good English around here." Mr. Collins, who rapidly became advertising manager, now gracefully passes along the accolade. "If I could be remembered for one thing," he says, "I'd like people to remember that I fostered and encouraged a brilliant group of young women at Macy's, and even brought some of them into the store. Stella McClure, book buyer, Mary Murphy, merchandise councilor . . . and in advertising, the copywriters . . . ah, the copywriters! Bernice Fitz-Gibbon, Margaret Fishback, Alice Hughes, Katherine Lowe . . ." Here Mr. Collins blissfully closes his eyes, recalling his little band of golden girls. . . .

Miss Fitz-Gibbon, who was to invent some of the most memorable advertising slogans of all time, came from a farm in Wisconsin and taught English for a time in Wisconsin schools. She wanted to be a writer, or at least to get a job in a publishing house, so she journeyed to Chicago where, finding editors and publishers cool toward her ambition, she went to work at Marshall Field's. Macy's in New York had

just organized its Training Squad, recruited largely from college graduates who were to be groomed into executives, and the idea had caught
on in other department stores throughout the country, including Marshall Field's. Miss Fitz-Gibbon was placed on the Marshall Field Training Squad where she spent half of each day selling and the other half
learning how to be an executive. . . .

At that time, in the early twenties, Macy's in New York was acquiring fame everywhere as the most "up-and-coming" store in the United
States, so Miss Fitz-Gibbon traveled on to New York and applied for
an appointment with "Jimmy" Goold, predecessor to Kenneth Collins
as advertising manager. When no appointment was forthcoming, she
got a job writing advertising copy for Wanamaker's. . . .

Her most famous contribution to Macy's came about in 1928, after
Goold had been succeeded by Kenneth Collins, and after Miss Fitz-
Gibbon herself had married Herman Block, an attorney, and had already applied for maternity leave because of the impending birth of
her first child. . . .

The Smart-to-be-Thrifty phrase turned out to be the most durable of
all Macy slogans * but not even a copywriter knows just what will
succeed and what will fail. Most of Miss Fitz-Gibbon's inspirations at
Macy's were sure-fire hits, as when she headed an advertisement of the
then-new strapless evening gowns with the artless query:

HOW DO YOU KEEP IT UP NIGHT AFTER NIGHT?

which was, of course, followed by the explicit information that Macy's
strapless gowns stayed up practically by themselves. But some of Miss
Fitz-Gibbon's most cherished wheezes fell with an unaccountable thud.
One ad, headed READIN' WRITIN' AND THRIFTMETIC passed right
over the heads of the public into oblivion. . . . The same thing happened with another play on words, DON'T BE AN INCOMEPOOP.

Errors—misquotations, printer's errors, or mistakes in fact—are
bound to creep into almost any printed text, especially when the text

* Editor's Note: Miss Fitz-Gibbon's "Nobody but nobody undersells Gimbels,"
which she coined about twenty years after the Macy slogan, has proved equally
durable.

comes off the presses as fast and furiously as Macy advertisements. Macy's, once terrified of such disasters, had come to treat them blithely. When an advertisement misquoted a passage in *Pickwick Papers,* an apologetic notice from Macy's two days later read:

GREAT SCOTT! WE SLIPPED UP ON OUR DICKENS! *

And when another ad, about taffeta dresses, attributed "Rustle of Spring" to the wrong composer, Macy's apology (also written by that illustrious pixie, Bernice Fitz-Gibbon) displayed a wild-haired pianist performing amid a storm of grace-notes, over a text which lightheartedly read:

WE MADE A MISTAKE ON THAT SCORE!

In a recent fashion advertisement (the apology continued) . . . we referred to the musical composition "Rustle of Spring" which we blunderingly attributed to Rubenstein.

. . . Immediately our dear and well-informed public pulled us up short—put us in our place. We've been twitted and taunted and scoffed at. Because it seems that Christian Sinding wrote "Rustle of Spring."

You see it was this way. We were thinking of—*da* dum de *da* dum de *da* dum de *do* . . . which any nit-wit ought to know is the Melody in F. What we should have been thinking of was this— *la* la la *la* la la *la* le . . .

As we were telling you when the slip occurred, TAFFETA'S BACK. We are sorry that we sinned against Sinding—so now we're rescinding! But the quaint new dresses with the little taffeta capes are as beguiling as if we had made no mistake. Come in and see them—they are in

THE BETTER DRESS SHOP—THIRD FLOOR
MACY'S

This ad was a terrific success, mainly because thousands of Macy's dear and well-informed public wrote letters and telephoned to inform

* This headline was written by Miss Fitz-Gibbon's lawyer husband.

them that they had misspelled "Rubinstein." When she is asked today whether it was deliberate, Miss Fitz-Gibbon smiles and says, "Wel-lll . . ."

It also set thousands, or possibly hundreds of thousands, of Macy's well-informed public on the trail of Christian Sinding, whom nobody had ever heard of. On that point, Macy's was strictly accurate. Christian Sinding did write "Rustle of Spring."

Macy's was a great one, in those days, for stimulating the public mind, for leading it up one path and down another and leaving it exhausted, but refreshed. . . .

There has been some speculation, it might be inserted here, as to the truth of the terrible "feud" which is alleged to have been going on between Macy's and Gimbels ever since Gimbels opened its store across the street from Macy's in 1910. Among the people who ought to know, some insist that it is a true vendetta, others say that it originated as a publicity gag, like the radio "feud" between Jack Benny and Fred Allen, or the "feud" between Bing Crosby and Bob Hope. Still others maintain that Eddie Cantor started it, unbeknownst to either store, when in a comedy skit his stooge urged him to reveal some dark secret or other and he replied with the now famous line, "Does Macy tell Gimbel?"

Macy's public attitude about competition from Gimbels is somewhat lofty, as if to say, "Who's competing?" Macy's considers itself, accurately, so much bigger in size and scope than Gimbels that it prefers to regard the other store's rivalry, outwardly at least, as so many pebbles flung against a rock. Gimbels, questioned about its own feeling in the matter, replied amiably through its president, Bernard F. Gimbel. Mr. Gimbel's words were these:

We congratulate Macy's on their 100th birthday. (They certainly don't look it.) We're only 115. (We certainly don't feel it.) Our public recognizes that the "battling for business" in midtown New York, good natured in the main, has helped build the most varied, the most accessible and most patronized shopping area in the greatest city on earth. Sometimes it has been a little rough on the contestants, but it has never been unpopular with the crowd. If the manners look a little better, it does not mean that the battle is

less real. (Neither store ever takes its eye off the other. What it sees,
it quickly translates into action.) This is the kind of competition
the customers love; and we have always believed that the customer
is the boss.

It is certainly true that rivalry exists, not only because the two stores
are close together geographically and offer rather similar services to a
rather similar clientele, but also because Gimbels has lured away some
of Macy's best talent to work under the rival roof. Bernice Fitz-Gibbon
was one Macy star who abandoned the Straus firmament, in 1935, to
go to Gimbels, where in due time she thought up her second most
famous slogan, one which was to contribute a fashionable phrase to the
American language itself.

That slogan was the famous "Nobody but nobody undersells
Gimbels." The first three words have practically supplanted the
one word "nobody." The slogan *Ne personne, mais ne personne*"
is plastered all over the Galeries Lafayette. Children use it. Stand-
up comics use it. It is prominently displayed in a framed ad that
hangs on the walls of the Tour d'Argent, one of Paris' most elegant
restaurants—the one where they number the ducks. "Nobody, but
nobody" has crept into the lines of several greeting card companies,
where it has become a classic.

III

How to get from here to there

All kinds of legends have grown about the Fabulous Fitz. Most of them are not true at all. Some are partly true.

It's not true that, because I outsold everybody in Macy's basement, I was taken up to the advertising department to write pots and pans.

It's not true that I peddled threshing machines door to door back in Waunakee, Wisconsin.

It's not exactly true that I scribbled Macy's famous slogan "It's smart to be thrifty" and handed it to my obstetrician as I was being wheeled into the delivery room.

It's not completely true that I'd hire for trainees only young males and females who came from Middle West farms . . . where they had had to roll out of bed at 5 A.M. to bring the cows up from the pasture.

And it's not exactly true that I turned down any applicant who did not read and admire E. B. White. But, as a matter of fact, every topnotch writer that I developed *did* read and admire E. B. White.

And it's not wholly true that I encouraged wealthy fathers to bring in their brainy daughters to learn advertising at my feet providing the fathers paid Wanamaker's $100 a week for each daughter that I trained.

An arch-tycoon, with a Phi Beta Kappa daughter on his arm, offered to do just this, when I was at Wanamaker's in 1936. He said, "I've researched females' futures. If a girl wants to get married right away, she should get into nurses' training. Nurses marry best. Advertising careerists make the most money and have the most enjoyable work. I hear that you are the only person in the U.S.A. who can teach people to write advertising."

I was tempted to accept the offer; but then I decided I'd better check with Wanamaker's top management.

Top management was shocked, and said, "It's against the law to let anyone in a store work for nothing!" I was disappointed; because I had envisioned building up a fat fund to use for better artwork to go with our superlative copy.

I mentioned my selling bank vaults and safes. That's important, because that's where I started to learn about business and how to sell. The farm sold only milk and hogs and firkins of butter. I had nothing to do with the selling of these.

Naturally I didn't set out to be a bank-vault saleswoman. I set out to be a reporter for a newspaper in Rockford, Illinois. But after a couple of weeks, I discovered something interesting. The city editor was making $100 a week, while the advertising manager (half his age) was making $200. I switched to advertising quick as a wink.

My job was to go around to the department stores, sell space, and then write the copy to go into the space. I was a sensational success. I became so famous (around Rockford, Illinois) that I landed the "plum" of selling bank-vault equipment. It was a plum because the commission was very large. Tootling around southern Wisconsin and northern Illinois in an old Ford, I developed a regular selling routine.

There's an old Irish saying that the way to get attention is to create a disturbance—shake people up, scare them. I created a disturbance. I shook people. I scared 'em.

I would walk into the office of a Swedish furniture manufacturer and stare in fascinated horror at the heavy old iron safe in the corner. "Surely, Mr. Johnson," I'd say, "you don't keep the company records in that thing?"

"I sure do," he'd answer with custard-calm complacency. "See how thick the walls are? Absolutely safe from fire."

Then I'd scare the bejabbers out of him. I'd beg him to take his papers out, quick, and stuff them into a desk drawer. "Wood is a nonconductor of heat. But iron is a quick conductor of heat. All your records would shrivel and disappear in that old iron safe." Mr. Johnson would sign up in a trembling hand for one of my trusty well-insulated metal safes. Did I feel guilty upsetting Mr. Johnson? Not at all. Every word I spoke was God's truth.

A good headline should create a disturbance. One of the best advertising jobs I ever did was a shoe campaign that in headline after headline scared the bejabbers out of parents about their children's feet. This was my argument: "Madam, do you know that nineteen out of twenty children are born with perfect feet? It's wearing the wrong size shoes, generally a size too small, that ruins eighteen out of twenty by adulthood." That campaign sold a lot of shoes. And I daresay saved a lot of feet.

After my safe-selling success, the green pastures of my native dairy country weren't green enough for me. I headed for Chicago and Marshall Field's, where I wangled my way into a training course for college graduates who wanted to learn about retailing. We trainees were supposed to spend half the day in one of the general offices—Personnel or Comparison Shopping or Publicity or Credit or some such—and the other half on the floor selling.

I spent my first half day selling in Field's street-floor ribbon department. The rest is legendary. I was not made for dispensing lengths of satin and silk. Nimble-witted is not nimble-fingered. Does it take one kind of brain to write a pretty sales check and another kind of brain to write a brilliant headline? It certainly does not. It takes the same kind of brain. A headline won't be brilliant unless it's chock-full of sell.

The morning was a disaster. I wound ribbon this way and that way—and then rewound it another way. Those ribbons were alive! I did loop-the-loops and figure eights and chased runaway bolts like a Wellesley girl on roll-the-hoop day. By twelve o'clock, the ribbon department was a shambles, and the ribbon salesgirl looked like a poor Guernsey caught in a Maypole on a windy day.

As soon as they unwound me, I went straight to the general manager. My selling record was good. My dollar volume was the highest of the whole college squad. Only my winding record was bad. I suggested that Field's take me out of ribbons and put me in a department where the store sold large uncomplicated objects placed far apart on the floor.

That's how I wound up in Field's furniture department. I was still just a trainee, kibitzing half day. But in my first week—half week, really—I outsold all the pros (all men, of course, who were working a full eight-hour day, six days a week). When I learned that the men were drawing big juicy commissions, I promptly insisted on the same. So instead of my puny $18 a week (Field's claimed it lost money paying $18 to the college squad members) I earned well over $100 a week from the day I started . . . to Field's consternation and my delight.

But my main interest in life was the putting of words on paper. Field's obligingly offered to let me write copy for the Field magazine *Fashions of the Hour*. Wonderful! Except that the copy pay in advertising was, at that time, $35 a week. I couldn't bear to go ahead *backwards*. So there was only one way to go—East.

So I never did get into the Field advertising department. But my selling experience in Field's helped me in my advertising copy job later in Macy's because I learned that the more you know about an article (even if it seems trivial and unimportant) the more it impresses a customer and the easier it is to sell.

Later, in the middle twenties, when I got the Macy job as head of all home furnishings advertising, I reported for work and was surprised that my first assignment was an ad on Hartz Mountain canaries. Don't ask me why canaries were listed under Home Furnishings. But they were, and perhaps they still are. Come to think of it, a canary is an appealing home decoration.

I was handed a pink sheet sent up by the Macy canary buyer, listing all the facts about canaries—or rather the facts the *buyer* thought would interest Macy customers.

Right off the bat I insisted on seeing a Hartz Mountain canary. There was pandemonium. The wearied head of the merchandise room of the art department burst out with "God help us! Now they've started hiring them as wants to *see* what they write about! We'll be crammed with livestock."

I stuck to my guns. I also had a tussle with the canary buyer, who said customers didn't want to know the difference between a roller and a chopper. I said *I* wanted to know. I also wanted to know if his canaries were ambidextrous. Could the rollers also chop? And could the choppers also roll? I put that and a lot more canary information in the ad. The ad ran. Results were phenomenal —best mail-order and floor response in canary history! My stock rose. While it was up, I persuaded Jimmy Gould, the advertising head, to put this sign in every copywriter's office:

> YOU MUST MIND THE ANCIENT LAW
> AND NEVER WRITE WHAT YOU AIN'T SAW.

This sign, rememberable because of its illiteracy, later went with me to Wanamaker's and Gimbels. Pretty soon Macy buyers started asking for that new copywriter who puts a lot of unnecessary stuff in, but sells a lot of goods. My salary jumped from $75 a week to $100 a week. I was on my way.

Yes, that canary ad was my first Macy triumph. How did I happen to know that telling a lot of petty unimportant details helps enormously in the selling of anything?

I had learned that in my very first selling job—when I peddled insulated safes and bank-vault equipment. In my next job I learned it all over again when I was selling furniture at Marshall Field's. The customer likes to know all the facts there are in connection with any item she buys, however useless the information may actually be to her. She wants to know whether the mahogany has been floated downriver to the tropical mill or dragged by elephant through the jungle; whether her Irish knit belt was knit on the toes of the Aran Islands men or on the fingers of the Aran Islands women; or whether the Thai silkworm that spun the heavy Thai silk is indigenous to Thailand.

One day a hefty woman, whose hat boasted a bright red geranium sticking straight up in the air, marched in to buy a table. She plainly knew the table she wanted—a walnut affair inlaid with leather. But the salesman who waited on her was called upon for the patience of Job and the erudition of Solomon. There was nothing about that table this woman didn't want to know. I overheard her asking about the varnish, the veneer, the joints, the glue, the wood, the design. After she had learned all the salesman knew about those things, she demanded an analysis of every blemish in the leather—the little rips and tears the top grain gets when the steer rubs against barbed wire or thorns. None of this information closed the sale. The factual facts were getting nowhere. "What kind of leg is this?" continued the woman, peering under the table.

I could see my salesman friend's lips start to form "Provincial" or "Empire" or whatever the table was. But then a look of malice flickered briefly in his eyes, convinced as he was that his long

recital of accurate information about the table had been in vain.
"That, madam," said he, with a wink in my direction, "is a fine
example of a Fitz-Gibbon leg." And then he went on into a long
song and dance about the great designer Fitz-Gibbon, who, he said,
was a second cousin of Hepplewhite's but who had remained ob-
scure and unknown because the dastardly Hepplewhite stole so
many of his designs. The customer stood spellbound. "A Fitz-
Gibbon leg! Why didn't you tell me that in the first place?" And
she bought the table on the spot.

Why didn't I make a beeline for New York right after I had
graduated from the University? I was scared.

I had a friend who was there already. She had a job in a New
York advertising agency, and knew all about the big city. Whenever she sensed that I was on the brink of taking the Twentieth
Century for New York, she would hastily wire or write, "Stay
away!" She convinced me that I could never earn my bed and
board in New York, because I was the "dreamy impractical" kind.

Well, dreamy impractical "Me" hit New York in the middle of
July in the middle of the twenties. I went straight to Macy's, because
Field's had told me that Macy's was the up-and-coming store. But
Macy's advertising director wasn't seeing anybody till fall. So, dis-
couraged, I went to Wanamaker's advertising director, Joseph
Appel.

Mr. Appel wasn't seeing anybody either, said his secretary.
Fired up by my furniture-selling success, I scribbled a little note.
"Miss Fitz-Gibbon of Marshall Field's can help you make your
August furniture sale a big success." Joe Appel saw me. He hired
me.

At Wanamaker's I was told to wander up and down the furniture floor and write my ads around what I heard—pull my headlines right out of the customers' mouths. That's when I learned to
listen. Most copywriters have tin ears, which is why most head-

lines are unbelievable. You've seen ads where a four-year-old holds up a can of tuna fish and says, "In our house we never compromise with quality." Or, "Mummy wants all our meals to have that Sunday-dinner excellence!" Double-jointed adjectives abound in national advertising. What woman ever said she wanted her boudoir to be garden-party pretty?

And I'm still haunted by an ad for boys' clothes I once saw in a Milwaukee paper. A chunky twelve-year-old was pictured saying to his mother, "Hey, Maw, all the other kids got ruggedness and comfort and authentic styling. Can't I have some too?" Nobody can convince me that that writer ever got within a hundred feet of a twelve-year-old boy.

Another illustration of how people don't talk is that commercial on Lark cigarettes: Who would ever mutter as he puffs on his Lark, "Richly rewarding—uncommonly smooth"?

There's more to writing copy than just listening. You have to improve on the average person's inarticulateness, but you must do it in a believable idiom. Listening to the furniture customers at Wanamaker's, I learned how people think and speak and turned it to my advantage. But I didn't headline my ads for eighteenth-century sofas with exactly what I heard, which was something like this: "Say, Myrt, that one over there's not half bad."

The Wanamaker furniture sale ended just before Labor Day. Joe Appel wanted me to stay on. I don't believe he ever realized that my entire advertising experience had been six weeks on Wanamaker's furniture floor.

I then took myself and a sample book filled with the Wanamaker furniture sale ads up to Macy's. That was all I had to show because I had never really been in advertising before, except for a few weeks on the Rockford, Illinois, paper, where I sold display space to the stores.

I got a job as head of all home furnishings advertising and stayed with Macy's for twelve years.

My salary started at $75 a week and ended at $19,000 a year. The last several years were at the higher figure—upped because an advertising agency offered me a job at that figure. The offer came after I had created the Macy slogan "It's smart to be thrifty."

IV

Anybody, but anybody, can

"Anybody, but anybody, can write advertising" is the theme of this book, and I sincerely mean it—almost. After all, most statements have to be qualified slightly. Take for instance a bathing suit ad: "Anybody, but anybody, can wear our swimsuit." Sure, anybody, but anybody, who has a fairly decent figure. Or "Anybody, but anybody, can eat our pastrami." Sure, anybody, but anybody, who isn't allergic to pastrami. So, as I have said, "anybody, but anybody, can write advertising" unless he's so bereft of the King's English that he has a poverty-stricken vocabulary and can't tell a synonym from an antonym. English . . . "Aye, there's the rub." There is only one way up to the copywriter's crow's-nest, and that is via the English language. If you confuse "desiccate" and "desecrate," give up now. Desiccate has to do with coconuts. It does not have to do with tombstones.

Once a young man showed me the title of the thesis he was working on: "The Importance of the Caesura in Milton's *Comus*." Imagine! Out of the lush, lovely centuries of English literature he was fascinated only by the caesura. Milton is bad enough. Milton's *Comus*, worse. Milton's *Comus*' caesura, still worse.

Roughly speaking, I believe that anybody can learn to write advertising. But I wouldn't take a chance on the girl who came in one day looking for all the world like a full-fledged beatnik complete with ponytail, and a volume of Proust under each arm.

No sooner had I finished typing the paragraphs about how I'd hesitate to hire a beatnik person because he would not be thing-minded, than my memory jumped back to the day I did hire such a person (masculine gender).

It was in the middle thirties that just such a non-thing-minded young man applied to me at Wanamaker's. Andrew was the son of a writer who had made a great commercial success. The big popular magazines vied for his novels, which were serialized. *The Saturday Evening Post* wanted every word that he wrote. Son Andrew was not proud of his father's career. He was embarrassed by it. He shuddered at any commercial success. He didn't even want to take money from his father—which was why he was applying for a job. Why Wanamaker's? Because he lived in nearby Greenwich Village. The word beatnik was unknown in the middle thirties, but that was what Andrew was. I explained that advertising was selling—the very word made him shudder.

I had to talk him into taking the job. He was revolted at the thought of selling anything. Andrew was an avant-garde poet, an intellectual snob. I played a trick on him. I started him out writing up a fabulous special purchase that Wanamaker's London office had made in men's sportswear, designed and made in England. The values were so extraordinary that even skeleton merchandise descriptions made them irresistible.

Andrew wrote every description. Andrew did more. He tried on and modeled for the artist every suede jacket and sweater and pair of slacks—and incidentally pirouetted before the big mirror in the art department. It was obvious that he fancied himself in every garment. He even got the men's-wear buyer to sell him some of the stuff at less than the usual employee discount price.

The ad ran. We gave it top position in our strongest paper. The response was spectacular. Gone was the superior cool intellectual. We planted a palpitating Andrew at the main Wanamaker door to help direct the horde we knew would pound in the minute the paper hit the street. The doors were mobbed. Andrew was thrilled —the ice melted; the superior cool one was jumping for joy. In minutes he was a convert to the free enterprise of our capitalist country. He was particularly thrilled with the fat juicy markup. He kept saying to the buyer, "Better mark this higher—up it a whole dollar. You can get it. Your cost of doing business is over 30 per cent—so you'll have to push up the price."

Andrew was a great success. When we didn't have spectacular purchases, he wrote our most elegant booklets and direct-mail pieces on budgeting, the children's back-to-school promotion, and the campaign opening a revolving credit account that Wanamaker's originated. He eventually became one of our best hard-sell copy-writers. Yes, anybody *can* succeed. Andrew's achievement was applauded by all the Wanamaker big brass. He was even introduced at a big rally meeting of the employees in Wanamaker's Philadelphia store, which was as elegant and successful as its New York sister store had become inelegant and unsuccessful.

He found that sales response excited him more than placing a free-verse poem in a small intellectual quarterly. (Wasn't it Robert Frost who said that free verse wasn't fair—it was like playing tennis without a net?)

Perhaps you are thinking that I and my beloved advertising spoiled Andrew, the intellectual beatnik, for serious writing. I don't believe it. I am sure that advertising writing helps, not hurts, other kinds of writing.

A trainee of mine, Fred Bermingham, became editor of *Esquire* and later produced some excellent books. And my other Bermingham trainee, Steve, wrote Gimbel ads by day and successful novels by night.

And back in the twenties, F. Scott Fitzgerald wrote copy for subway cards.

Copywriting will help, not hurt, other kinds of writing. So, start in a retail advertising department, and experience the thrill of selling. As J. Walter Thompson has always said, "Every product contains an element of excitement. Look, listen and dig into the product to find that excitement. And then promote it." Andrew did just that . . . and you can too.

Of course it is better if you are naturally thing-minded as most people are. If not, you can cultivate "a passion for possession." To be a success in advertising you must want to fill other people with a passion for possession. You can learn to do that too. I believe that every person has a potential passion for possession.

Diogenes would not have made good in advertising. *He* didn't want *anything*. Every day he was wheeled into the marketplace wearing nothing but a ragged tunic. He carried a wooden mug. Then one day he saw a man drinking out of his hands, so Diogenes threw away his mug.

Besides this passion for possession and an eagerness to fill other people with it, you need technical skill. This book should help you develop that. It can't make you into a writer. If you aren't sure of your grammar, you'll need to buckle down and study a textbook on the subject, with exercises to do and lots of good and bad examples.

The best place to polish and exercise your English—and your husband's and your child's—is right at the dinner table. If Father isn't good enough in English, then let Mother, since women are the culture carriers of the race, be in charge. How dreary the dinner-table conversation that is limited to baseball scores and re-hashing of the latest episode of the Munsters, and the baby lispings of "Look, Ma—no holes." (This latter, in case you don't know, is a bread commercial verbatim.) Try a few word games. Have a spelling bee. Give the kids a chance to learn a word they can air at school. Have you any idea what a thrill a child gets when he is the only one in the class who knows what a "century" is? My daughter Elizabeth shook the Manhasset, Long Island, primary school to its foundations when, in the second grade, she used properly the word "apocryphal."

Let your young son learn a fresh insult or two. I have a grandson who gets his English along with his lamb chop. He got into a hot argument with his dearest friend who kept yelling, "You're a sap! Sap! You're a dope!" Steve nigh unto bust but finally with a mighty heave blurted out, "Do you know what you are? You're trite." Pretty good for a nine-year-old. I had often overheard these insults that he and his best friend periodically hurled at one another. I had told Steve not to use all the old hackneyed words. I said, "Don't repeat what John calls you—'sap' and 'dope' are hackneyed. Call John a 'lunkhead' or a 'ninnyhammer.' Then you won't be trite." But smart Steve said, " 'Lunkhead' and 'ninnyhammer' are polysyllabic. I'll call him trite. It is better to use monosyllables."

A study was made not too long ago (my clippings are gone or I would give you the exact date) of eighty geniuses who became high achievers when they grew up. What had these brilliant children in common? Color of eyes? No. Weight? No. Build? No. They were neither all ectomorphs nor all endomorphs. Number of siblings? No. Income of parents? No. Environmental background? No. What, then? It was found in every single case that the parents had great respect for the English language. They loved English, were smitten by words, used them brilliantly, precisely, imaginatively. This had rubbed off on the children, broadened their base of learning so that they were far ahead of their peers.

I used to hire copywriters on the results of a synonym test. I'd give them a word. They'd give me a synonym. If they ran out of synonyms too fast they'd never get on my staff. But, if they were smart enough to protest that there was really no such thing as a synonym, because every word had a different meaning, I'd *hire* them.

Male and female copywriters took these tests, worked for me a couple of years and went on to bigger things.

I think it is accurate to say that wherever I was—at Macy's, Wanamaker's, or Gimbels—that place became the most successful launching pad in the whole field of advertising. Of course it was Kenneth Collins, head of Macy's advertising, who first gave Macy's this distinction. Collins' brilliant regime at Macy's provided me with a model. In both Wanamaker's and Gimbels I tried to run the advertising as I believed Collins would have done it. B.C. (before Collins) Macy's advertising department was a fretful, worrisome spot. A great child psychologist once defined a happy family as a place where everybody was looking for a laugh—a place where everybody was having a good time. Kenneth Collins' booming laugh shook the whole thirteenth floor at least once every thirty minutes.

I never had the top advertising job at Macy's—Collins had it. During my first six years I was head of all the hard goods (hard goods is just what it sounds like—furniture, housewares, large and small appliances, lamps, pictures, mirrors, rugs—in fact all home furnishings).

During my last six years I was head of the other half of the advertising: all the soft goods—all fashions, hats, underthings, infant's and children's wear, all fashion accessories, and so on.

I was talking about the three stores—Macy's, then Wanamaker's, then Gimbels—being the greatest launching pads from which the young career-minded advertising trainees took flight into orbit and landed some of the best jobs in New York—mostly in advertising agencies or with big industry or mail-order houses.

When my ex-cubs went out to look for more lucrative jobs with agencies, they were hired because of the excellence of their retail store samples. One young man went to J. Walter Thompson and after three years moved to Young & Rubicam. He got the Young & Rubicam job, not on his work at J. Walter Thompson but on his sample ads from Wanamaker's and Gimbels. And again, later on, he moved to another agency and was hired not on the work at Young & Rubicam, or his work at J. Walter Thompson, but on his old and yellowing samples from Wanamaker's and Gimbels. So you see, it will be worth your while to start in a retail store. But first you must learn to put words together in an interesting way (I'm assuming you write correct English). And you must learn to look and listen. And you are never too young to begin, or too old.

I well remember the first time I got the idea that I could put words together that would interest people. I was about eight years old.

My father and I were seated on one side of the dinner table. Opposite us sat three neighboring farmers. In the middle was Art Ruhl, a newcomer. His farm was directly across the road from our front gate. The farmer on his left was Hank Kessenich, the one on his right was Pete Ziegler. I remember thinking that they were seated in the same order in which their farms lay. Mr. Ruhl's was between the Ziegler and Kessenich farms. Suddenly Hank spoke up: "Art Ruhl here has promised to help me with clover hulling." Then Ziegler said, "I hope Ruhl will help me with clover hulling too." I piped up, "Of course he'll help you—it'd be a poor Ruhl that wouldn't work both ways."

There was a silence. Then a big guffaw from my father. Everybody clapped. I was in seventh heaven.

Those few words were the turning point in my life. I realized immediately that I could say things that made people laugh, that I could say and write interesting things, that when I grew up I would write for my living. I wouldn't be a farmer's wife. But where would I write? Not on a farm. Maybe in some city where people pay good money to other people for writing things.

It wasn't just the applause. It was the realization that I was pretty darned clever and that I had cut quite a figure. That's why this "round the dinner table" study of English is good for everybody's ego. Take the timid soul. There's one in every family. Imprisoned in many a quiet person is a gay abandoned one wildly signaling to get out. And then, someday, this person says something clever and cuts quite a figure. All of a sudden something wonderful happens. Everybody laughs. And he's got it made! That sleepy somnolent August noon (dinner was at noon on the farm), with a rush and gush of self-confidence, I realized that *I* had it made!

Of course, my clever pun went to my head. I was intoxicated with my own brilliance. A tall brunette Norwegian, who had just moved into our neighborhood, walked into the dining room. I called out, "Oh, Mr. Peterson, aren't you a Norse of a different color?" Later, my father tried to explain why this second pun got only a titter instead of a guffaw. I learned that there were puns and puns.

Most real writers like to play with words. I found that the people who look down on puns generally cannot make a good one. Puns are fine.

The dinner-table hour was the high point of our farm day. Nobody wanted to miss it. What did we learn in this permissive easygoing atmosphere? Everything. Better English, grammar, anthropology, ornithology, zoology, natural history, literature, spelling, puns, metaphors, similes, mythology, history, simple economics. And most important of all, the fact that one must never stop studying.

Speaking of similes and metaphors . . . everybody at the farm dinner table worked on creating apt rememberable ones.

The Arnold bread people have been featuring a poor simile on the air: "The bread that tastes like breakfast." Well! How does breakfast taste? Lots of people won't even eat breakfast. When the coiner is lured by alliteration, the result is usually mediocrity. "The salami that tastes like supper."

Bugs Baer is a master of similes. After I had read his "as short as a crow's walk," I watched crows walk. Their very short legs collapse after a couple of steps.

The best metaphor of this century, the "iron curtain," was created by the old master of English, Winston Churchill.

My grandfather claimed the creation of a dilly of a simile. It goes back to his teen days in Ireland where the boys would gather on the pub steps, standing on the corner watching all the girls go by.

The Irish lads would line up to leer at the passing virgins—sizing up ankles especially. When a thickish ankle would pass, Grandfather Fitz-Gibbon would mutter, "Beef to the heels like a Mullingar heifer."

Much later, when I was in the little village of Oola, near Limerick, a cattle sale was going on in the main street. I noticed a wagon with a sign MULLINGAR HEIFER FOR SALE. I noted the cow's ankles —they were beef to the heels, all right. This beautiful phrase is still used by the Fitz-Gibbon clan—usually as a warning to someone who is putting on weight: "Mullingar heifer—beef to the heels."

Creating similes drives one to the dictionary. And there were dictionaries all over the farmhouse. We were always looking up words. Christopher Morley said that reading the dictionary can be turned into one of the most interesting indoor sports. The study of words, their derivations and meanings, can be as exhilarating as an adventure story. Learn to read the dictionary for fun. Learn the derivation of words.

It is almost impossible to forget the meaning of a word if you know its pedigree. Take the word "curfew." It comes from "cover the fire." It was used centuries ago in France and England—each evening at eight or nine o'clock a man would ring a bell, which meant that you should cover the fire, put out the lights and go to bed. About that time, on the farm, my father would ring a bell, shake down the big coal stove with its rosy glow of coals gleaming through the isinglass and call out "Curfew." Who would ever forget the meaning of the word "curfew"?

My own children learned the meanings of hundreds of words through the fascinating books of Margaret Ernst. Get some of the Ernst books—maybe start with *In a Word*. Here is how James Thurber describes it in his Preface to the 1954 edition: "The primary purpose of this compendium is to entertain, to fascinate, even to astonish word lovers, but it is my personal prayer that it will also serve to impress them with the importance of *accurate speech*, *careful writing*, and *true meaning* [my italics], in a period of the world's history when those virtues of communication are becoming more and more essential to the security, such as it is, of Man on earth."

My children never forgot the meaning of the word "tawdry." The word comes from the celebrations on St. Audrey's Day in England. The boys would give their girl friends cheap trinkets and bracelets. Such gifts became known as "Tawdry Gifts."

My nine-year-old grandson will always remember what the word "sincere" means because he learned the derivation at the dinner-table English lesson. *Sine* and *cere*—without wax. Long ago dishonest cabinetmakers concealed the imperfections of their work and their woods by applying a cover-up coat of wax. Honest cabinetmakers were sincere—their woods and their work were pure, unadulterated, unvarnished, honest.

And did you know that the word "lady" comes from an Anglo-Saxon word meaning loaf-kneader? Or that "capricious" comes from the Latin word for goat? And "dunce" comes from Duns Scotus, a brilliant teacher of the Franciscan order. He was brilliant but unpopular, so his enemies called anyone stupid a "dunce." See what fun you can have finding the origins of words?

If I were a housewife I'd start right now to turn the evening dinner into a cultural education center. One of my aims would be *to make the family literate*. Literacy and correct pronunciation will probably be our next status symbol: That's already true in England, and the United States often follows England in adopting status symbols.

What you are is determined by *heredity* and *environment*. You cannot do much about your heritage, but you can turn your home into an atmosphere conducive to learning. "When you're born you're done for" is a lugubrious fact in many fields. Take grand opera for instance: You could probably never reach baritone excellence without having been born with a certain width of palate, or special throat formation, or gorgeous gullet, or something. Probably you'd need to have been born with very special genes in order to be a great scientist or a great historian. Not true in advertising. The beauty of advertising is its ability to let you zoom to the top no matter what you were born with. All you need is to develop an observant eye, an attentive ear, and then, through diligence and study, acquire the technical skill to record what you see and hear. It's all learnable. Advertising is a craft, not an art.

The dining room or family room adjacent to the dining room should contain:

1. A large unabridged Webster dictionary (Second Edition is better than the Third.)
2. A regular stand on casters for this dictionary
3. A smaller college dictionary that can be passed around the table
4. Also on a nearby bookcase, Warringer's *Grammar and Composition*
5. Margaret Ernst's *In a Word*
6. *The Fables of Aesop*
7. *Bulfinch's Mythology*
8. Fowler's *Modern English Usage,* or a recent revised and edited edition of Fowler's *English Usage* by Sir Ernest Gowers

9. Margaret Nicholson's 1957 *Dictionary of American-English Usage*
10. Roget's *Thesaurus*
11. Pears *Encyclopedia*
12. Plenty of pens and writing pads

If you can find a copy of Barrett Wendell's *English Composition* in a secondhand store, get it. Be sure to read Fowler in some form or other—the original or Gowers' revision or Nicholson's American revision. Read Fowler for fascination or pure delight. And read Bergen Evans and Rudolph Flesch for more pure delight. A good investment that would spur excited, delighted learning in any member of the family would be three books by Theodore Bernstein, the assistant managing editor of *The New York Times: Watch Your Language, More Language That Needs Watching,* and *The Careful Writer.* They will raise the cultural status of the whole family. And they will do it so entertainingly that nobody will be aware of how much he is learning.

My father did not concentrate on grammar. Most of the time he stressed *observation.* He always said, "Don't say 'I saw a bird.' Tell whether it was a woodpecker or a goldfinch, a titmouse or a canary." He would constantly point out things that were so close that we didn't even look at them. He tried to develop our powers of observation.

This developing of one's powers of observation became a family trait. My grandson, six-year-old Geoffrey, once said to his brother, "Don't say you want grapes, Steve. Be spethific [he has a slight lisp]. Say you want Thompson's Seedless. You might just as well, for that's all we've got."

To test our powers of observation my father made everyone give an impromptu description of his or her own room. He told us the story of the architect who was obliged to pass a badly designed house on his way to work every day. The horrible lines of the ugly house so grated on his artistic eye that he knew he would have to do something about it. Finally he solved the problem. He bought the house, lived in it, and it never bothered him again—because he never saw it. Something close to you can become so common that it becomes invisible, like the postman. It was this imperviousness to the wonderful world around us that my father didn't want us to acquire. He wanted us blessed with a Holy Curiosity. That was why he made us compete in describing our rooms and everyday surroundings. The winner got the biggest piece of pie. We had to include the placement of doors and windows and a description of the pictures on the wall, the color and pattern of rug, bedspread and curtains.

This dinner study at our house was a combination of new-fashioned and old-fashioned teaching—a kind of progressive-square education. Square, because we learned by heart gems from authors as square as Henry Wadsworth Longfellow, Tennyson, and Wordsworth.

When my father was chided because he let the children "hog the limelight," he said, "That's all right. I don't want docility. Docility is the virtue of asses." My mother would speak up. "Say 'docility is the virtue of dunces'—that sounds better."

My father was dead right on the undesirability of docility. Medical research has recently revealed that a two-months-old baby who roared with rage when his bottle was snatched from him developed into a competent, independent six-months-old baby. But a two-months-old baby who submitted meekly when his bottle was snatched developed into a whiny dependent individual when he was six months old.

There was no authoritarian rigidity at our dinner table. My father did not believe in turning us into little memory machines. He was a stickler for correct grammar and correct pronunciation. The poems and doggerel I learned around the dinner table have been of great value in writing advertising.

If I hadn't memorized A. A. Milne's "The King's Breakfast" when I was teaching it to my own children, Gimbels wouldn't now have its "Nobody but nobody" slogan. And if I hadn't memorized Longfellow's "The Children's Hour," I wouldn't have been able to present to Coca-Cola a slogan verse which it *almost* bought. It was based on the fact that for decades Coca-Cola has publicized the word "pause," as in "the pause that refreshes." My slogan verse went:

> *Between the dark and the daylight*
> *When the night is beginning to lower*
> *Comes a* pause *in the day's occupations*
> *That is known as the* Coke-*tail Hour.*

"The Coke-tail hour" is a very promotable and charming bit. And the whole idea has a kind of unstodgy morality about it that teenagers would take to. What happened? Well, some Coca-Cola higher-up said that the board of directors felt that the word "Coke-tail" was too close to "cocktail," which would offend Coca-Cola's conservative top brass. Perhaps my price—$25,000—was too high. And there you have it—Coca-Cola, Longfellow, and Fitz-Gibbon killed by a twist of lemon—the executive kind.

Everybody at our farm dinner table, from the five-year-old on up to the grandaunts or granduncles, learned that the mastery of the English language was a very good thing to have.

I know of no better way to impress you with the importance of literacy than by telling you the story of Stanley. Here is the case of a young man who leaped to the top of the heap after he had achieved this priceless skill. I hired Stanley as office manager at Gimbels. He had a dreadful inferiority complex. He had only one year of college and he was in a department where all the secretaries and even the messengers were Phi Beta Kappas. He had no self-confidence at all. Stanley wouldn't say "Boo" to a goose. I suggested that he study basic grammar. He bought the book. He did more! He actually enrolled in a basic English grammar course at night. He learned all the things that used to be taught in grades five through nine. Maybe they are not being taught at all now. By the time Stanley had finished the grammar course he was a changed person. He was bursting with self-confidence. Each morning he brought a list of the bloopers in grammar and punctuation he had noted the night before—in print ads and on TV and radio.

According to Stanley's count, everybody—north, south, east, west—misuses the words "imply" and "infer."

Don't let the sun go down today without conquering this error. You will shine like a white candle in the murkiness of illiteracy. Here we go:

"Imply" is active. One who implies is one who says something or writes something.

"Infer" is passive. One who infers is not the doer. He hears something or reads something from which he draws or deduces a conclusion, an inference.

When you say that the speaker implied that the Democrats were to blame, you say that the speaker suggested or intimated that.

When you say to the speaker, "I infer from your remarks . . . ," you are saying, "I gather from your remarks . . . ," which is correct. Keep thinking of "gather" as a synonym of "infer."

I suggest that you start teaching yourself and your family right now all about the English language.

The director of the dinner hour doesn't have to be Mother or Daddy. If big brother or Aunt Avis has a love affair with the English language, that person should take over.

Occasionally the only near-egghead in our family (there were no real eggheads), Uncle Edward Fitz-Gibbon, who was superintendent of schools in Dane County, Wisconsin, would take over the English hour. You may say, "All this is impossible because our children are too young—four to thirteen." Perfect. When I was four I had picked up quite a bit of "riches on the side." I am sure that I knew all about the Pied Piper, Johnny Appleseed, Pandora's box, Scylla and Charybdis, William Tell and his apple-on-the-head son, and Achilles sulking in his tent and his vulnerable heel, Procrustes and his bed for travelers, and the Augean stable—which, of course, was very understandable to a farm child. I picked up these riches not because I was particularly gifted but because I couldn't escape them. Riches on the side were all over the farmhouse.

By four I am sure that I also knew I should say "this kind," not "these kind," unless I was prepared to say "these apple." (This very day, I noticed an expensive four-color page by Kraft using the word "kind" with a plural verb!)

To this day when I dine I look for riches on the side. My dining area, overlooking New York's East River, has a large unabridged Webster's dictionary on a rolling dictionary stand, simply because I cannot conceive of sitting down alone to eat without a dictionary nearby.

This book cannot be big enough to cover a "how to write" course, which should include exercises to do and correct. Even if I could squeeze in a "how to write" course, I'm not an expert. I'm pretty good at grammar; but I'm not all that good. I got so I always turned to Stanley. What everybody needs is a Theodore Bernstein of *The New York Times*, or a Bergen Evans, or a Rudolph Flesch, or an Edwin Wooley (Wooley dates me). Get Bernstein's most recent book, *The Careful Writer*. I'm sure that if you read this book thoroughly you'll never make that evangelist's error. You must have heard him say, at the end of every sermon, "God bless you *real* good." And Long John on WOR radio ends every program with "Sleep *real* good." (And what about the dress that looks *well*? A dress has no eyes, so it can't *look* in any manner at all. But the dress can look *good*.)

Real is an adjective—never never never an adverb! When I hear it misused, I really wonder whether the eight parts of speech are still being taught in school. Illiteracies are all over the place. Here is one of the most appalling I heard recently on TV: "The beauty of this country belongs to all *we* Americans." We! Many people are frightened of *us* . . . indeed frightened of the objective case. And just this very day a TV commentator said, "The White House invited my husband and I."

My nine-year-old grandson Steve would be able to correct a sentence like that. He'd say, "If the lady who was speaking had thrown out the words 'my husband,' she would have known that it was wrong to say, 'The White House invited I.' " Stephen is getting the feel of the structure of an English sentence. Like Stanley, my old office manager, Steve is building up his own self-confidence —confidence at the core.

The worst errors are those that show that the speaker is trying to be refined and elegant and failing wretchedly. That's worse than out-and-out violating all the rules. "Me and him are friends" is less grating on the cultured ear than "the differences between Mary and *I*," for example.

People have said to me, "Fitz, you're just plain lucky. Your plain direct style just happens to be the fashion these days. What will you do when convoluted circuitous writing comes into style?" It won't. It can't. It never will.

Carmel Snow, the legendary editor of *Harper's Bazaar*, once tried to get me to go to Paris with her to write up the Paris openings for *Harper's Bazaar*. "Fitz, I want your good blunt Gimbel manure English. I want to throw out of the *Bazaar* every word of that awful flowery fashionese which is so unfashionable."

The hardest copy to learn to write is fashion copy. Even a good writer sometimes ends up with insipid fashionese. There is one superlatively good writer whom you could adopt as a model. Her name is Eugenia Sheppard. For years she had been fashion editor of the New York *Herald Tribune*. She is now fashion editor of the

New York *World Journal Tribune.* Dig out her stuff in a library and study her word sorcery. She writes clearly, crisply, and objectively. She is not on a fashion magazine staff, although her pieces often bob up in all the magazines. Analyze her cool intelligent way of presenting fashion. And you'll never produce simpering silly stuff. Eugenia writes as sensibly about fashion as if she were analyzing the Common Market—never a twitter, never a flutter.

My father had a theory that the only way to get the heavy polysyllabic words *out* of your vocabulary was to get them *into* your vocabulary as early as possible. He'd announce, "Tonight is polysyllabic night—everybody must use long show-off words." Or perhaps we would have a sesquipedalian Monday night or a monosyllabic Tuesday night.

Sometimes he'd start off with "Gerald, did you perform your matutinal ablutions?" Even when my brother Gerald was very young we knew that that was silly talk and that "Did you wash your hands this morning?" was better English. That kind of pompous, big-word talk at ten is all right. At thirteen it's enthralling. At twenty it's all wrong. At thirty it's appalling!

Or Father would sing his own version of "Three Blind Mice," changing it to "Three Rodents Destitute of Vision." Then he'd sing his polysyllabic version of "Home, Sweet Home," as "Residence, Fine Residence." All this taught us that one should use short, simple, direct words, because they were better than fancy show-off words.

Father also called our attention to the hired man's show-off phrases. Eddie, our hired man on the farm, had had no education at all. But he'd picked up a couple of fancy bits that he'd hurl when he wanted to impress people. We were all tickled pink when Eddie, with a nonchalant shrug, would say, "A mere bagatelle, Mr. Fitz-Gibbon, something at which I'd never take umbrage." "Bagatelle" and "umbrage" gave Eddie self-confidence.

When my ten-year-old granddaughter, Betsy, who is more

sophisticated than her nine-year-old brother, Stephen, and her six-year-old brother, Geoffrey, tells the boys that it's better to call dinner "dinner" than to call it a "Lucullan feast," Stephen and Geoffrey chime out with "We know short words are better. We're just getting those big words out of our system now so that we won't use them when we grow up."

The late Kenneth Collins, who came to Macy's from a professorship of English at Harvard, was a master of crisp simple monosyllabic English. But he was not above throwing polysyllables at a recalcitrant Macy buyer. I recall the fabric buyer complaining about a word in an ad. "Well, Jim," answered Kenneth, "I put the word in for verisimilitude." "Oh, I see. That's perfectly all right, Ken," said Jim.

I looted a leaf from Collins (over the years I looted millions of leaves from Collins' book) when the same buyer popped up a few years later at Gimbels. I said in answer to his criticism of my ad, "Oh, I couldn't do that, Jim. You wouldn't want me to pile Ossa on Pelion, would you?" "Oh no, Fitz, of course not," he said.

Along with the hilarious polysyllabic words, my father would tell us about mixed metaphors and euphemisms. My daughter and her lawyer husband are carrying on the traditional English-lesson dinner hour out at their home in Denver. Stephen and Betsy (nine and ten years old) were convulsed with mirth over a Winston Churchill euphemism. Churchill had called his opponent in the House of Commons a liar. He was forced to retract. Which he did by saying, "My worthy opponent is a purveyor of inexactitudes." My grandchildren are getting a good grounding in English syntax and vocabulary around the dinner table every night. Whenever they learn a new word, they spring it on the family. Which is good. That's what a family is for—to practice on.

At a party, Geoffrey, aged six, sidled up to a guest and said, "You can call this party a bash if you want to. But don't call it a wingding. Because that's been said before." "Yes," added Stephen, "it's such an obvious pun on our name Wing and we think it is pretty hackneyed."

Does this awareness of correct vivid English produce little show-off monsters? Not at all. They are all delightful and devastatingly diverting. I quote my own grandchildren's sayings and I quote my own ads—not because they are brighter than other people's ads and grandchildren, but because they are available.

You'd think it would be easy to put words on paper with clarity and power. Well, it isn't. The gobbledygook passed around on office memorandums in most organizations is as bad as the hilarious officialese that has come out of government bureaus. Stuart Chase in his book *Roads to Agreement* quoted a honey:

A foreign-born plumber in New York wrote the Bureau of Standards that he found hydrochloric acid fine for cleaning drains, and did they agree? Washington replied: "The efficacy of hydrochloric acid is indisputable, but the chlorine residue is incompatible with metallic permanence."

The plumber wrote back that he was mighty glad the Bureau agreed with him.

Considerably alarmed, the Bureau replied a second time: "We cannot assume responsibility for the production of toxic and noxious residues with hydrochloric acid, and suggest that you use an alternate procedure." The plumber was happy to learn that the Bureau still agreed with him.

Whereupon Washington wrote: "Don't use hydrochloric acid; it eats hell out of the pipes!"

This pompous polysyllabic padding is called "pudder" by the English. Learn to write simple direct sentences—the placing of little, simple old words in a fresh order makes a fresh thought. Always remember that the concrete word is better than the abstract. Always prefer directness to circumlocution. Always resist the horrible lure of rippling or reverberating polysyllables. Develop a simple direct style—as plain as a butter tub. You'll never find any woolly padding in a great stylist like E. B. White of *The New Yorker*.

Before I'd hire a writer I used to ask him to write a paragraph of nature description. Like the French, I believe that the adjective is the enemy of the noun and I always want to eliminate the heavily adjectival, purple-patch style of writing. When I came across this kind of creamy prose—"with a grandiose swish of her brush, Mother Nature dips into her palette"—the writer is quickly put out of the running. And I was always against "rosy-fingered Aurora" or "rosy-toed Aurora." Steer clear of flossy syntax. Pithy compact sinewy sentences will do much to push you up the ladder even if you are a brand-new cub.

One day I came across a delightful composition by a child of ten. (It is in H. Allen Smith's *Write Me a Poem, Baby;* Mr. Smith says Edward Weeks found it in the works of Sir Ernest Gowers.) Woolly padding seems to be a morbid condition contracted in the early twenties. Children show no signs of it. Here is the composition:

The bird that I am going to write about is the Owl. The Owl cannot see at all by day and at night is as blind as a bat.

I do not know much about the Owl, so I will go on to the beast which I am going to choose. It is the Cow. The Cow is a mammal. It has six sides—right, left, upper and below. At the back it has a tail on which hangs a brush. With this it sends the flies away so that they do not fall into the milk. The head is for the purpose of growing horns and so that the mouth can be somewhere. The horns are to butt with, and the mouth is to moo with. Under the cow hangs the milk. It is arranged for milking. When people milk, the milk comes and there is never an end to the supply. How the cow does it I have not yet realized, but it makes more and more. The cow has a fine sense of smell; one can smell it far away. This is the reason for the fresh air in the country. The man cow is called an ox. It is not a mammal. The cow does not eat much, but what it eats it eats twice, so that it gets enough. When it is hungry it moos, and when it says nothing it is because its inside is all full up with grass.

The writer had something to say and said it as clearly as he could, and so he unconsciously achieved style. But as someone has pointed out, why do we write when we are ten, "so that the mouth can be somewhere" and perhaps when we are twenty "in order to insure that the mouth may be appropriately positioned environmentally"?

Gilbert Keith Chesterton said, "Dignity is the last resort of mediocrity." Dignity is close to pomposity. And pomposity always breeds polysyllabism. And polysyllabism results in obscurity. So you don't get through . . . and nobody knows what you're talking about. Even the smart P. T. Barnum, after his show was over one night, said, "The festivities have come to a conclusion." Nobody moved. He repeated his words. Still nobody moved. Then he said, "It's all over. Go on home." Everybody went.

A leading industrialist, in answer to the question "What happened?" came out with "Nothing has eventuated as yet." He's the kind of guy who would also say "The answer is in the affirmative" instead of "Yes." And a big store that should know better recently ran this headline: OUR CARPET ENGULFS PRACTICALITY WITH ELEGANCE. This pompous padding I call "haggis." What is haggis? Haggis is a thick lumpy Scotch pudding made of liver and lights and oatmeal and suet all boiled together in the stomach of a sheep.

Here are two writing rules to remember:

1. Use short simple blunt words (preferably of Anglo-Saxon, not Latin, derivation).
2. Place your short simple words in a natural direct way—the way a primer is written. Subject—verb—object: "I see the dog."

Inversion is effective in Scripture and the parables, but we are not composing parables. For instance, the unjust steward said, "To dig I am not able. To beg I am ashamed." Very effective in the New Testament. Not effective in advertising, which should be straight as an arrow.

H. G. Wells said, "I write as I walk because I want to get somewhere, and I write as straight as I can just as I walk as straight as I can, because that is the best way to get there."

I once worked with a fashion stylist who had three pet words. If an ad contained any one of these three she was as content as a kitten full of cream. The words were *ineluctable, meticulous,* and *inordinate.* I find that fashion people love words of Latin derivation, generally polysyllabic. They like to say a thing is "imbued with." They like words like "acquiesce" and "distinguish"—dry, rusty, decrepit words. Many of them are hipped on heavy erudition. Advertising writers know that blunt, simple, monosyllabic writing is good fashion. They know that the placing of little simple old words in a fresh order makes a fresh thought.

Be sure you know the meaning of the words you use. The original meaning of "enhance" was to make larger. Don't say "This girdle will enhance your figure."

Stylists should learn that "begin" is better than "commence" and that "happen" is better than "transpire" and that "sleep" is better than "slumber" and that "bloody" is better than "sanguinary." If you stuck a pin in a stylist she would be "sanguinary" and not just plain "bloody."

A snobbish men's-wear campaign ran this headline: ACT LIKE YOU'VE ALWAYS WORN WORSTED-TEX. YOU'LL GET USED TO BEING A LEADER. Better if the copywriter could act as if he'd learned his grade-school grammar! Then he would have known that "like" is never a conjunction. (Webster's Third Edition doesn't tell you that only illiterates use *like* as a conjunction, but its Second Edition does. And so does the Oxford English Dictionary. And so does Fowler.) United Air Lines says, "Our stewardess smiled *like* she meant it." And a gasoline ad says, "Your car starts *like* it's summertime." And the Dash detergent ad: "makes your automatic washer clean *like* it's 10 feet tall."

Even though we bent over backward at Wanamaker's trying to produce fastidious English, occasionally an error would get past a careless proofreader. We were mortified when a flurry of letters arrived, criticizing our using "like" where we needed the conjunction "as."

Mark Dall wrote the apology, which we ran in a prominent space with his inspired headline: WE NEVER SAW THE LIKE.

Our clever apology delighted English teachers. So if you need to clear up "like" and "as," do so, and you'll raise yourself in your own estimation.

Stanley was always able to point out an illiteracy in a print or radio or TV ad, such as this headline in a big *New York Times* ad for a Miami hotel. Here was the headline under the photograph of a freckle-faced boy:

ME AND SIS
ARE TAKING
MOM 'N' DAD
TO THE AMERICANA

The writer of this ad was trying to achieve a folksy cuteness, a palsy-walsiness, by being illiterate. The body copy was just as bad: "We'll all enjoy things together like for a swim or dinner or something." That "for" in the sentence reminds me of my six-year-old grandson Geoffrey, who announced, "I never look at that birthday program on TV because," he said, "the man who runs it makes awful mistakes in grammar." The commercial ran like this:

Happy birthday today
Happy birthday today
We're going to have a party
You're invited for to stay.

Geoffrey explained proudly, "He shouldn't say '*for to stay.*' He ought to throw out 'for'! He massacres the King's English."

Now, Geoffrey at six doesn't know that "for" is a preposition, but his sister Betsy knows it along with the other seven parts of speech. Nothing, but nothing, equals the surge of self-confidence that mastery of English grammar can give you. *Confidence at the core*—that's what it gives. And that's all you need to get to the top. Confidence at the core does more for you than anything else in this world—more for a girl than long eyelashes. And it can do more for a male than a Discobolus physique.

Stanley also noted the bad habit of adding the suffix *ize* or *wise* to words:

Don't say accessorize or hospitalize or finalize or advertising-wise or anything-wise.

It was that impeccable writer, E. B. White, who said, "We'd just as soon simonize our grandmother as personalize our writing." By the way, a book you should buy and keep is *The Elements of Style* by William Strunk, Jr., and E. B. White. You'll treasure it all your life, and read it for sheer enjoyment as well as information.

Why does a mastery of English fill one with so much self-confidence? Because when you know in your bones that you can never misuse *lie* and *lay* and never misuse *sit* and *set* and never misuse *good* and *well*, that knowledge makes one feel secure enough to relax and indulge in a little elegant carelessness, when words spill out with abandon in vigorous, economical expression that has charm and vigor. And that's what makes good talk and good writing.

The difference between *sit* and *set* was cleared up for me when I was very young. One day I came into the house and told my father, "There's a hen in the haymow. I tried to shoo her off a big bunch of eggs. But she wouldn't go. So I suppose she's a 'setting hen.' "

This, he explained, is what I should have said: "There's a

Plymouth Rock hen in the haymow sitting on a clutch of eggs. I couldn't shoo her off, so she must be a 'sitting hen.' Your mother sets the hens. 'Set' is a transitive verb and takes an object, *hens*. What the hen does is sit. *Sit* is an intransitive verb. It can't take an object. You can't sit anything."

Then he went on, and cleared up *lie* and *lay*.

If you have ever been in a hospital, you'll notice that everybody there is mixed on *lie* and *lay*. Not only do the nurse's aides and nurses say, "Lay on your left side." Interns and doctors make the same mistake—as does everybody on TV.

By now you will have noticed that since it is impossible to include a thorough section on grammar I have been just spreading a little smorgasbord table before you based on my own likes and dislikes.

The quickest way to become literate is to enroll in a good grammar course. If your grammar is shaky, this book can only exhort you to start immediately to acquire a command of English. And who will be your teacher? Ultimately you. As Clifton Fadiman said in one of his *Holiday* columns, "All true education is a delayed action bomb, assembled in the classroom for explosion at a later date." And, in the same piece, he says, "A teacher says certain things that create *another* teacher. This other teacher is the one hidden inside the student . . . the newborn professor inside the student takes over and with any luck the process of education continues till death." Of course, we forgot most of the specific things we learned around the farm dinner table, but one lesson we never forgot was that we'd have to continue to observe intently (with our eyes and ears) and that we'd have to continue to study English for the rest of our lives.

A practical reason for turning your dinner hour into an English lesson is getting your children into college. This dinner hour, devoted to words and their derivations, will turn children into ravenous readers. And it looks as if the world of the future will belong to those who read as the hungry eat—from real hunger.

The omnivorous reader will be able to get into college and stay in college . . . and pay his way via scholarships, if he needs to. And if his life work is advertising after he leaves college, he'll continue to read and learn as long as he lives.

Who knows? Maybe this whole helter-skelter of my ideas on the writing of English may be terribly dated. Maybe there's a New Grammar similar to the New Math. Maybe it isn't eight parts of speech any more, but seven or nine. Even if I am behind the times, as I well may be, I think the suggestions here are all sound for advertising.

I must confess I can't read Proust. I haven't tried very hard. My idea of a good simple declarative sentence is: "Scrod is baby cod." Just as plain and simple as that. I can't read Joyce. (But I am going to have another go at Joyce because he makes beautiful puns.) My idea of music is melody, so I don't know what Hindemith is about. Or e. e. cummings. My favorite poets—Emily Dickinson, A. E. Housman, Robert Frost, Yeats. I even like rhyme.

Old-fashioned? Probably. After all, I date so far back that our grammar teacher in the convent, Sister Clement, had us put a wiggly line under the subject, a straight line under the verb, two straight lines under the object, and a wiggly line over a straight line under the predicate noun.

When I come to involuted writing à la Henry James, I always feel like the critic who reviewed one of his novels. Maddened by the delicate involutions, he finally said, "Out with it, out with it, speak up, spit it out in Papa's hand." Much of the flossy institutional advertising makes one want to yell, "Come on, out with it, spit it out in Papa's hand."

What ever happened to Stanley? He is now in a big agency where he sits with the mighty. He no longer does little clerical administrative chores. He even speaks up at creativity meetings. Of course, Stanley was intelligent and attractive. But he owes his rise to one thing only—impeccable grammar.

Whether I am out-of-date or not, I have reported accurately on what an understanding of old-fashioned English grammar did for my office manager, Stanley. He learned to write what he meant quickly and clearly. "Go thou and do likewise."

And let us not burden advertising with the blame for proliferating the vulgarisms, banalities, inanities, verbosities, pomposities, and idiosities one often hears in TV advertising today.

V

A horse looks like a violin

I once hired a young cub, a Dartmouth graduate. He went on to become editor of *Esquire* magazine and author of several books just because he said, "A horse looks like a violin from above." How did he know? He had climbed up in the rafters of a barn and looked down. And a horse *does* look like a violin from above.

His name was Fred Bermingham. He was just out of college, but college had nothing to do with it. Often *rigor mortis* of the powers of observation sets in very early. Often older people who have never been to college can see circles around the conventional young.

I have always had an eye out for the offbeat person who has a fresh, sharp sense of observation. George Meredith said, "I've made bread from the bump of wonder: That's my business, and that's my tale." Making bread from the bump of wonder is a good definition of advertising. (It's also a good definition for most other businesses, certainly for any kind of creative merchandising.)

As I look back over thirty-five years of writing advertising and helping young people and middle-aged people and older people break into advertising, I really believe that one of the common de-nominators among the successful ones has been this sense of wonder —this Holy Curiosity.

Who is the darling of the gods? He who keeps curious is the darling of the gods. I have never known anyone who bounced out of bed in the morning, delighted and astonished by the world in which he found himself, who was not a success. A vibrantly alive curiosity and a perceptive awareness will put you right up there with the best of them. This intense interest in people and things —this sense of wonder—*can* be acquired.

The best teacher for those who want to find their lost sense of wonder is Gilbert Keith Chesterton. Chesterton went through life startled and astonished at the little common everyday things, be-cause he looked at them with a fresh unjaundiced eye. He bewailed the fact that the attribute of wonder had atrophied in most of us. He tells us that we shouldn't be surprised if the sun doesn't rise some morning, but that our hair should be standing on end and our eyes starting out of our heads in awe-stricken wonder that it *does* rise every morning.

A three-year-old who had not yet lost that Chesterton gift for vivid observation said this when her foot went to sleep: "My foot feels like ginger ale."

An advertising writer whose income was way, way up in five figures once ran this headline in a shampoo advertisement: "Your hair will be so clean that it will squeak." That's observation. Be-cause clean hair does squeak.

But the average person never listens to the still small squeaks in life. He has a hackneyed idea of how a thing looks and sounds, and so doesn't bother to look or listen.

The first person who called a baby's hand a starfish really looked; because a baby's hand does look, for all the world, like a starfish.

We would all get more out of life (and better jobs) if we learned to be scrupulous lookers. It's hard work to look at a thing. You can shirk looking at a thing by letting ready-made phrases and clichés take over for you. This is just a form of indolence—letting everybody else do your looking for you. Loose looking is lazy; clear looking is hard to do.

Watch a woman walk along the street. "Walk" is a vague umbrella word that covers all kinds of perambulation. How does she really move? Does she strut, or mince, or waggle, or waddle, or teeter, or lope along like a country doctor's buggy?

If you do not learn to look at a thing sharply, whatever you write will seem vague and phony. If you develop into a sharp looker, your writing will come to life, and this reality will make what you write believable. And believability is far and away the most important requirement of advertising.

"Observe" means to take note of, to be aware of. That's what that highly paid copywriter did in describing the results of a shampoo. She noted, and tucked away in her memory, that clean hair squeaks. The reader of her ad will note that clean hair does squeak. So the reader will believe every word in the ad or in the TV commercial. And when she believes, she buys.

Sharpen your powers of observation. Learn to look at a thing as if you had never seen it before in your life. Most people, young and old, seldom really look at a thing. They see through a film of prejudices, which is why they express themselves in old clichés and hackneyed stereotypes.

I remember a chic young thing who came in to apply for a job in fashion writing. She had clipped a smart photograph of a woman in a dashing checked suit. Her headline said: HOW TO LOOK LIKE A MILLIONAIRE EVEN IF YOU ARE ONLY A THOUSANDAIRE. Under it she had written a few words of vague generalized description. I asked her, "What kind of check is this?" Her answer was "Well, it's just a check—a check's a check."

So we got out *Vogue* and *Harper's Bazaar* and noted the difference between a gun-club check and a hound's-tooth check and a shepherd's check.

She caught on quickly. "You know, I really have never *looked* at a check." And then she added, "I can see that it's more important to *look* at a thing than to do what I've been doing—just sitting trying to dream up words like thousandaire versus millionaire."

How can you develop a keen sense of observation? Practice. For the next week make a game of sharp looking. And play the game at the dinner table. Do what my father used to do: ask anyone at the table to describe his or her own room. How many doors? How many windows? What does each window give on? Describe the shade and curtain on each window, the dresser. What was on the top of the dresser this morning? What color is the bedspread? The rug?

The dinner table can be the place for testing the sharpness of all the senses. What are the outdoor sounds at seven in the morning? At noon? Is there a twelve-o'clock whistle? This game can be played by everyone at the table from the three-year-old up to the great-grandmother. Developing keen observation will not only bring you lots of money; more important, it will make you a more interesting person to everybody including yourself.

Good creative people (whether they're in advertising or merchandising) are both *in*quisitive and *ac*quisitive. They are curious about people, curious about new products, curious about everything.

They are not like the old farmer who, when he backed out of his driveway into the swift-moving traffic, was asked, "Don't you look?" "Sure I look," he said, "but I don't see good." They "see good," because all their senses are sensitive to newness, freshness, and little nuances of difference.

Write what you hear, not preposterous statements. My father's lessons in observation also included observing with one's ears. He wanted us to be able to recognize birds and bugs and bees by ear as well as by eye.

I remember his stopping the horses one day while we all craned our necks out of the surrey to observe a skein of wild geese flying south. He said, "Be very still and listen, they gossip and chatter all the way south." I still can hear their faint gabble.

Today when I see a skein of wild geese flying down the East River, from my New York apartment high in the sky—it's almost all glass on the north, east, and south—I always try to hear the faint gabble-gabble. But I don't even though I am seventeen stories high. The muffled sound of the city, the drumbeat of the city, drowns it out.

I remember another lesson in observing with our ears. Father told us if we listened carefully we could hear the heavy breathing of our ponderous Clydesdale horses plowing in the "back-40" field that must have been 2,000 feet away.

And I remember how amused my father was when I called a Clyde horse a buff Cochin—because of the heavy feathery look of the Clyde's feet.

Father had all kinds of ways to trick us into observing things. He told us that the proper time to plant peas was when the burr-oak leaves were the size of a mouse's ears. And he said that he would count on us to watch and tell him when. We scoured the 250 acres for a mouse and then decided to creep into the granary (mistakenly pronounced *grainery* in the Middle West). We couldn't find a mouse in the granary so we moved to the corncrib. We finally got a fleeting glance at a mouse as it scurried across the corncrib floor. Its ears didn't seem any bigger than commas. We raced to find Father. And all hands helped to get the peas into the ground.

I can still see the inside of that corncrib—corn yellow and a soft dull pink—the yellow of the corn and the dull pink of the exposed cobs where the corn had been nibbled off.

Years later, when I had my own agency, I handled the Stroock Fabrics account. I had to think up a name for a color. I came up with corncob pink. The client said, "Not corncob pink, Fitz. Everyone will think it's yellow." But everyone didn't, because we made it clear that it was pink. And Stroock's corncob-pink promotion was a great success. Everything's been grist for my mill.

I remember one of our dinner-table English hours at which Aunt Alice was present. She had one expression that always convulsed us with mirth. She would say, "Face up to things—don't stick your head in the sand like a kangaroo." It seems she had been saying that for years before I first noticed it. Father explained why I had not noticed it before. "You were not listening. She has always said kangaroo instead of ostrich. But you *expected* her to say ostrich and so you heard ostrich. Most people don't really look—they see what they expect to see. And most people don't really listen—they hear what they expect to hear."

Then he told us about the ancient painters of horses who always put eyelashes on the lower lids of horses. Actually horses don't have eyelashes on their lower lids. But the painters expected them to have the eyelashes so they painted what wasn't there.

Even now, over the years, little memories—little observations of eye, ear and nose—float back to me, such as one of my earliest memories when my father gave me my first lesson in learning how fascinating commonplace objects can be. I was very young. I had picked a violet for my father. He told me to peer deep down into the violet and see the queen washing her feet in a tiny tub. Only the other day I looked into a violet and saw the queen washing her tiny feet in the tiny tub.

Winston Churchill, speaking of his painting in *Painting as a Pastime*, tells how he learned to see the delicate tracery of an icicle-covered twig on a tree. Here is what he said on observation in relation to painting—but it is even more meaningful in connection with writing:

Just to paint is great fun. The colours are lovely to look at and delicious to squeeze out. Matching them, however crudely, with what you see is . . . absolutely absorbing. . . . Painting a picture is like fighting a battle; and trying to paint a picture is, I suppose, like trying to fight a battle. It is, if anything, more exciting. . . .

In all battles two things are usually required of the Commander-in-Chief: to make a good plan for his army and to keep a strong reserve. Both these are also obligatory upon the painter. To make a plan, thorough reconnaissance of the country where the battle is to be fought is needed. Its fields, its mountains, its rivers, its bridges, its trees, its flowers, its atmosphere—all require and repay attentive observation from a special point of view. One is quite astonished to find how many things there are in the landscape . . . one never noticed before. And this is a tremendous new pleasure and interest which invests every walk or drive with an added object. . . . I found myself instinctively noting the tint and character of a leaf, the exquisite lacery of winter branches, the dim, pale silhouettes of far horizons. And I had lived for over forty years without ever noticing any of them except in a general way, as one might look at a crowd and say, "What a lot of people!" . . .

The whole world is open with all its treasures. The simplest objects have their beauty. Every garden presents innumerable fascinating problems. Every land, every parish, has its own tale to tell. And there are many lands differing from each other in countless ways, and each presenting delicious variants of colour, light, form, and definition. Obviously, then, armed with a paint-box, one cannot be bored, one cannot be left at a loose end, one cannot "have several days on one's hands." Good gracious! what there is to admire and how little time there is to see it in!

No wonder Churchill is called the greatest man of his century.

Yes, the ability to observe sharply, accurately, will make advertising writing easy as pie. Because you can actually look at a *thing*. In sustained creative writing (a novel or play, for example) you have nothing in your hand to look at. You must dig deep in your conscious or subconscious. That probably is not learnable.

Now let me get down to the actual writing of copy. My first suggestion would be that you write longhand. Amateurs often say, "I don't need to write longhand; I can do just as well on the typewriter." I do not agree. Remember that words are your materials and you have to toy with them, polish them, and play with them to make them come out right.

Some writers can dictate. Dictated copy at its best is natural, easy, and direct. At its worst—and usually it is at its worst—it's dull, hesitant, and repetitive. Which is not surprising, because, even in conversation, you will note a tendency in yourself to start a sentence not really knowing how it will end. In advertising you need to know what the end of your sentence will be when you begin it.

The amateur will sit down and bite up pencils racking his brain for a headline. Why, the headline should almost write itself! At least it should emerge from the copy. After the raw idea, as it were, stands up in the text, it has to be rewritten—words shifted, words substituted, action introduced, polished, and generally rehauled. I recall, as an example, after toying around with the word *weed* for garden equipment, "Weed 'em and reap."

So every writer has to be a good observer. It has been said of Hemingway that he looked at everything as though it were his last day alive. That's how you should look at everything you see and hear around you.

So if you want to be a successful advertising writer and have a lot of fun working and make a lot of money while you are working, all you need to do is:
1. Sharpen your observation.
2. Become a master of English writing—so that you can convey vividly your keen observation to the reader.

Think how dull is this sentence: *I participate in many sports.*
And see how interesting this is: *I ski, I skate, I swim, I pole-vault.*
Good writing should always evoke a picture: *old as the doges—
new as a peeled egg.*

Ideas are supposed to be scarce as hens' teeth, and people who
have ideas are supposed to be scarcer. Maybe. But everybody really
has a pretty equal chance in the idea department, since very little
in the world at this point is new. The trick always is to latch onto
somebody else's .old idea and make from it something new. This
takes sharper eyes than wits, and almost everyone can be trained
to look sharply. I'm thinking of the Lord & Taylor buyer who was
being propelled down the Grand Canal in Venice in a gondola. She
happened to notice the gondolier's glamorous slippers—pointed
toes with black velveteen tops and black felt soles. Gondoliers have
been wearing them for centuries. The buyer whisked a pair off to
America, had it copied for men, women and children, named the
slipper "the Gondolier," and turned an idea as old as the doges
into fresh new profit.

Then there is the story of a department-store buyer who rolled
up quite a portion of fame in her field (and probably a big bonus
too) by taking heed of something that everybody else had looked
at heedlessly for decade after decade.

Lord & Taylor and other stores had been sending boatloads of
buyers to Europe for years. For years they had been staying in
Paris hotels, and for years they had been taking baths in Parisian
salles de bain. In the good hotels of France when you get out of the
bathtub you don't reach for a towel, you reach for a great volumi-
nous robe of thick white terry, which hangs on the bathroom door.
You put it on, hug it to you and you're dry whole minutes before
the people in America who rub themselves dry. Well, American
buyers in Paris had been blotting themselves dry for years in these
terry robes. Did anything click? Nothing. Then one day off to Paris

sailed Lord & Taylor's negligee buyer, wide-eyed and palpitating, on her first trip. Everything in Europe was breathtaking and new. Old hands at the buying offices in Europe were amused at her naïveté. They were also amused when she insisted on buying one of those luxurious wraparounds right off the bathroom door in her hotel. How blasé can you be? A few weeks later Lord & Taylor burst into the papers with a faithful copy of the French "blotter." That was years and years ago. And ever since, Lord & Taylor has been selling more "blotters" than you could shake a stick at. And all because somebody had the bright idea to transplant somebody else's bright idea. One sharp look—one keen scrupulous observation—can send you scooting up the ladder of success.

One more illustration of the value of sharp observation: The Wanamaker curtain buyer came up to my office with his arms full of ruffled sheer organdy curtains. He said, "Now is the time to advertise these, but every other store will have a sheer organdy promotion too. What can you say in the ad to make people order ours instead of Altman's or Stern's?" So I examined the organdy. It was very sheer. I could almost read a newspaper through it. All of a sudden I remembered my father's perpetual exhortations to observe things. One time he said, "See the blue jay up in the maple tree? Did you notice the pink veins in his foot?" We peered again and saw them. So I ran the ad with this headline:

WANAMAKER'S ORGANDY CURTAINS
SO SHEER YOU CAN SEE
THE VEINS IN A BLUE JAY'S FOOT

The buyer was right. The paper was full of organdy curtain ads. But Wanamaker's had the best response. One woman sent in this note with a big order: "I am ordering your curtains, because they're so sheer I'll see the veins in the blue jay's feet. All the other ads emphasized sheerness too. But I believed your ad. The other ads said 'Sheerer than sheer.' That sounded to me like all that nonsense about the detergent: 'whiter than white,' 'cleaner than clean.' But your simile made sense to me. I could just see how sheer your curtains were."

It was the combination of a sharp eye and a sharp nose that had looked and sniffed years earlier that enabled me to write one of the most successful blanket ads ever written.

Here is what happened back in the middle of World War II, when, you'll remember, there was a shortage of wool. A blanket company came to Gimbels and said, "We can give you thousands of virgin wool blankets, but there's a fly in the ointment—the color. And they're *all* this color—a muddy off-pink." I looked at the dirty pink. By no stretch of the imagination could you call it shell-pink or cloud-pink or baby-toe-pink. Well, what did it look like? Then it all came to me in a nostalgic wave of fragrance—the perfume of a big kettle of strawberry jam bubbling in my grandmother's summer kitchen on the farm. That was it, all right, not the pink of the strawberries but the mauvy off-pink of the fuzz: the scum that rose to the top of the bubbling berries.

In our ad we were very frank about the dirtiness of the muddy pink color. Indeed, I believed that this one drawback was a help, not a hindrance. It provided a believable explanation of why Gimbels, in the teeth of a shortage of virgin wool, could offer this great bargain. Like most women, when I am offered a bargain I want to be given a reason—just one good reason.

I did mention the fact that mauve was the favorite color of the great painter, Whistler, and that Whistler had once said mauve was pink trying to be purple. The ad was really charming. Of the four Gimbel stores, Gimbels, New York, was the only one to buy the pink blankets. The other three Gimbel stores, along with most of the blanket departments throughout the nation, had turned down the promotion because of the bad color.

The ad ran. A woman out in Iowa wrote all the way to New

York saying, "I need blankets like I need a hole in the head, but I couldn't resist the pink of the fuzz that rose to the top of the strawberry jam. I too had a grandmother and she made her strawberry jam on a big wood-burning range in her summer kitchen." (Only a genuine farmer knows what a summer kitchen is—it's an extra kitchen tagged on to the regular winter kitchen and reached by a twelve-foot outdoor walk.)

Thousands of orders poured in—many of them on a wave of nostalgia for the good old days that were themselves rosier and pinkier. All the blankets were sold within a few hours.

VI

Don't throw the book out the window till . . .

You can't throw the book out the window until you know the book. By "book" I mean the grammar that contains all the rules of correct syntax, analysis of phrases and clauses, spelling and pronunciation—all the tried-and-true, old-as-the-hills rules for writing.

People have said things like this to me: "You have a reputation for being hard to work for. You expect your writers to spill out their thoughts with originality and spontaneity, and yet you hit the ceiling if there's the tiniest mistake in grammar or spelling. How can you reconcile wild abandon with painstaking care and caution about observing all the rules? You can have one or the other, but isn't it incongruous to expect these contradictory virtues?"

It's not incongruous. On the contrary, it's much easier to write with that what-the-hell abandon when you know and observe all the ground rules. Working within a rigid framework of guidelines makes it easier, not harder, to be original and spontaneous.

Actors understand this. They prefer a director who is a stickler for the observance of basic rules of acting; that enables the actors to relax and spill out the words and gestures with spontaneity.

Musicians feel the same way about the conductor of an orchestra.

Speaking of rules of rigidity and guidelines—there's nothing more rigid than the laws of a sonnet. But the rules haven't kept poets from writing sonnets.

Mother Fidelia was our English teacher in the convent. (The convent was Sacred Heart Academy, also called Edgewood Villa, on the outskirts of Madison, Wisconsin, giving on Lake Wingra, the smallest of the Madison lakes. This estate was given to the Dominican nuns early in the 1900's by a former governor of Wisconsin, Governor Washburn.) Mother Fidelia was a holy terror when it came to the observance of the ground rules in writing, syntax, word selection, spelling, and punctuation. Some of the freshest, most unconventional writing pops up in a convent. In ours it was safe to make mistakes of over-originality, over-exuberance; but woe betide you if you broke the basic rules of English composition.

Yet Mother Fidelia, for all her severity about the rules of syntax, punctuation and spelling, certainly had an open mind. As open as that of the Mother Superior to whom George Bernard Shaw wrote many of his famous letters. Each letter started with this salutation: "Dear enclosed nun with the unenclosed mind."

The best advertising writing, like the best any other kind of writing, requires an "unenclosed mind" disciplined by a thorough understanding of basic writing rules.

My training in the convent convinced me that an error in English was a mortal, not venial, sin.

At Gimbels we used to give each applicant a brief test: grammar as well as literature and mythology and so on. Here is a sample test:

Who was sulking in his tent, and why?
What was the Buddhists' law of karma?
What is the Plimsoll mark?

Who was Lucullus?

What was the name of Don Quixote's horse?

Why did Alfred let the cakes burn?

What was Veblen's theory of conspicuous consumption?

Who was Caligula?

Why did Diogenes carry a lamp?

Explain Scylla and Charybdis.

What is a Judas goat?

Locate the Flea Market, Rotten Row, Epsom Downs.

Why did Thales fall into the well?

What is a Pythagorean theorem?

The question missed oftenest was "What was the name of Don Quixote's horse?" Nobody ever remembered Rosinante.

The most often missed question in the syntax test was "What is a gerund? Illustrate."

So keep at your syntax until every word is crystal-clear. For two reasons:

1. You will be literate—and that's a rare distinction these days.

2. And as I said before, nothing else will give you the same surge of self-confidence that knowing the English language will give you.

A smattering of grammar, syntax, spelling and punctuation is being taught in the schools in the early grades. Then all the children who have never really understood it are passed on. Junior and senior high-school teachers assume that the children have already learned the basics, so they do nothing about it.

Rigid training and clear explanations could be fun for the children. Learning correct English will not make them stilted or artificial. They'll relax, because they will be filled with self-confidence. They will increase their vocabularies. They will become omnivorous readers, and will be drawn to books as a bee is drawn to a ripe plum.

They will be intoxicated with words. Why are words so important? Psychologists have discovered that we think with words. We don't have the thoughts first and then seek for words to express them. We have to have the words first; then we can think the thoughts. Perhaps this explains why one of the common denominators found among successful people is a large *and precise* vocabulary.

I learned a useful lesson in word precision in my convent school. This convent was set in the middle of a hundred-acre farm. There were lush pastures, hickory groves, and a small lovely willow-bordered lake. And there were chickens. The chickens were the most fun, because the old hens were always stealing nests and sitting in the empty manger boxes in the barn. Carefully hidden in the hayloft, we children would toss handfuls of hay down on the sitting hens—all the while emitting demoniac Phyllis Diller shrieks.

One time the sister in charge of the chickens (we called her "the chicken nun") chased us for the hundredth time out of the barn. As we scampered off, highly indignant, we met Mother Fidelia. "Sister Sabina's mean," we complained.

"Mean?" said Mother Fidelia. "Do you mean she's *humble* or *inferior*? Or perhaps you think she is *stingy*?"

Well, no, we didn't know whether or not she was stingy.

"Well," she said, taking a pad and pencil out of the capacious pocket in her white habit, did we mean *tart, testy, churlish, cantankerous, huffy, pettish, peevish,* or *disgruntled*? Or did we think Sister Sabina was irascible?

We shook our heads violently at "irascible," because it sounded blasphemous.

After Mother Fidelia had rattled off another dozen synonyms, explaining the nuances of meaning, we were ready to make our choice. We finally decided that Sister Sabina was "waspish." She agreed that Sabina was sometimes waspish.

The final choice was unimportant. But the Mother Superior's

insistence upon the right word was. She might have scolded. She might have lectured us on respect for a nun, and that (to mix a couple of clichés) would have rolled like water off a duck's back in one ear and out the other. But, instead, she made us word-conscious. She put over a tremendous lesson in vocabulary by stressing the necessity of selecting each word *precisely*—not sloppily using one word to cover a dozen gradations of meaning.

Everybody can take a leaf from Mother Fidelia's book. He can train himself to look on every object with an unprejudiced eye, and to select the word which most closely suits his impression. In other words, he can learn to *say* what he means and *write* what he means.

Mark Twain put it this way: "A powerful agent is the right word. Whenever we come upon one of these intensely right words in a book or a newspaper the resulting effect is physical as well as spiritual, and electrically prompt."

I had one lucky break. I grew up in a family that was fascinated by words. I'll never forget the day I went down to my Uncle Jim's farm to help his sister Eliza put on the dinner for the threshers. The threshing crews out in Wisconsin were made up of the neighboring farmers plus the two owners of the threshing machine. They were all good solid folk living nearby, usually reserved, calm, and polite. But on threshing days, at dinnertime, these mild-mannered men turned briefly into savages. Like the Gadarene swine rushing down the cliff into the sea, they stormed into the house at the stroke of twelve, tore into the big dining room, grabbed chairs, and, chins down on the tablecloth, began spearing with their forks the corn bread and pickles and everything else spearable, guzzled and grabbed and grunted, and in eleven minutes flat flung out of their chairs and retired to the side hill. They lazed about gossiping casually as though they had all the time in the world until the machine was fired up again. The threshers' dinner had to be on the dot! Any farmer's wife (or spinster sister) in the neighborhood would rather die than frustrate the threshers in their mad lunge for food.

Aunt Eliza and I got to work early. We baked eight pies—four pumpkin, two apple, and two mince. We mashed turnips, scalloped potatoes, baked ham, basted meat loaf, sliced tomatoes—the works. Along toward late morning, while everything was cooking, baking or marinating, we started to get things on the table. Eliza happened to remark that she felt like a "restauranteur" and I, delighting to trip the erudite Eliza, said there wasn't any "n" in "restaurateur." "Oh, yes, there is," said Eliza. "Oh, no, there's not," said I. The argument was on.

Aunt Eliza, like many of the country schoolmarms of those days, was a purist. Her rhetoric was flawless, her syntax shining. I had lost every argument we'd ever had on pronunciation or word derivation or grammar. But not this one. For once I was right. I plumped the big old Century Dictionary right down in the middle of the dinner table and pointed proudly to "restaurateur." Considerably nettled, Aunt Eliza adjusted her bifocals and thumbed through Marshall's *Compendium of Every-day Knowledge*. She still couldn't believe that she could be wrong. She also dragged out Murray's *Historical Principles*. Then, back to the parlor again, and, grim of jaw and stony of eye, she deposited on the dinner table Fowler's *Modern English Usage* and two French dictionaries. By then you couldn't even see a glimmer of the heavy cut-glass dishes of watermelon rind and tomato preserves. Just then the big kitchen clock boomed twelve and the maddening horde descended on a table strewn not with dinner but with a mountain of lexicography. We *never* lived it down.

My prospects as a potential dairy wife were considerably dimmed, but little matter. By that time I had already resolved to become a word merchant. The interminable sparring with Aunt Eliza and other members of our word-addicted clan provided just the background I needed for advertising writing.

My daughter and her husband have been carrying out these round-the-dinner-table English lessons. They have been very successful. I am sure children are being born brighter than ever before. I am sure that at ten I was not nearly so bright as my ten-year-old granddaughter, nor was my vocabulary so large as hers is. Here's proof of Betsy's deep understanding of the basic meaning of a word.

Betsy's mother had asked her to sweep a walk during a light snowfall. Betsy swept away the flakes . . . and more flakes fell. Finally in a burst of revolt, she cried, "This is a Sisyphus job . . . or should I say Sisyphean job? It's impossible. It's undoable! I keep finishing it up and it keeps on becoming unfinished." She had understood more than the literal rolling up the stone which continually rolled back. She understood more than the literal story. She understood the word's basic meaning.

Last summer I tested her on the twenty-five words most often misspelled by college graduates. She got 100 per cent and knew the meaning as well as the spelling. What an advertising copywriter she'll make!

No school, all by itself, can educate your child. The home must help—and help early. So start a nightly English-lesson dinner hour. Not only will it be fine preparation for an advertising career; it will do much more. The only real riches you can keep for the long haul are what you carry between your ears.

VII

Most copywriters are made . . . not born

You can make yourself into an engineer. You can make yourself into a lawyer. Can you make yourself into a novelist or poet or playwright? I suspect not.

But I do believe that you can make yourself into a creditable advertising writer; because advertising writing does not require that rare kind of talent that sustained writing requires. Advertising is a craft, and a craft can be learned. Shaw's advice to would-be writers (somebody said that it was off the top of his head, but even the top of Shaw's head was better than other people's whole heads) was to the effect that a would-be writer should write a thousand words a day for five years—that he should learn to write as he'd learn to skate: by staggering about and making a fool of himself. So write something every day of your life.

Your job in a retail advertising department will make you write *every day*. That probably would not be true in an advertising agency, where, I hear, dozens of trainees are always "waiting in the wings" where they cool their heels for months before they ever get a chance to put a word on paper.

The exigencies of life in a retail store and the necessity to get out dozens and dozens of different ads every day are likely to hurl you into the fray before you are ready. That's good. And that's one reason why you move swiftly up in a store.

The materials a copywriter uses are words. His tools are a thesaurus and a large unabridged dictionary.

A copywriter should actually read the dictionary—go through it in the evenings as if it were what it is: an interesting book. He should make the job a form of recreation.

The point is to dig up fresh new words that have not been worn threadbare.

Take the phrases "bright red" or "bright blue"—isn't the effect more graphic if you say "shrill red" or "sharp blue"? Of course, the skilled writer will use few adjectives and adverbs and many verbs and pictorial nouns. He will also use little surprising words. Instead of saying "it wears like iron," he may say "it wears like pig iron." "Pig" makes it sound more durable.

When I had my own agency we once ran an ad with this head-line: ADVICE TO THE PECUNIOUS AND IMPECUNIOUS. "Pecunious" is a good word which had not become hackneyed. (Incidentally, "hackneyed" comes from the English and French. A hackney was a common ambling horse for hire. In other words, something much used, mean, hence trite, vulgar, commonplace.) I note that although Webster's Second Edition lists "pecunious," the Third Edition does not. I prefer the Second Edition to the Third. Although the Third includes more new words—recent coinages, new technical words, and current slang—it has thrown out some good old words like "pecunious." (Also the Second Edition is prettier typographically and much easier to read. And the illustrations of word usages are culled from the most beautiful English ever written.)

I have always delighted in using surprising twists on old words. Here's part of an ad that was addressed to the trade: to media buyers in advertising agencies when we worked on the *Seventeen* magazine account:

Did you know SEVENTEEN MAGAZINE invented the Teen-ager? Yes . . . we invented her right from scratch. In pre-SEVENTEEN days, being between thirteen and twenty meant you were a void—to be avoided. Like the albatross, nobody loved ya. Department stores ranted on about your being a plague on the market. Decent dress designers never heard of you. There were no teen clothes, no teen sports wear, no teen cosmetics, no teen hairdos. Sensible, sensible shoemakers made sensible, sensible shoes to let you grow in . . . and groan in. You were left by your lonesome and then some. Then along came smart, brash SEVENTEEN MAGAZINE and turned the tune. In our own sweet, unabashed way we found the forgotten foundlings and gave them a magazine all their own. We researched teens' needs, teens' shapes, teens' measurements. Then we went into the market and *made* the market create what the teens had been missing.

We found teen-age girls unkempt and we left them kempt.

We found them inept and we left them ept.

We found them inert and we left them ert.

We found them a bit uncouth and left them couth.

We found them disgruntled and left them gruntled.

We found them maculate and left them immaculate, poised, fashionably dressed.

We found them peccable and we left them impeccable.

We found them insipid and left them sipid.

We found them outlandish and left them landish.

We found them idle and left them busy.

We found them indigent and left them digent.

We found them trepid and we left them intrepid.

We transformed the uncouths into couths, the unkempts into kempts, the inerts into erts! We did it all by speaking to teen-agers on their own terms and in their own language. We learned to teach without preach, and reach the millions of teen tycoons more effectively than any other magazine on earth ever had.

I thought "teen tycoons" summed up rather brilliantly the incredible teen market. I urged *Seventeen* to register the words, even if we had to create a new coined word to do it—such as "Teen-Tykoons." (The "k" instead of the correct letter "c" makes the phrase eligible to be registered as a trademark. The law does not permit a manufacturer to lift regular words out of the language and monopolize them by registering them for his personal use.)

One of the words in the *Seventeen* trade ad quoted above I got from my small granddaughter, who said, "Since the word 'intrepid' means brave, fearless, I suppose that if you dropped the 'in' the word 'trepid' would mean 'scared, shaky.'" That sent me to the dictionary, and, sure enough, I found that's just what trepid means. Of course I should have known it myself from the word *trepidation;* but I didn't.

It's never too early (and never too late) to start playing with words. Because analyzing a word sends one straight to the big unabridged dictionary. And that's the place to go, if you are bent on success, because an enormous, precise vocabulary is one of the only proved common denominators of success. The bigger your vocabulary the more successful you will be in any field—banking, advertising, medicine, real estate, *anything*!

So acquire an enormous vocabulary.

Even if your college sheepskin came from way back near the tail of the sheep, or even if you never finished the eighth grade, you can still be the possessor of a rich, wide, tremendous vocabulary.

Investigators, eager to test captains of industry who had scanty formal educations, approached one tycoon who refused to take a vocabulary test.

He said, "Frankly, I'm scared. I quit school after the fourth grade. I couldn't have much of a vocabulary. I don't want you to show me up before all those smart college fellows who work for me."

He was finally persuaded to take the test, along with the Ph.D.'s in his company. Of course he came out way on top.

You'll notice that humor and lightness go right along with "soft sell." I get pretty sick of those sober pontifical denunciations of advertising copy that is fresh, bright, light, clever, juicy, exciting or witty. I think it's a case of sour grapes. The critics criticize clever ads because they are not clever enough to write clever ads.

Let's just take these adjectives one by one. The opposite of fresh is stale. The opposite of bright is dull. The opposite of light is heavy. The opposite of clever is stupid. The opposite of juicy is dry. The opposite of exciting is humdrum. The opposite of witty is solemn.

A good ad should entertain as well as inform and propagandize. In fact, it can't inform or propagandize unless it *does* entertain. You know it was the Jesuits back in the seventeenth century who made the startling discovery that is the nub of modern progressive education: namely, that you cannot learn unless you are interested.

You can't be interested until something stops you or stirs you or tickles your fancy. No ad is ever sought out and read by anybody except the person who wrote it or the one who paid for it. Copy must cut across the reader's complacency and rivet his attention.

"There's money in mirth," said the cartoonist-humorist-adman-author, Don Herold. In *Humor in Advertising and How to Make It Pay*, he claimed that humor in advertising is so effective it makes most other techniques look extravagant. He believed that grim, solemn advertising was so ineffective that it was unprofitable. In this same book Mr. Herold paid me a compliment that I still treasure, because I have always had such respect for his opinion. He referred to me as "the long-time genius advertising manager of Gimbels."

Speaking of humor and lightness in copy . . . Louis Kronenberger has summed up this matter of the witty versus the solemn in his introduction to *Cavalcade to Comedy*. Mr. Kronenberger says:

The truly insane (because utterly unsound) theory that what is amusing must be less significant than what is ponderous or grim; or that what is witty must be more superficial than what is sentencious or sober; or what is fanciful contains less truth than what is factual—all this is part of an age-old conspiracy whereby those who plod rather than leap, who ponder instead of react, seek to discredit their betters. It was one such plodder, I feel perfectly sure, who first circulated the fable of the hare and the tortoise.

A good ad should be good reading. It should be un-lay-downable. It should also be very pick-up-able. You've heard about the books that "you just can't put down." But you can't put them down until you pick them up.

My motto, with a bow to Hilaire Belloc, has always been:

> *When I am dead, I hope it may be said:*
> *"Her sins were scarlet but her ads were read."*

People said that Fitz would hire only Middle West farm girls and boys. That was not true, of course. I had learned that New York City girls and boys, if they had worked in their childhood, turned out to be just as successful as the country crop. Delivering hot rolls at daybreak or running one's own newspaper route was just as good a working background as was milking cows.

The founder of Wellesley once said that he'd rather have one calico girl than two velvet girls. So would I. Calico carries the connotation of a lively, hard-working, fast-moving doer. Velvet stirs up a vision of a dilettante languidly hovering over a brandy Alexander at four o'clock any afternoon.

One day after I went to Gimbels, *Life* magazine phoned to say it would like to do a piece on Gimbel advertising copywriters since everyone was saying that Fitz would hire only young people who had grown up on a farm and had had to roll out of bed before 5 A.M. to fetch the cows up from the pasture.

So *Life* came down to Gimbels, rolled in its cameras, and a beautiful piece with many pictures appeared shortly. The calico girls were Ruth Timpe, a blond Phi Beta Kappa from Kansas, and Joan Epperson, a brunette from Missouri. It didn't hurt a bit that both happened to be exceptionally pretty. Both girls had not only gone after the cows, but milked 'em!

I have been called the corn-fed, cow-milking copywriter. Corn-fed, yes. Cow-milking, no. It isn't that I haven't tried. But I don't have the digital dexterity to take milk, as the Swiss cheese ads say, "fresh from the cow." Milking requires a rhythmic wrist—which, you will remember, I didn't possess earlier in my career when I was trying to wind bolts of live ribbons at Marshall Field's ribbon counter.

I suppose that one reason I was flooded with publicity is because of the startling juxtaposition of me and advertising: me, a hick girl from a dairy farm; and New York advertising, glossy, flossy, and fashionable. Several articles on me appeared in big-circulation magazines in this country and a few on the Continent. When I announced that Gimbels would interview only Phi Beta Kappas for copywriting jobs, letters of congratulation poured in from university presidents and heads of English departments as well as many Dear-Sir-you-cur-type letters from enraged students. *Time* and *Fortune* and most newspapers ran a paragraph or two on Gimbels' advertising snobbishness. Applications, of course, quadrupled. I believe we had more applications than all other New York advertising departments put together.

You are probably thinking, "No wonder everybody who worked for Fitz-Gibbon was successful—look at the talent pool she had to choose from."

Yes, that probably helped. But when we were obliged to fill a copy vacancy overnight, we picked someone almost at random. And those at-random trainees were all successful too. I am certain that copywriters who pride themselves on high creativity—the ones who always insist that copywriting is an art, not a mere craft—will be infuriated at my idea that high success can be achieved by a pedestrian attribute like assiduity. But it's a fact nonetheless.

Don't worry too much about not being original

I have noted that the biggest stumbling block for most people—male and female, young and old—who would love to break into advertising is the feeling that they are not original enough. They say: "Don't you have to be terribly unusual?" Or "Even though I think I could think up a brilliant sample book that might get me hired, my lack of brilliant fresh ideas every day would soon get me fired. Having to think up things that no one else was ever bright enough to have thought up would be a dreadful daily strain." Or "I'd think of something and then find out that someone had thought of it before me." Don't worry. The word "original" means "that of which anything else is a copy or reproduction." How much completely original thinking is there in advertising or merchandising or politics or medicine? Not much. Not too much is independently conceived in its entirety.

"What I thought I might require, I went and took." And *I* didn't do that. According to Kipling, it was Homer who went and took what he thought he might require. Which brings us to plagiarism. Plagiarism has been defined as "giving birth to an adopted baby." I have never been greatly concerned about people's lifting my advertising copy and ideas. I've already mentioned the fact that my "Nobody but nobody" slogan has been used by the Galeries Lafayette in Paris. For years people have been telling me that they saw it in the Galeries' store displays, window displays, and delivery trucks. A good slogan, like that one, creeps insidiously into the language, and people often lift it unawares. And if they don't actually lift it, they often adapt or adopt it unconsciously. I am thinking of the wonderful Avis Rent A Car campaign. One of the early headlines in the campaign was:

AVIS IS ONLY NUMBER TWO IN RENT A CARS

Over twenty years ago I ran an ad on Gimbels' fashion. At that time Gimbels' fashion reputation was nonexistent. Macy's fashion departments ran rings around ours at Gimbels. I thought it would be smart for Gimbels to come right out and, in a disarmingly frank and humble way, admit that we were not number one in fashion —that we were only number two. The Avis campaign came much later. I'm a pretty good salesman, but not in a class with William Bernbach. He sold his client on being number two. I softened the blow to Gimbel vanity by comparing Gimbels with Sir Thomas Lipton: Here is the Gimbel headline:

WE ARE NOT NUMBER ONE IN FASHION
WE ARE ONLY NUMBER TWO,
LIKE SIR THOMAS LIPTON WHO ALWAYS CAME IN SECOND
(NOBODY EVER REMEMBERS WHO CAME IN FIRST)

But my clients, the merchandise managers of Gimbels' fashion departments, gave out roars like the roars of a wounded bull. They said, "You'll murder us. Stores always have to pretend they are fashion leaders whether they are or not." Which was silly. With the Gimbel fashion performance, it would have been miraculous if I could have persuaded New York that we were a fast, dependable number two.

Another campaign that might have stemmed from a Gimbel one of that period is the Berlitz campaign of teaching foreign languages. I am not saying that Berlitz is a copycat. Let's use one of the current euphemisms. Berlitz' present campaign is "evocative" or "reminiscent" or "derivative" of our Gimbel one on foreign-language records. Our opening headline for the campaign was:

like Sir Thomas Lipto

(the world's greatest No. 2 man),

Gimbels never gets its paws on the cup

Five times Sir Thomas sailed the Shamrock. Five times he came in second. (By the way, what were the names of the sporting gents who came in first?) Neither Sir Thomas nor Gimbels ever won a prize for sailing a yacht, plunging a neckline, or renovating a Look. Unlike Sir Thomas, we've never tried to come in first—in creating fashion, that is. We leave design to the designers. We've never had the urge to out-Sophie Sophie; we've never aimed to be a super-Hattie. But just as nobody beat Sir Thomas when it came to tea, nobody beats Gimbels when it comes to thrift. Sir Thomas may have brooded about his near-misses; he may have needed a brisk spot of Orange Pekoe as consolation brew. But Gimbels is proud of always coming in a fast second. Just let high fashion be high fashion for a wink, and we've pounced on it. That's why you find smart cashmere coats at Gimbels . . . not at $100, not at 89.50, but at $80. That's why you find the silk prints pictured lower left, not at $25, not at $15 but at 10.98. Thrift is Gimbels own cup of tea! (And when they start giving out Oscars for being first with the bargains, we believe that Gimbels will get that Oscar.)

OF COURSE YOU CAN LEARN TO SPEAK RUSSIAN
MILLIONS OF TWO-YEAR-OLD RUSSIAN BABIES
SPEAK RUSSIAN

Like as not, Berlitz, along with Doyle Dane Bernbach, never heard of our ad.

I have long noted that copywriters are like couturiers who often, without any communication, get the same ideas simultaneously—even when they are continents apart.

Besides, it's like the Vikings-versus-Columbus argument. Even if the Vikings discovered America first, it was Columbus who nailed down the discovery which ushered in the modern world. And to Columbus the credit belongs.

I have noticed that the adapter or adopter often does a better job than the person who had the idea in the first place. As the man said, "My wife is a genius with leftovers, it's the original meal that's so bad."

I cannot think of anyone (in retail or national advertising) who has the Doyle Dane Bernbach gift of protesting humility—but not too much humility—in such a delicate charming way.

So even if I had had the merchandise managers' blessing on Gimbels being number two in fashion, I probably couldn't have nailed it down as Columbus did the discovery of America. Like Lief the Lucky or St. Brendan, I'd have been earlier than anyone else . . . but, like them, I would have been unsung and uncredited.

And, many years ago, I presented to William E. Robinson (then publisher of the New York *Herald Tribune*) this slogan: "Who says a paper has to be dull to be dignified?"

A later *Herald Tribune* slogan was certainly reminiscent of mine. The moral: It isn't the flash of the original idea, so much as its steady, sound development. And in steady day-by-day, over-the-years promotion of a product's excellence national advertising beats retail advertising all hollow.

you can have your carriage trade

we're a Horse and Buggy store

(We've always been a horse and buggy store. Even in the dear old days when a "carriage" trade was considered something to be thankful for. Nice old sway-back dobbins trundled up to our door where chestnut geldings and slick landaus slithered up to others. Then, as in these days, we were a mighty plain store. We sold our bombazine and our plush sacques and newmarkets and havelocks without a single fancy frill. We knew then — as we know now — that the customer pays for fancy frills. (Now that is a bit of horse sense worth chewing on.) These are horse and buggy days. This is a horse and buggy store. (We've been horse and buggying for 100 long years. And never in that 100 years have we been horse and buggyer than we are right now. Never have we been so shorn of non-essentials — of be-braided doormen, of dream wrapping paper, of amusing (and expensive) little show case displays.

Thursday starts our gigantic 100th anniversary sale. You'll find our ten great floors burgeoning with bargains. You won't find them burgeoning with beauty. We can't afford to burgeon with both. And you can't afford to let us. A bargain isn't a bargain when the price tag has to include mauve haired mannequins and red satin chairs and carpets with a pile as high as your ankles. Giddap to our once in a century Spring sale. Giddap from Westport and New Rochelle and Roslyn and Maplewood and Bay Ridge and the Bronx. WHOA! (Come in and marvel at the plain, unvarnished, unadorned, ungarnished values in this 100 year old horse and buggy store!)

GIMBELS 100ᵗ SPRING SALE

What I was trying to do with plain old Gimbels was to build credibility for our low-price policy by coming out and admitting frankly to a shortcoming—a shortcoming that couldn't be concealed anyway.

That was not original with me. Twenty years earlier Kenneth Collins had horrified Macy's by breaking a long-time rule. For years the advertising department had been forbidden to mention the tremendous crowds at Macy's, because it was thought that crowds would deter people from coming. In the teeth of this sacrosanct ruling, Kenneth Collins came out with a full page with the headline:

SRO STANDING ROOM ONLY AT MACY'S—
BIGGEST HIT ON BROADWAY

Of course this crowing over crowds didn't keep people away—it helped bring greater crowds.

Just as the Ohrbach editorials today admit that Ohrbach's is an uncomfortable place to shop, not enough salespeople, crowds, an elbow in your ear, no delivery. These admissions all help—not hurt—Ohrbach's.

Just as my ad on plain old Gimbels, describing its strange assortment of smells and peculiar arrangements of merchandise, lured more and more people to Gimbels. One ad I remember had this headline:

WHEN LIEDERKRANZ LAST IN THE DOOR YARD BLOOMED

The smelly cheeses in the grocery department were alongside the Arpège perfume in the cosmetics shop.

Admitting an imperfection is often the shrewdest kind of positive selling. But it takes a good client to appreciate the value of negative advertising.

VIII

How to break in sneakily

Where? New York? Or in your home town? New York, if possible; because just as New York is the capital of everything else—finance, music, painting, theater, retailing—it's also the capital of advertising. But, if you settle on New York, be sure that you have saved enough money to see you through the first year. As a beginner you can't earn enough.

Of course a little financial worry won't hurt—it may even be good for you. You'll be like the rabbit in the old fable. The dog was criticized because he couldn't catch the rabbit. "Well," he explained, "you see *I* was running for fun—but the rabbit was running for his life!" In a way, I was running for my life when I hit New York in the middle twenties. Things had not gone well financially at the farm—in the early twenties. Then when the 1929 stock crash came, everything got worse.

We were in danger of losing the farm that James Fitz-Gibbon had managed so profitably in the middle 1800's. The Prudential Insurance Company held a huge mortgage. Wreathed around the farm deed were about a dozen or more littler mortgages.

Of us four children, it looked as if it would be up to me to make money. My older sister didn't want a career—she just wanted to be a housewife. One brother wanted to be a farmer. The younger wanted to be, and later did become, one of the best basketball players in the Middle West.

So it was up to me, as it had been up to the rabbit, to run for my life. I did. And the dog didn't catch me: I told you earlier how I managed to squeeze into the Wanamaker advertising department.

Things are different today. There are thousands of bright young people for every opening—at least for every copy opening. Competition wasn't that sharp in my day.

How can *you* be that one among thousands?

Well, suppose you want a little experience before you enter the big-city competition. You might think of starting out in your home town or in some largish city not too far away. The odds won't be quite so much against you there.

Be prepared to use all the pull you can. Maybe your rich grandmother runs up a huge monthly charge bill in a local big prestige store. When she is paying her bill, she could ask the credit manager to get you an appointment for an interview with the advertising head. (I have known that to work even in New York City!) A credit manager is very important. And so is any affluent store customer.

Whether you choose your home town or New York City, apply my old test—put yourself into the shoes of the guy you will apply to. Ask yourself, If *I* were the advertising head of Blank & Co. Department Store, what would I want an advertising applicant to say and do? The answer is obvious. He'd want help. Help from a callow, inexperienced beginner? Yes . . . help from anybody.

I always wanted the applicant to have researched thoroughly me, my store, its competitive place in town—and then come up with a sensible helpful suggestion.

Let's suppose your sister's sister-in-law is married to a chap who is assistant buyer in the women's suit department of a big important store. Meet him. Question him—so that the information you get (superficial though it may be) will still lift you out of that low plateau of complete callow ignorance. Ask him questions. How much volume does his department do? Will his immediate superior, the suit buyer, aid in getting you an interview? Or will their immediate superior, the merchandise manager, help? What are the idiosyncrasies of the advertising head, and of his top writers? Of the president of the store? (For instance Bernard Gimbel prefers headlines that contain the word *you*.) How many suits did Blank's sell from the ad in last Sunday's paper? Was that a satisfactory response? (In New York a direct merchandise ad is supposed to bring in—in the two days following the ad—ten times as many dollars as the cost of the newspaper space.) When you apply, you should indicate that you know that. Also let it be apparent that you know a tabloid paper contains 1,000 lines (5 columns, on 200 lines deep). And that a full-size paper contains 2,400 lines—8 columns on 300 lines deep. It would make you appear on your toes to know how much the store pays for space—the price per line in each of the papers. Any little fact about retailing or a retail advertising department lifts you a little above the general competition. A New York store always measures space in lines—not in inches.

How to get an interview

Since every person in a position to hire advertising writers (in department store, advertising agency, or industry) has at least one hundred applications for every opening, it behooves you to stand out in your letter of application.

Enclose a brief résumé (no more than one third of a page) covering all the salient data: place and date of birth, any distinction in high school or college. In a separate section list any employment, even summer vacation employment, arranged chronologically. Don't work backwards.

Your letter must be brief, crisp, impeccable in appearance, syntax, spelling, punctuation. Here is a letter that once impressed me:

Dear Miss Fitz-Gibbon:

I want to write copy for you.

Not only am I able to put words on paper with power and charm, I am also sensational in selling.

I know you have hundreds of applicants, but you don't have anyone just like me. Because I can earn my keep from the day you put me on the payroll.

I have wonderful legs. I can fetch and carry. I'm a demon for speed. If you hire me, I could make it from the advertising office to Miss Hoff-stretter's office in your basement girls' dress department to get her OK in nothing flat. And there'll be nothing flat in the copy I take to her to OK. And it won't contain any irrelevant whimsey; because I know that every store buyer is primarily concerned with her bonus which depends on the volume I can help her bring in. I agree with Winston Churchill, "when there's a serious point to be made, forget humor and whimsey. Make your point with a piledriver."

You see I've been a selling sensation all my life. For eight years during my brownie days in the Girl Scouts, I sold more cookies than any other scout in all Denver.

Money? Anything you can afford to pay me. I well realize that at this point you can do more for me than I can do for you. Pay me peanuts now. But be prepared to pay me pots of money later.

How can I earn my keep right off the bat? I'll wager I am a better typist than anyone in your whole department . . . 85 words a minute . . . never an error, typographical, punctuation, spelling.

Here is my idea: Right now, late in December, you are preparing pages for your big annual February furniture show. I am well aware that your store does not run the usual February furniture *sale;* but you do feature page after page of furniture and rugs. You run thousands of rug listings.

Who will type those thousands of rug listings? Not your razzle-dazzle star writer! Me, lowly me. Or rather I, lowly I. After I type them, I'll race down to the rug department to get them OK'd and race back to your production department—as I did all last summer for Bloomingdale's advertising department.

Why did I suggest rugs? Because rugs are a big profit maker. Like other soft goods, rugs roll up into small storage space. And they don't drop suddenly in value from fashion changes as other merchandise does. Since I want to make a lot of money eventually, I'd like to write copy for a big profit-making department.

I'm your girl, all right. If you can see me at 10 A.M. tomorrow (Wednesday) I could be sitting at your typewriter by Wednesday afternoon.

> Sincerely yours,
> Mary Elizabeth Carter

P.S. How come I know so much about soft-goods profit makers? I have made it my business to know. I read and study every issue of *Retailing Daily*.

What happened? I hired her, of course. I had been feeling guilty; because I knew that *I* should be studying *Retailing Daily*—and wasn't. I figured that having Mary Elizabeth around would teach me many things I needed to know about the merchandising of home furnishings. A letter like this one will do what a good ad does. It'll persuade the reader that keeping his money is less attractive than exchanging it for the product . . . and the product is *you*.

I always used to ask out-of-town applicants, as well as New Yorkers, what they thought of local advertising. I asked them to name the best ads run in New York during the last two months. The smart ones invariably named the best ads. The others dodged the question with "Well, you see I live out in Nebraska and never see New York papers." But the smart ones knew (no matter where they lived); because they had made it a point to follow the New York papers in their local libraries.

Research the store before you apply. Talk to people who work in the store. And research the competitive stores. Talk to people who work in the competitive stores. Be prepared.

Opportunity strikes only the prepared.

While at Gimbels I got a letter from Wilroy, who was teaching English in France. He was a junior Phi Beta Kappa. His letter said that he was wild about advertising, and would come running the minute there was an opening at Gimbels.

We were crammed to the gunwales with Phi Betes, so I had to turn him down. A few months later, this letter arrived from Florida:

Dear Miss Fitz-Gibbon:

If you can't take me on as a copy cub, how about hiring me as your secretary? I offer flawless English, flawless shorthand, flawless typing, and flawless driving. I never get a ticket. I hear that you drive yourself in from Manhasset [28 miles] every morning.

My family owns citrus groves in Florida. I spent all my childhood as a hand in the groves. I get up early in the morning. I learned that in caring for our citrus groves. I could grab an early train at Penn Station, be at your house in time to drive you in so that you'd be at your desk at 8:30 in the morning . . . and you wouldn't be delayed by parking problems.

I hope you find this irresistible.

> Very truly yours,
> Wilroy M.

Did I hire him? Of course; wouldn't you have done the same? He made the product he was trying to sell irresistible. No more parking lots for me.

Like many others, Wilroy was an almost instant success. He was a work grabber, and was turning out some of our best ads while simultaneously breaking in his successor-secretary.

Moral—make yourself irresistible. Offer some extra skill (even a mundane one like typing or driving) that will put you a peg or two above other applicants.

Wilroy stayed with us till his father died and he inherited a million-dollar citrus fortune. But he sorely missed Gimbels. And mostly he missed the stimulating copy department. He used to drop in often, arriving in his chauffeur-driven Rolls-Royce.

40 miles an hour and 50 words a minute

Perhaps you may be thinking, Learning to drive and learning to type would take months and months. This is not so.

I learned to drive in a most dramatic way (I don't mean that I drive dramatically, but that I learned dramatically). Until the day I learned to drive, I had scarcely ever been in the front seat of our old farm Ford. And I had never steered anything in my life, not even a bicycle. While I didn't antedate the invention of the bicycle, in my youth it wasn't the fashion for farm girls to have bicycles.

On this particular day, I remember, my brother Wayne and I were alone on the farm when he was thrown from a horse and broke his ankle. In great pain he crawled to the car and managed to work his way into the back seat, all the while yelling for me.

It was plain that Wayne couldn't drive himself. And it was equally plain that he had to get to the hospital at once. I cranked the old Ford, which, as you cranked it, always crept forward and nuzzled up to your ear. Then I ran around to the door, jumped in, chugged out onto the highway, drove into Madison and into the teeth of Madison traffic, and pulled up neatly at the hospital door —ten miles from the farm. (Wayne now insists that he had to tell me everything to do, but his recollection is clouded by the pain he was in.)

I learned typing quickly too. The city editor of a St. Paul newspaper offered me a reporter's job. But he was about as fond of the hunt-and-peck system as Katherine Gibbs. Every cub who went to work for him typed touch system or didn't go to work for him. I had forty-eight hours before I was to appear as a bona fide touch typist in St. Paul, so I rented a typewriter for two days. I memorized the keyboard, and then I practiced typing for the next forty-two hours of the forty-eight. I practiced in the bathtub, while I was eating lunch, and on the train to St. Paul. I practiced while I was going to sleep. I slept only six hours of the forty-eight, but I think I practiced in my sleep. My fingers were tapping out words whether I was in front of the typewriter or not. So were my toes. When I got to St. Paul, I could rattle along at a 40-word-per-minute clip. Come to think of it, it was more like 50 words a minute.

My crash program for driving turned out better than my crash program for typing. So I don't recommend the latter. Today I am an erratic typist. I never learned the figures. So I hope I won't be snowed under with protests from business schools who recommend a more leisurely program.

It wasn't till World War II that my secret of learning how to learn things was discovered by the Navy. The secret can be stated this way: You learn by doing. But much of the time the thing you're learning to operate isn't around to operate. So therefore you have to practice driving whether or not you're in a car, flying whether or not you're in a plane, and Mozart's sonata in B flat major whether or not you're before a Steinway. By going through the motions constantly—on a bus, during a lecture, in the meat market—you may appear to be off your rocker, but you are learning all the time.

Apply this technique to advertising—live it, sleep it, eat it—and you'll write it, brilliantly.

We'll assume that your letter of application proves to your prospective employer as irresistible as the letters quoted here were irresistible to me. So you have your interview.

The retail advertising manager to whom you apply may well say something like this: "Our merchandise copy seems to be all right. But we are weak in institutional copy. Our store policies are very fine; but when we state them in an institutional ad somehow they sound stuffy and not believable. For instance, when we say that this store will be happy to take back anything you buy if you are not satisfied with it, we come right out and say that this company is dedicated to the highest standards of storekeeping and that we do not consider any transaction final until it is completed to the satisfaction of the customer. There must be a better way to say it."

Then *you* speak up and say, "There *is* a *much* better way to say it. Just let me have a sheet of paper and a typewriter for a few minutes and I'll write it for you."

In less than ten minutes you hand your prospective boss something like one of these, which we once wrote for a Denver store:

RETURN OF THE PRODIGAL SUN . . . LAMP

. . . Store X had a sun lamp. Mrs. Y wanted a sun lamp. So she bought it and brought it home. But through coincidence or clairvoyance, Mr. Y had already bought his wife a sun lamp. "Prodigal" means "wasteful" in Webster—and an extra sun lamp is certainly wasteful. Mrs. Y didn't want an extra sun lamp. So she took it back to store X. Did she get cash or credit with a happy smile? Ah, no. She got a fishy eye and a glacial greeting. The floor manager fired questions at her that would have done him proud if he'd been a Department of Internal Revenue man probing for tax evasions. It's so different here. We greet our prodigal progeny (returned merchandise to you), if not with a fatted calf, at least with a fat credit slip or cash. So, if you've bought anything that doesn't fly right or lie right or play right or stay right or sit right or knit right or soothe your psyche, bring it back. We'll show you that we love you, need you, want you—faster than it takes to dash off a credit slip!

BRING 'EM BACK ALIVE OR OTHERWISE!

. . . Some stores are as happy to see you walk in with a "return" as
with a twelve-foot boa constrictor. They eye your package with the same
horror, fear, and suspicion. They poke at it, jab at it, turn it gingerly
this way and that. You feel like an asp-in-the-grass for bringing the
thing back—just because it didn't fit right or sit right or cook right or
look right with your puce portieres. But we're different. We're no more
ferocious than a day-old kitten. We wouldn't dream of drawing a beady
eye on a lady with a credit or exchange. Whatever the reason—a flaw
in the product or simply a flutter of your woman's prerogative—you
can always bring it back to . . .

DARKEN OUR DOORSTEP ANYTIME

. . . As we say: Some stores are hard as nails about taking merchandise
back. They're like an irate poppa with an erring daughter. They never
want to see the poor thing again. It's not *their* fault if it's imperfect.
It's not *their* fault if it's irregular. But we're a push-over. We're beam-
ingly paternal about anything we sell under our roof. It's our baby.
It bears our name. And we'll take it back any day in the week, except
Sunday. After all, if *we* don't want it, how can we expect *you* to?
Naturally, we think our family of fine famous brands is the greatest in
the world. But, if any of them misbehaves—well, you just come tell
Poppa.

Of course you cannot use these actual ads; because I have already
sold them to a Denver store and they have been run. But they all
prove my point—that for a story to be believable it must deal in
concretes. And these concretes must sound as if they have or might
have happened. Use these as models. You can write one just as
good. You'll notice all three are believable because they are interesting and are not written in the dull talk of the usual institutional
message. Our Denver store reported a flurry of thank-you notes
from customers who said, "Now we know you mean it. Now we
won't be scared to bring something back."

Store heads reading this may think that it will encourage re-
turns. Yes, but that's good. Don't forget that the most successful
profit-making stores in the nation (like Rich's in Atlanta and
Marshall Field's) take *anything* back! Maybe that's why they make
so much money.

One day a smart girl walked in cold and said, "I understand
Father's Day business is terribly important. I hear general store
volume jumps about 20 per cent in those two weeks. I have an idea
for a fresh promotion. Here is the headline: THE OLD GRAY LAIR
AIN'T WHAT IT USED TO BE. The idea is to do Father's den all over
for Father's Day. There is no excuse nowadays for an ugly, old-
fashioned 'den.' A smart store could roll up a huge increase in
furniture, lamps, rugs, draperies, etc., sales by becoming the town's
headquarters for remodeling the old gray lair into a lounging room
or hobby headquarters or sewing center or library-study. It would
be brilliant to make available the services of a smart handy-man
for shelf-putting-up, etc. To coordinate the entire store in this
operation would be the final coup."

We hired her. She had the right idea—she was trying to help.
That's what every store advertising head wants—help. So learn to
look and to see what is needed. And you'll learn to help.

Another applicant walked in once with this headline for Columbus Day:

WHERE WAS CHRIS' MISSUS IN 1492?

We hired her too.

Others may ask, "When I apply for a trainee job, what kind of
writing should I show?" Poetry? No. Not serious poetry. Gay light
amusing doggerel, if it's amusing enough, often makes a good impression. The average big store likes to use a light humorous ap-

proach in advertisements, direct-mail booklets, catalogues, and other printed matter. But no serious philosophizing verse. No blank verse. No free verse.

Occasionally lighthearted verse sells products better than a serious straightforward ad. We ran such an ad at Gimbels at the tail end of World War II. It was about Gimbels' hard-water soap. You are thinking, perhaps, "Of course an ad on soap would sell because soap was very scarce at that time." That's true. But we had run the same size ad, a humorless, no-nonsense direct ad, on the same soap, same prices, only a week before, with only a middling response. But the lighthearted rollicking verses seemed to delight the public, and the sales response was astonishingly high. They were written by Mark Dall, who was a navigator in World War II. Why did Mark's verses sell so much more soap than our solemn ad had done? Perhaps its lightness matched the people's mood of the moment. On the other hand, who really knows what sells anything?

HELL-BENT FOR LATHER

The cumulus is scattered, and we're over Biarritz,
But I'm not so scared of Jerry as I used to be of Fitz.
I'd rather meet a Stuka in a Hermann Goering rage
Than to hear the dread commandment: "Rewrite the Tribune *page!"*

   Hardwater Soap is the only soap for me,
   And I need soap terrifically.
   It's silky as my parachute, it's flawless as a rivet.
   One giant cake, they say, will purify a civet.

   Hardwater Soap! Hardwater Soap!
   Good old Gimbels will give you all the dope.
   Sixteen flavors, fresh as all outdoors
   To glamorize the debutantes, to sweeten all the pores.

Send your son a carton if he's fighting overseas.
One cake will bring a lassie from her high horse to her knees.
Send some soap to Iceland—it's too cold to wash the dirt,
But the Eskimos adore it—it's their favorite dessert.

Buy some soap for Malta and the prisoners at Crete,
The price is like the Allies—almighty hard to beat.
Send a box to Greenland (you know—where all the ice is),
And loudly shout hosanna for Gimbels' lower prices.

Hardwater Soap from the Suez to Gibraltar,
Dramatic at a burial, magnetic at the altar.
Hardwater Soap from Vine Street to Park Ave.
That's what the boys in the bathroom will have!

Hardwater Soap—lemon or gardenia?
For the mighty Army, Navy, or Marineia.
Lave the tired ligament. Suds the frontal lobe.
Hell-bent for lather right around the globe!

Now I see the Channel: a welcome, silver stream.
So I shall fly and fight again, and coming home I'll dream
Of precious jools and step-on stools—sic transit glorium—
Of objets Hearst and liverwurst at the Gimbel emporium.

In any case, it will do you good to learn to write amusing doggerel. Clip the best you can find. Robert Louis Stevenson once said
he had "played the sedulous ape" to several writers. Why shouldn't
you? Try to emulate good writing by other people—in prose or
verse. It won't spoil your own individual style, and will be good
practice writing.

IX

Landing a job on your first call

Earlier I told you how I got a job at Wanamaker's when I first came to New York. I had had no appointment with Joseph Appel, the advertising director. He sent his secretary out to tell me there were no openings on his staff, and that he wouldn't even see applicants till after Labor Day. I scribbled a little note to him. In ten minutes he had hired me. When I returned to Wanamaker's in the thirties, it was to take Joseph Appel's job—he had just retired.

I think it wise to try to push through on your first call. Have a short, crisp, clear résumé in your hand, listing your education and jobs.

One time at Wanamaker's, a cute young applicant came in. She had no appointment, had never worked before, so her résumé showed only the details of her education. My secretary suggested that she make an appointment for a few weeks hence. She demurred. Then, like me, she scribbled a note.

The note said, "As I walked through your housewares department just now, I noticed that you have a large assortment of birdhouses. I haven't seen you advertise any. But here is a headline, nice and short—the way you like headlines: HOUSE FOR WREN."

I told my secretary to let her come in. When she got inside my office she said, "I just thought of a better headline. How do you like this? THE WREN IS DUE THE FIRST OF THE MONTH."

I said, "Is that ornithologically correct?"

"It's right on the button," she said. "The wren outside my bedroom window always comes about two weeks from now. Doesn't it take about two weeks to prepare a retail advertisement for the paper?"

Of course I hired her. I couldn't resist her. Like practically everybody else I have hired in some thirty-odd years, she was very successful.

Would I have hired her a month later? Well, maybe—but who can tell? That would have been too late for the wren house. Would Joe Appel have hired *me* a month later? I doubt it. It's always easier not to see people than to see them. I might easily have canceled the appointment. Or Joe Appel might have canceled it. So push in on your first visit, if you can do it without appearing too pushy.

In my Wanamaker period, I taught an evening copywriting course in the Tobe Coburn School. I had just heard that the only common denominator of success was the possession of an enormous vocabulary. So I made a rash promise to my copy class—all of whom wanted to break into advertising. I said I was going to give a difficult vocabulary test, and I'd hire the one who got the highest mark.

The winner was about the unlikeliest person you can imagine— a sad-faced widow in her middle forties, mother of five, who had never written anything more elaborate than a note to the milkman. I kept my promise and hired her. For these past many years Mrs. X has been holding down the top female job in a big advertising agency. Like everybody else, she again proved that writing advertising is learnable for any intelligent person.

Another widow that I hired in my Wanamaker days was a woman who worked as a shopper in the store's comparison office. She didn't even care for advertising; but when she discovered that it paid better than her shopping job, she persuaded me to let her try. Of course she was successful. She was blessed with normal intelligence. She finally ended up with her own bridal consultation business, for which she did all the advertising and promotion, and did it very well.

Perhaps you are thinking, "Isn't everything too rosy? It's hard to believe that everybody was successful." Well, I can think of a couple of people, both young men, who have been only moderately successful, when they should have been outstandingly successful. But their not reaching the dazzling top was the result of personality quirks. One was a genius—a junior Phi Beta Kappa who graduated at the top of his Yale class. He is now in an agency doing well. But he should be earning $50,000! He's a mathematical genius; he's bursting with originality. But he doesn't want to work. He says frankly that he hates to work at anything. Loathing work of any kind can be quite a deterrent to a dazzling success.

My other genius, Mark Dall, turned out to be the best copywriter I ever had. An agency hired him from his Gimbel copy job—at twice his Gimbel salary. Mark was the father of four and had just bought a house and a lot of land in Connecticut. Instead of continuing his wildly original stuff (which was the reason the agency had sought him out), he turned conservative. He was so eager to keep his big agency job—what with four children and all—that he curbed his wild abandon. And that curbing had held him down.

How fast can a smart girl climb? Well, take the case of Edith, a Phi Beta Kappa, who came to Gimbels after she had a six months' fling abroad. She was barely twenty. We started her as leg girl in the proofroom. In less than three years Edith was making $200 a week. Remember $200 a week then was much more than it would be today in our peak prosperity. Then she up and had a baby and decided not to take a permanent job again.

Edith lives in a Connecticut suburb, and free-lances. She can pretty much write her own ticket. Stores want her to write institutional ads for them. Agencies call her. And the top fashion magazines beg her to free-lance fashion captions and editorials. So far she has been content to write a couple of ads a week—for which she generally gets about $200. With most of her week to herself and her baby, she can make as much as she did on a full-time job.

Is Edith a good advertising writer? She is terrific. Could she write fiction? I doubt it. Advertising, I maintain (many people differ), is much easier than sustained serious writing. How long can Edith keep it up? Won't she need to get back into a regular job to keep in touch with what's going on? I don't think so. The newspapers and magazines keep her in touch in a superficial way. But most important of all, the normal down-to-earth life she is living keeps her in touch with all womankind fundamentally. Edith is living life at firsthand, not vicariously.

One of the great mistakes that many women in business make is to deprecate domesticity. When a woman adopts the sketchy bachelorlike existence of her male office associates, takes her recreation in theaters and nightclubs, she is living an unnatural life that gives her no insight into the lives of the people to whom she is appealing in her advertising. Women have an especial value in advertising, and that value consists of their intimate firsthand knowledge of the lives of other women. When a woman copywriter isn't writing copy, chances are she's trundling a cart through the supermarket, or running orange peels down the disposal unit, or cutting out a sheath, or whipping up a soufflé. That is what all the other women are doing, too. And doing women's work establishes a rapport, an easier communication, among women. Women do most of the buying. Women control more than half the wealth of the country and have the spending of most of the other half. Advertising writing is selling. Doesn't it stand to reason that a woman is more likely to know what will appeal to other women?

A myth persists that women advertising executives live in penthouses high above Park Avenue and spend all their time that they don't spend at the Colony driving between Madison Avenue and Southampton. Not true. Most successful women copywriters are just as embroiled in everyday living as my former cub Edith, who, as I told you, lives in Connecticut and free-lances. Do you know why Edith is so good? Because when an agency calls her to talk about advertising, Edith will interrupt the conversation with "I'll have to call you back—Peter is yelling." And, sure enough, you can hear Peter's little wail all the way from Connecticut. (And, sure enough, the agency will see the fine fruits of Peter's wail in Edith's next piece of copy.)

How domestic am I myself? Very domestic. A few years ago I was written up in *Good Housekeeping* as "Cook of the Month." I'd much rather whip up a batch of my thistledown griddle cakes than spend that time in a nightclub.

And I am a terrific cook—limited but terrific. My excellence is of a negative nature. I merely remove flour. I take a dependable recipe and make it over and over and over—each time shaving the amount of flour. In the case of griddle cakes (pancakes back on the farm) I turn out a thistledown product that is practically flourless. It is a time-consuming, painstaking process. There has to be a smidgen of flour, otherwise one would be pouring maple syrup on scrambled eggs. Which would be preferable to pouring it on thick floury cakes. This shaving down the amount of flour in my sunshine cake once won me a distinction at the Dane County Wisconsin Fair.

My repertoire is not large—griddle cakes, sunshine cake or any other kind of cake and every kind of cookie. And absolutely impeccable gravy. I know that the French brown their meat without benefit of flour. I find that hard to do. So here is my recipe for roast leg of lamb and gravy.

Take a smallish leg of spring lamb. Rub with salt, freshly ground pepper, sage, and garlic. Pound into the skin little pellets of parsley. Rub in 2 level teaspoons of sifted flour—not a powdery particle more! Place in a shallow open roasting pan in preheated 450° oven. After 15 minutes, turn oven down to 300°. When done, place roast on platter. Add 4 cups of strong black coffee to the sputtering brownish goo in the roasting pan. Scrape off the goo and mix thoroughly into the coffee.

I still shudder at the thought of a store-bought cookie or a store-bought anything in the bakery line. Also I never serve anything on damp circles of bread or moist toast points.

This cutting down on flour also results in my making the best piecrust in the world. It is rich and delicate, and it flakes horizontally—never vertically.

I just put a smidgen of flour in a bowl, and then, with silver knives, I cut lard-and-butter into the flour, adding it fleck by fleck, gingerly, sparingly—stopping the minute the mixture becomes handleable.

And, of course, any soft pie filling must contain no flour at all and no gelatin at all. What will thicken it? One or two egg yolks.

A little cognac-and-rum improves pumpkin pie filling.

Remember—just keep your flour down to a fleck, a mite. Then your pie will have that lovely messy collapsible texture. With a silver fork prick the bottom piecrust. Then put the pie into the oven at 350° and bake for one hour till the filling is settled.

I am sure Gold Medal and Pillsbury will never come knocking on my door.

Betty Crocker, your job is safe.

Nevertheless, there are a few things I know. One is to beware of *the pie that came in from the cold*. In other words, beware of refrigeration. Cold ruins food. All cake and pie should be served warm—some right out of the oven, some lukewarm. Never put pie or cake into a refrigerator. The same for most fruits. I'm always shocked to hear people order "ice-cold melon." A melon should be warmish and fragrant—as if it had just been ripening in the sunshine when plucked. Iced tea is the only thing that should be really cold.

Am I as good in all-round housekeeping as I am in cooking? No. But I'm a good all-round houseworker. I am a wizard in basic rough cleaning. I'm a clean-as-a-whistle, down-on-all-fours scrubber. But I'm no good at all in general tidying.

In my suburban days (after the children had gone off to Smith and Annapolis—and the nurses and the young career-bound housekeepers had departed) Wilhelmina, a wonderful Dutch housekeeper, kept the place spic-and-span, closets and bureau drawers and kitchen cupboards organized.

For the past several years Wilhelmina has been living in retirement upstate. But about twice a semester she comes down to New York and organizes me. My desk, always a chaotic mess in my advertising department days, still is a chaotic mess. It takes Wilhelmina about six weeks to straighten out me and the desk. She organizes every inch of the apartment. She pastes up charts in every closet and drawer telling me where everything is and where it must be returned after I have used it. She charts the course my ship should take, but the problem is I keep running into storms. Every time I have an idea, no matter where I am I jot it down, and the result is that there are hundreds of little jottings all over everything—all carrying priceless gems of wisdom. But which piece has what gem? Without Wilhelmina I'd be a ship lost at sea. I cannot live without her tidying genius. And the thought of her forthcoming arrival always bucks me up tremendously; because I know that soon everything will be straightened out.

My complete ineptitude for handling detail explains why I hired only Phi Beta Kappas. Many people have asked me, "Why only Phi Beta Kappas, Fitz, since you weren't one yourself?"

I knew that Phi Beta Kappas were tidy. They'd have to be tidy. You can't get papers in on time unless you're tidy. And retail is detail. Since I am wretched in detail, it behooved me to buttress my advertising department with tidy organized minds.

Things move swiftly in a retail advertising department (where the divisional copywriter is an amalgam of marketer, researcher, media buyer, stylist, as well as copywriter). It was a relief to have people around who could remember that Miss Hamburger's girls' cotton dresses had run in the *Daily News* but not yet in the *Journal-American*.

Didn't our brainy Phi Beta Kappas grow restive and bored when they had to turn out so many unimaginative hard-sell ads (white sales, housewares, clearances, etc.), which are necessary in the overall promotion of a big department store?

They did indeed become restive and bored.

The unimaginative Phi Betes did not stay with us long. They generally moved into agency positions where many of them shone with distinction. Even our elastic hours and two months' vacation could not hold them. But we were eternally grateful to them, because their well-organized work habits and their tidiness of mind were godsends in the bedlam and melee of running dozens of newspaper pages every day of the week. And their presence in the department was a real comfort to me because they never released ads to the wrong papers, as I once did at Macy's: I put the high-priced article into a tabloid and the low-priced one in the elegant Sunday *Herald Tribune*. The heavens didn't fall. Nothing untoward happened. The items sold equally well (considering the cost of the space) in the wrong papers. But each buyer sobbed on my shoulder, feeling that the response was only half what it would have been but for my blunder.

People have asked me, "Wasn't it harder to find the 'wild abandon' type of writing among the Phi Betes?" Not really. The percentage of pedestrian plodders and sizzling soarers is just about the same in the brainiest stratum as it is in the lowest stratum. The original, imaginative Phi Betes we cherished and clung to. They were so sensationally good that they soared to the top and could write their own tickets in agencies, industries, the magazine field, and even in radio and TV.

Anyway, you don't need a Phi Beta Kappa key to be a success in advertising. Probably you don't even need a B.A. to be a brilliant copywriter. But it is better to have higher education. This country is so sold on higher formal education that you need a degree even to get an interview for an advertising writing job.

But if you can't get a B.A. or feel that it is too late to get one now (it never is), don't be downcast. Educate yourself—as did a certain doctor I know. The smartest man I know owes his meteoric rise in general medicine and surgery to the fact that he had practically no formal elementary education. He feels that the lockstep procedure in late grammar school and high school holds up mental development: "Avoiding all that gave me such a running start that nobody has ever caught up."

Of course he did get an education. And he probably inherited good genes. His father was head of the mathematics department of the University of Texas. So he had a fine home library at his command. So well did he go through his omnivorous reading and studying that at age sixteen he wangled his way into a Middle West college of engineering, where his performance in engineering was so sensational that he was admitted to M.I.T. He turned down M.I.T. Instead he chose Western Reserve Medical School, and later transferred to Physicians and Surgeons at Columbia, New York, where he finished near the top of his class. And he's been on top of everything ever since. Both friend and foe concede that he has no equal in his field. He is famous nationally and internationally. He is in his middle seventies now, is a topnotch golfer, threads a needle without glasses, has all his hair and teeth, and is trying to retire; but his patients and their daughters and granddaughters won't let him. His words: "I shiver to think what would have happened to me if I had lolled through a fashionable prep school and Princeton."

He appears half his age, and looks as if he could kick a fly off a wall. That was the test of masculine agility out around Waunakee, Wisconsin.

A formal education is not an absolute requirement for copywriting, but you'd better have one before you go knocking on the doors of retail advertising departments.

I owe a good deal of my success to the cooperation of the English departments in colleges all over the country. They kept me supplied with fresh original talent.

At the suggestion of the head of the English department at Syracuse I once hired a gal who shot to the top immediately. This was at Macy's. In a year Frances was just as good as any of us. We knew it and she knew it.

And I mustn't forget Beth. She had managed to get into the advertising department of a commonplace store in a small town in New Jersey. One day she barged into Gimbels clutching a clipping of a Gimbel ad, and her rewritten version of it. Of course her ad had the Gimbel ad skinned a mile. Before she had rewritten it, she had shopped the merchandise in the Gimbel ad, as a customer, and examined it thoroughly. She had cornered the assistant buyer in the department and found out all he knew. Then she dug into dictionaries and encyclopedias. She probably knew more about that particular piece of merchandise than anyone in New York City. Of course I had to hire her. She had a grown son at the time; so she must have been pushing fifty. She holds down the best woman's job in one of the top agencies in New York.

She too managed to get into my office on her first visit. Be pleasant but firm—don't let secretaries tell you to return later.

I once hired a writer for no other reason than that she could type 80 words a minute. Previously we had had a policy of interviewing only Phi Beta Kappas, figuring that we would save time by letting the colleges do the sifting and winnowing for us. Occasionally we were so dazzled by a fresh, original, limber mind that we grabbed him without checking up on mundane things like accurate typing. Then my copy chief came in one day, saying, "I'm desperate with the new Phi Beta cubs. Let's hire the next good typist that walks in, even if he or she has a face like an ostrich." A young thing who did not look the least bit like an ostrich walked in. She had never been to college, but she could type 80 words a minute. We hired her as a copy trainee. She was a terrific success. We did not know, when we hired her, that she was John Kieran's niece. And, of course, she possessed many, many talents besides the ability to type competently. In short, she was prepared.

One person who's got to be resourceful is a retail store copywriter. At 9:30 of a Monday morning the poor dear is faced by an assortment of buyers with a desk lamp, a vacuum cleaner, some thingummy from the notions department, and maybe an umbrella. From this conglomerate assortment she must shape an alluring advertisement. Don't think it doesn't take resourcefulness, originality, ingenuity, *and* vitality to do it. Suppose a buyer from the basement came to *you* with a bare-root (not even balled, mind you) scragglywaggly three-foot apple tree(?) and asked you to write an ad. What would you do? Let me tell you what a student in my class did. (You well may read closely—I hired her.)

Eleanor had graduated from Wellesley about fifteen years before I bumped into her in the evening copywriting course I was teaching. At the time I was advertising director of Wanamaker's, and the assignment I gave the class was to write an advertisement for some crab-apple trees we were selling in our annual garden sale. I brought one of the little trees into the class—the usual scrawny, dried-up, twiggy thing that never gives an inkling of its future glory. The ad Eleanor wrote showed that she had a talent for the "wide blue yonder" school of advertising writing. What she did was the same thing the people who advertised the old Jordan car did. The Jordan automobile ads were full of everything *but* talk of automobiles. The ads roamed deliciously over winding highways up the bosoms of hills and down through leafy glades, past mountain panoramas, and across plateaus under vaulted arches of azure sky. Did Eleanor picture the scraggly twig we happened to be selling? Did she create a verbal picture of a twig stuck in a clod with some burlap wrapped around it? Needless to say, she didn't. Eleanor indicated her art to be a lush, full-grown, full-blown, heavily laden tree. Her headline was IN THE SHADE OF YOUR OWN APPLE TREE. And the tart, tangy copy fairly sang:

IN THE SHADE OF YOUR OWN APPLE TREE

Big trees from little trees grow. We believe that firmly. That's how we grew. That's how we expect our crab-apple tree to grow when you plant it. Our crab-apple tree costs a mere $1. It's a bit on the smallish side now (three feet) but it gives promise of mighty things to come. Of soft pink blossoms massed against a bright blue sky. Of little red apples set in a mosaic of green leaves. Of quivering pink crab-apple jelly (on hot biscuits). Of snow-covered gnarled branches outside your windowpane. Our little tree isn't very photogenic at the moment; but the photograph above will give you an idea of how it will look some years from now. Better order this minute while transplanting season is on. It isn't every day you get the makings of a great giant crab-apple tree for a measly little dollar bill.

We ran the ad at Wanamaker's, and the trees were gone in the first hour. We also hired Eleanor. Later she went to Gimbels. And then big advertising-agency money lured her away. Her life became glamorous; she married a big wheel and finally got to the rare point where she was having so much fun when she wasn't working that she stopped working.

Remember that for the fifteen years before Eleanor wrote her crab-apple ad, she had been doing nothing but secretarial work. Generally, though, secretarial work doesn't offer a whit of the preparation for writing advertising that changing diapers, ironing husbands' shirts, packing school lunches, coaching the baby sister on the meaning of Suzie's gurgles, and shopping at the local Sears does. I'm convinced that many housewives would make brilliant advertising writers.

And I must tell you about Anna Maloney and the gas stove. Anna was a housewife from Boston—a graduate of Simmons. She couldn't get a copywriting job anywhere in New York. The only opening she could find was a dreary clerical job in the art division of Macy's advertising department. When a buyer came up with a hat or a toaster or whatever to be advertised, Anna accepted the merchandise and gave the buyer a receipt. After the artists had sketched the stuff, Anna phoned the buyer, who came up, collected the article, and returned the receipt. What a ho-hum occupation for a brilliant college graduate!

But Anna kept an eagle eye on the ads that were run. When she saw a feeble ad, she would run down to the department in her lunch hour or relief period and check on the activity of the cash register. Generally the response to a poor ad was poor. Then Anna would rewrite the ad. One day she selected a particularly bad example—an ad for a special purchase of gas stoves.

The bored copywriter never bothered to look at the gas stove, and just lifted her copy right out of the manufacturer's dreary brochure. The ad was a dud. Nobody even came in to look at the stove.

Anna went down to the floor, and examined the neglected sample stove surrounded by idle salespeople. That night, at home, she wrote an ad and marched in with it the next day. The copy was so good that we ran a second ad for the stove immediately. Anna, in a rhapsody over the oven, had included her pet recipe for rhubarb pie. She told exactly how to make it, how one must never paw the pastry, how icy the water must be, and how to cut in the lard and butter with silver dinner knives in order to get a delicate, rich pastry that would flake horizontally. We, said Anna editorially, wouldn't give the time of day to pastry that flaked vertically.

Then she painted such a tantalizing picture of the heavenly pink mess running over the sides to burn and bubble, making a ruin of the shiny new oven, that no woman reader could think of baking such a masterpiece in her ruin of an old oven. Every last stove was sold.

Of course Anna Maloney, who went on to a great advertising career, had more than alertness to the main chance—she had an observant eye. Her rhubarb-pie recipe was so irresistible (and that irresistibility carried over to the stove) because of the particular pinkness with which Anna endowed the rhubarb—the distilled pink of springtime itself with its trilliums and the faint dying pink in the west at the end of a May day.

When I've told this story, young people have said, "I couldn't do such a snide thing. I wouldn't want to rewrite an ad that would get somebody fired."

Don't worry. A copywriter who does a dull routine ad won't get fired just because an applicant presents a better version.

She will be jogged into doing better work, but she won't lose her job.

So fill your sample book with rewritten ads. It's the best way to land a copy job.

If your sample book doesn't wow your prospective boss in a department store, put on a show of wild enthusiasm on your first interview. Department-store hirers often succumb to just that. Here's a case history of another girl who did well:

Ellin came to New York to make her fortune in retailing. She knew that she could go further faster if she were able to get on the college training squad of Bloomingdale's, Abraham & Straus, or

Macy's. It's extremely hard to get on a college training squad. The competition is sharp. Scores of the country's most attractive and intelligent college graduates compete for each place on the squad—which is very costly for the store to maintain. Indeed the investment in each trainee is so great that the store loses money unless the person stays at least two years. The weeding out of the applicants is done through a series of difficult tests.

Ellin was a good student but she didn't shine in math. She was sure that she would flunk the math test—she always flunked math tests. But, luckily, she had a friend who had made the Macy squad a couple of years before. Barbara told her, "There's a trick to it, Ellin. I can tell you how to get in, even if you flunk all the tests. Just pretend you are back in school as cheer leader for a big game. Get enthusiastic. Work up a wild, impassioned frenzy over retailing. Act excited and intensely interested. Lean forward, your eyes wide, pupils dilated, and your lips parted a little, and drink in every word the interviewer says; then summon up all the zest and ardor and fervor that you can manufacture over storekeeping and hurl them all at her."

Well, Ellin practiced all evening—eyes wide, pupils dilated, lips parted, in a transport of elation at the idea of working in a department store. She took the tests at all three stores. She flunked the math at all three stores. But all three wanted her madly. And the personnel departments in the stores she turned down called on her repeatedly to reconsider.

Enthusiasm is always appealing but particularly in a retail store.

Isn't putting on a show, as Ellin did, immoral and insincere? No. Because as I have often noticed, if you want something to be so, pretend it is, and your acting as if it were will make it true. You really will be sincere—it won't be just an act.

So, if your sample book doesn't make you irresistible, let your enthusiasm make you unbeatable. Remember, you'll do all right in advertising copy once you're inside a department store.

Then there was Robert, an attractive young man with a Phi Beta

Kappa key, a B.A. and M.A. all from Harvard. Robert applied to me after I had opened my own advertising business. He said, "If you take me, I can't stay with you long, because I plan to teach English and I'll need to go back to Harvard for my Ph.D."

Practically every 4A agency wanted to take him on as a trainee. Robert said, "I'd rather come to you for two reasons: one, I hear that the big agencies keep the trainees in the mail room for months, and two, although my writing is correct and clear it hasn't that what-the-hell abandon that you like; it's too stiff and conventional."

Robert had analyzed his writing well. It was stiff and conventional—no little explosions, no fireworks, no vivid imagery, no abandon.

We started Robert out helping to write speeches and proofreading my ads. His job was to cross out an imprecise word and substitute the exactly perfect one. He did just that to the ad I wrote for the Northwestern Life Insurance Company. It was a testimonial ad, giving my reasons for having bought an insurance policy for my brand-new grandson, Stephen.

Here is the copy:

I WANTED STEVIE TO BE ABLE TO SAY BOO TO THE BOSS

It looks as if my grandson Stevie, age two, is practicing for it right in this picture. That's fine with me. I don't want Stevie to be a bashful thrall when he gets out into the business world. I don't want him to be shivering in his boots, just because he's afraid there won't be anything to fall back on if the boss blows his top.

I want Stevie to know he does have something to fall back on . . . not so much that it will spoil him . . . just enough to give him some feeling of independence. If Stevie knows he can say "boo" he won't have to say "boo." And I want the same for the girls . . . Lisa, three, Betsy, three, and Gretchen, six.

Nobody but nobody, not even a grandmother, can absolutely guarantee a child security . . . life is too chancy for that. But a grandparent . . . or aunt or uncle or godparent or parent . . . can make sure each child holds a life insurance policy as soon as he can hold a rattle.

Robert's contribution was just one word. In my original copy I had used the word "oaf," which he changed to "thrall." He said "oaf" had the wrong connotation—that "oaf" meant a "lubberly dolt" and that "lubberly" meant "clumsy especially in the handling of a boat." He said, "What you really mean is that you don't want Stevie to be a captive. *Thrall* means *captive*."

Of course I knew what thralldom meant. But I had never heard the word "thrall" before.

Robert was right. He did a good job for us. We *brightened* his writing. He *tightened* ours.

All that fuss over one little word! Was that any way to run an advertising agency? You bet it was! We made money hand over fist, and we had a good time doing it. I was teaching Robert an essential of good writing—how to "let himself go." Robert was teaching me another essential—logical organization of material and precision in choosing words.

Last time I heard from Robert he was teaching English at Harvard.

X

How to write a retail ad

This book wouldn't be worth the paper it's printed on if it didn't tell you—no, *teach* you—how to write a retail ad; how to create copy, what to do about headlines.

There are two kinds of advertising. One, called retail advertising, is very simple. It is a method used by retail stores to sell. The other is a little more involved. It is called agency advertising. It requires a lot of time and planning and a lot of cash and patience in waiting for results. In retail advertising you advertise on Sunday; on Monday you may be sold out. In agency advertising, you allow six months to a year to achieve the same ends.

Now, if you're really serious about this advertising business, you'll settle down and pick up a pencil and take a stab at your first effort—Ad A, a sale ad. Sale ads are the ones that are handed out to cubs anyway. Why? Because they require little of the copywriter. The sale price puts the copy across. You don't have to entice the customer, or wheedle him. The very thought that he can save umpteen dollars on the purchase price of a broadloom rug sends him into a state of excitement. Actually he reasons, "The more I buy, the more I save." So all your ad requires is the head-line with the word SALE as big as your layout will allow it and a comparative price as high as honesty permits. The results should be something like this:

ONCE IN A LIFETIME SALE
BROADLOOM
$9.98 SQUARE YARD
REGULARLY $16.97 SQUARE YARD

Thick lush broadloom of the richness you find in a rug at a much higher price. Aztec blue, mink, vin rosé, Peruvian purple, citadel gray. All cut to room sizes. Wanamaker's 6th floor.

Don't think that I am holding this up as the ultimate in good ad-vertising. I am not. This, however, is the kind of advertising you'll be doing more often than not, when you start out in the average store.

Ad B requires a more suave approach. It is strictly a merchan-dise ad. The word "sale" is *verboten* in such an ad. But you want to create the impression of value, or worth, and probably of fashion. And don't forget fashion is just as much a part of home furnishings as it is of clothes or hair coloring.

All right—the buyer brings in a pair of side chairs. They're a combination of fruitwood and caning. They are $150 a pair. You gather up the layout man and the artist and show how the chairs are to be pictured—one on either side of a French Provincial table in a hall. Now you do a bit of delving in that well-stocked brain of yours and come up with something like this:

THEY MIGHT HAVE COME FROM AMBOISE

FRUITWOOD SIDE CHAIRS $150 FOR TWO

You might have seen these chairs in a little inn at Amboise or perhaps in some small château farther down the Loire. Their gently curved frames of applewood or pearwood show up superbly against toiles or damasks in muted colors. You get these two beautiful chairs for very little more than the price you might expect to pay for one. Use them as side chairs in a dining room. Use them in a conversation grouping in your living room, or in the foyer. Furniture, Seventh Floor.

(And don't forget the floor. A customer wants to know where to go.) There—you've created a mood, an atmosphere. French Provincial at high prices is being sold the length of the land. Here's something closely akin and well below museum prices, *but* the customer feels that he's really in the know when he recognizes for himself the words "fruitwood" and "château." This sort of "atmosphere" goes for clothes as well as furniture. Travel provides a great background for this kind of ad; so do the magazines—if your junkets are strictly the fireside variety.

Advertisement C is an ad that is based solely on facts—on a bit of research that you do perhaps in the library, talking to the buyer, and finally at your desk. Actually the first thing you do before writing any ad is to look at the merchandise under a microscope, as though you have never seen it before. You find out every living thing about it you possibly can.

Let's go back to that broadloom ad. This time instead of a sale price of $9.98 it's the regular price, $16.95. You have to use a very different approach. You don't mention "sale." What then? The broadloom is wool—all wool. This is the story and you find out everything you can about the desirability of having wool in a rug.

BROADLOOM
$16.95 A SQUARE YARD
THAT'S EVERY INCH WOOL

What makes the thickest rug? Wool.
What makes the heaviest rug? Wool.
What makes the warmest rug? Wool.
What makes the sturdiest rug? Wool.

As far back as Bible times rug makers have been weaving their rugs of wool. And rightly so. Wool has the qualities that make the perfect floor covering—the perfect broadloom. These qualities are listed above. What we have not mentioned is that wool takes dye as no synthetic possibly can. This broadloom is woven so closely a pin can't penetrate it. The threads are packed tightly and evenly together for smoothness of all-over wear. Our decorator consultant will help you with your selection of colors. 6th Floor.

At this point you're probably saying, "Why, anybody could do *that.*" Yes, as I have been saying, *anybody* could. *You* could. Just remember the story is right there in the merchandise and you won't go wrong. Here, however, is something a little more creative. We'll call it Ad D. It's an ad that's used to sell a whole department *and* a merchandising theme—maybe a fabric, maybe a color, maybe a style. Here is Lord & Taylor's charming and creative way of handling a fabric—twill in the store's Teen Shop. A cute teen-ager is being shown by an attentive beau how to handle a gun in a shooting gallery. An array of silhouetted ducks swims across the page. The headline is SPORTING TWILLS—BIG GAME FOR TEENS. The ad is gay, lighthearted, and fashionable.

I remember doing a similar ad at Wanamaker's. This time just for a china department—no central theme. We looked at shelves and shelves of china and came up with this headline: AMERICAN CHINA IS OUR DISH. It was illustrated with a sketch of a big corner cupboard with plates, tureens and platters. The approach was historical, telling of the early days of Pennsylvania slipware and coming up to the beauties of the loveliest of American china, Lenox.

You are probably thinking, "Nothing clever about that headline—anyone could think of something as commonplace as 'American china is our dish.' "

Exactly. But the ad won women. Because the writer included a terse history of Pennsylvania slipware, the heavy pottery with the beautiful glaze. The average American woman is delighted with herself if she can show she knows more about slipware than her neighbors know. And Wanamaker's helped her in her reach for status superiority.

Don't put any puns in your sample book, by the way. Most beginners' puns are terrible.

In a luggage ad don't say: "We've come to grips with the weight problem."

In a low-cut dress ad don't say: "Take a plunge."

Forced funniness is terrible. Don't try to be funny for your first several weeks. Just try to be clear and concise and convincing. You may say, "How will I know if my pun is hackneyed?" If it came easily, you can be sure it's threadbare. You'll learn to feel it in your bones when something must have been used before.

One of the most brilliant men in advertising is Paul Smith, who has the research to prove that creative people are less screwball than the non-creative. They make more sense. And they make a bigger profit for their bosses. David Ogilvy proves this in his wonderful Hathaway, Puerto Rico, and British Travel campaigns. Every word, every fact, is masterly selling.

Don't worry if you don't write easily, fluently, abundantly. People come out of a church faster when the church is almost empty than when a crowd is at the door. A master of language has a mind so full of ideas he is apt to hesitate over the choice of words to clothe his ideas. The empty-minded never hesitate. That's why they write so easily, so rapidly . . . so meaninglessly.

How to write a food ad

Cut down on adjectives. Use vivid picture nouns.

The Irish Tourist Board had a lovely ad on an Irish breakfast. I'll give you the copy because it proves my contention that the noun is almost always superior to the adjective. The copy below would make you want to grab a plane for Ireland, get out into the country on the open road—and knock on the door of a whitewashed stone cottage.

. . . fat little Irish farm sausages. Bacon that tasted the way bacon did before they started rearing pigs in factories. A loaf of sweet-tasting soda bread as big as a curling stone. Tea, strong enough to bend a teaspoon. Eggs and scones and good farm butter and fresh-made jam. The cost was three shillings and sixpence. In our language, fifty cents.

True there are a few adjectives. But it is mostly filled with picture nouns that make you see that breakfast, and taste it too.

Here is a good headline for Apricot Nectar drink: DID YOU EVER DRINK AN APRICOT?

Here is an idea for a stocking promotion:

Voltaire said, "Any woman, without an actual hump, can marry whom she pleases." Perhaps he was right. But we *know* this is true: Any woman with beautiful legs can marry whom she pleases. These Cantrece nylons fit your legs like liquid chiffon. . . .

Of course you wouldn't use this type of copy if your story were Cantrece nylons reduced 30 per cent.

And here's how to write an ad on tents (you can approach it negatively or positively):

Negative approach
    Putting up a tent used to be like grappling with an octopus.
Positive approach
    This tent goes up in ten seconds flat.

I like the negative approach because you can use a startle spot showing a man grappling with an octopus—with good shock effect. It will stop a person in his tracks as he riffles through the paper.

Never forget you have to fight for attention. The average person is assailed by 1,500 other sales pitches daily. So you must stop him in his tracks.

When I was at Wanamaker's, the children's buyer phoned his copywriter to say that he was coming up about an ad on girls' and boys' clothing.

He said, "I'll use most of the ad for girls' stuff and the rest for boys. You can just say across the top, 'Smart warm clothes for girls and boys.' "

Up came the buyer. I called in the copywriter and the art director. I had just come across an interesting statistic in a trade magazine. The gist of it was: In America's under-twelve age group there are one million more males than females. "Aha!" I thought. "Everybody neglects the boys. Maybe I can get Mr. X to take a large ad just for boys!"

It turned out that neither the buyer nor his merchandise manager knew this statistic. It was a surprising one, since we all hear so much about there being more females than males in the population—which is true in the older age groups.

Finally I sold the buyer and the merchandise manager on the wisdom of taking a big space. One shout is worth a thousand whispers when you've something to sell.

The copywriter spoke up, "Let's come right out and say that boys have been neglected. They're the most poorly dressed segment of the population. Women have fashion. Men have fashion. Little girls have fashion. Babies have fashion. Poodles have fashion. But boys have leather jackets and faded dungarees and run-down Keds, saggy sweaters, and shiny chino pants."

"Yes," I said, "there's the copy, all right."

"But," remonstrated the merchandise manager, "mothers will resent being told that they are neglecting their sons."

"We'll tell them that tactfully," I said. "They'll really be grateful, because they'll know Wanamaker's is telling them the truth. Let's run this headline: MADAME, YOUR SON IS SHOWING. We'll start right out with some direct truths. It is no longer smart to be a slob. Elegance has trickled in. Suburbia used to be full of females with shirttails hanging out over blue jeans, sling chairs, bucket chairs, low coffee tables made out of old doors, driftwood lamps, window drapes made of mattress ticking, bookshelves made of red brick and blond wooden planks, and block parties and barbecues. Casual living used to be in full bloom with plastic mats, stainless steel knives and forks and TV dinners. But things have changed.

"Now we have sterling silver in an old rococo pattern, English bone china with a rose motif, French Provincial furniture, pale area rugs on dark stained parquet floors. And black-tie parties. And caviar with sour cream and chopped onion, Bibb lettuce, artichokes, champagne, and above all a glittering chandelier. Wanamaker's has sold hundreds of glass chandeliers so far this year!"

"But," said the buyer, "nobody'll read that much copy."

"They'll read *Wanamaker* copy," said I.

"But all that talk will take a lot of space," said the merchandise manager. "I don't want to spend that much money."

"How much do you want to spend?"

"About $450."

"Let's take 1,500 lines—that space will cost $900—but I'll pay half of it," said I, "out of my private kitty."

I always insisted on a private kitty to be used when I felt a good big ad was necessary to increase the luster of the Wanamaker name in a certain category of merchandise.

The next morning the buyer and his stock boy came up with all the merchandise to be pictured. The copywriter saw that they were comfortably seated, and then he questioned them on each piece of merchandise.

"How do you know that that toggle coat is exclusive with Wanamaker's? Maybe the manufacturer sold it to some stores outside New York, in which case you must say 'Only Wanamaker's in all New York has it.'

"How can you prove that your chino pants are the best quality?

What count is the cotton? You say that Looks Brothers are selling the same chino pants for $2 more than you. We can't say that any store is selling it for more unless you get a sworn statement from Wanamaker's comparison shopper." And on and on and on.

Retail advertising people will note that this way of getting information from buyers differs from the way it is done in most stores. In the average retail store whenever a buyer wants an ad, he sends the merchandise up to the copywriter accompanied by a "blue sheet" or "pink sheet" on which he has filled out the details of merchandise, the value, the exclusiveness—everything!

This is a mistake—because the buyer starts to write. I have found over the years that it's a mistake to let a non-writer ever put pen to paper. Once a non-writer puts pen to paper (whether he is a buyer in a store or a client describing his product to his agency) he is carried away by a feeling of authorship. He gets to love and defend words—particularly his own words when he sees them on paper. And his own are seldom the best.

The copywriter and I went on dictating hundreds more words than we could possibly get into the ad. If your space permits two hundred words, there should be two thousand words in your mind. And at least one thousand in your first draft. We wanted the reader to feel that Wanamaker's knew more about boys' clothing than all other stores in town combined.

As I've said, a merchandise ad should bring in ten times the cost of the newspaper space in the first two days after the ad runs. Ten times $900 would be $9,000. Usually there is a price appeal (a reduced item) to get a big response.

Why build up the New Elegance of the suburbs? To make Mother realize that her son has been shabbily dressed and to jolt her into turning over a new leaf. Status symbols and snobbism are powerful sales urges.

Obviously Wanamaker's customers were buying boys' clothes of a much cheaper type than they should have been buying—considering their incomes and social position. They *were* neglecting their boys—possibly spending too much on the girls. A good ad should be like a good sermon: It must not only comfort the afflicted—it must also *afflict the comfortable!*

The result of the ad? It put Wanamaker's back into the boys' clothing business. Manufacturers bought up extra proofs of the ad —sent it out all over the country. Trade papers reprinted the ad. And Wanamaker's boys' business volume increased steadily week by week.

You'll go farther faster in retail than in national advertising

A savage attack on retail advertising was made by E. B. Weiss in *Advertising Age*, a leading trade monthly. Here was the title of the piece: "Why is retail advertising so horrible?" The writer went on to list the reasons: A store cannot attract or hold brilliant talent, a retail ad department underpays employees, overworks them in sweatshop conditions, is torn by internal intrigues, is a veritable den of iniquity, never permits real creativity, produces ads that are dull to read, dirty to look at, and resemble the ads of all the other stores.

This wasn't the picture at Macy's or Wanamaker's or Gimbels. If there was any political intrigue in any of these three stores, I was unaware of it. I was never smart enough to catch on to who was on which side. I am pretty sure though that there wasn't any internal intrigue. There's time for that sort of thing in an agency. But not in a store. Everybody is too busy turning out ads that bring response *bang!* the minute the paper hits the newsstands.

Don't start your career in that never-never agency land

Agency ads often have a strange unreality and seem to float in a never-never land. Agency talent seems to poke along so slowly that there's no sell in the ad. It's all been washed out by the interminable revisions caused by kowtowing to the client, niggling, revising, and revising the revisions, compromising. Not only is there no sell left; what is odder still to a retail person is that neither the agency nor the client who pays the bill *expects* to sell from the ad. Let me illustrate:

There's a radio station in New York that has a dozen daytime programs: talks, interviews, debates, and the like. This station commands the biggest daytime listening audience. During each program ten or twelve different products are on each of the programs all day long. Talk about saturation! It would be similar to a store's running a blouse ad on page 3, and repeating that same ad on pages 4 and 5 and 6 and 7 and 8 and 9 and 10. The paper would be peppered with the same blouse. But of course a store would never do that. Why? Because its first and only small blouse ad would sell out the blouses. So why repeat it on every page of the paper? Apparently not only do an agency's radio ads not sell but nobody even *expects* them to sell. My proof?

I listened acutely over many months and tried to buy some of the products that had had such saturation promotion on the radio. I couldn't. Either they never had existed, or, if they existed, nobody had bothered to distribute them. They weren't for sale in any stores. Indeed, the stores had never even heard of them! If that sort of thing happened in a retail store, the roof would fall in. The buyer of the advertised item would be pounding on the copywriter's door to find out why the ad had brought no response.

Here were the products plugged on radio that couldn't be bought, or even found, in the whole of New York: Energee bread, Uncle Sam's cereal, Brandywine mushrooms, Brandywine chicken livers. When the clients discovered that their expensive commercials hadn't brought a single response, why didn't the clients raise hob as the department store buyers would have done? Apparently the clients didn't even *expect* to sell anything.

Of course I realize that some national advertisers do this kind of thing deliberately—spend vast amounts of money advertising stuff that has never been distributed or possibly has never even been made! It's called market testing. But what shocking waste of a housewife's time and energy. And housewives today are far busier and more harassed and harried than their mothers and grand-mothers ever were.

After many many months of nothing for sale a little distribution occurred for the Brandywine products, which now can be un-earthed after assiduous searching. It still is almost impossible to find the bread or the cereal.

And that's why you should start your advertising career in a retail store.

Remember—if you don't sell, you won't soar, so start your career in a store

The first thing a store copywriter learns is that nothing happens till a sale is made. Nobody makes a cent of money until something is sold. And when something is sold, everybody begins to make money—the manufacturer, the wholesaler, the store president, the copywriter, the artist, the delivery man, everybody! The writer learns that there's an element of excitement in every product and that he must discover it and promote it.

"The moving finger writes and having writ, the thing moves out"

Or it ought to move out. And it does move out of a store. The biggest thrill of our private enterprise system is selling. So if you can't get a retail copy job right away, get behind a counter and sell something. Sell anything. Sell Girl Scout cookies. Don't waste time in an agency where writers don't sell—where they don't even *expect* to sell.

So start your advertising career in a store—a department store. A department store carries practically everything. A big mail-order house would also give you a chance to write about all kinds of things. A specialty store would limit your experience to just fashion goods. However, if you can get into only a specialty store, grab the chance. If you can write a good ad about one thing—be it hat or breakfront or stocking or gas stove—you can write about anything. The only thing you need is to have learned how to look at a thing—closely, peeringly, as if you had never looked at a similar thing in your life. You possibly haven't.

Then pick up your pencil and write down what you saw. Everything. Hundreds of words. Why would anyone want to own this thing? Would you exchange your hard-earned money for this product? What can you promise the prospective buyer? Will parting with her money for this thing make her look younger, prettier? Will it impress her neighbors? Will it make her or her family or her husband more important in the community? Will it be good for her children? And so on and on.

One of my ex-Gimbel cubs has created a sensation in the two agencies she has been with since she left me by appearing a day or two after a copy assignment with fifty-four pieces of copy, instead of handing in one piece after six weeks of mulling.

It's this absence of mulling that makes retail newspaper ads seem

fresher and sprightlier than the ads you see in the national magazines. Retail advertising has a quick spontaneity about it. This is
because it isn't reworked and kneaded and prodded by a whole
bunch of people before it shows up in print. Advertising agencies
have a good many cooks or kooks hovering over the copy. Every
ad is likely to be tinkered with by the media analyst, creative director, art director, psychologist, motivational researcher, client,
sales manager, typographer, photographer, and the president's wife.
What comes out is a camel (old saying: a camel is a horse created
by a committee). Fitz-Gibbon's Law applies here: Creativity varies
inversely with the number of cooks involved with the broth. Or one
head is better than two—or three or four or more. Retail stores
know that two can't think as *cheaply* as one. They can't afford a
committee, so when they want a horse they get a horse—not a
camel. Tepid, reworked advertising is like George Jessel's description of tepid, reworked acting in the movies: "Everybody is working for an Academy Award. Let's say you got a scene where an
actor is saying, 'Mother, Mother, don't die! You can't leave me
now!' Well, first time he does it, it's fine. He's wonderful. He tears
your heart out. Then the cameraman steps in and says there's imperfect tone around the guy's head. Nobody'd notice but another
cameraman. But we have to do it over. Then somebody else steps
in. By the time we shoot it twenty times the actor doesn't give a
darn if his mother is dead or alive, and his acting shows it."

Which brings to mind the story of Penelope, the faithful wife
of Odysseus, in Homer's *Odyssey*. During the twenty years
Odysseus was gone from home and given up for dead, great pres-
sure was put upon the young and beautiful Penelope to choose a
husband from her many suitors. She promised to do so, but only
after she had finished weaving a funeral pall for her father-in-law,
Laertes. Every day, all day, she would knit one, purl two; but at
night she would unravel what she had knitted. In such a fashion
she put off her suitors for twenty years.

All this knitting by day and unraveling by night reminds me

of what a bunch of non-writer executives in an advertising agency can do to a piece of copy. The copywriter weaves all day. The executives unweave the next. Edit. Revise. Revise the revision. Words are fragile things. They can easily be hacked at and haggled over until nothing fresh is left. Once wool or words are pulled apart, they get all kinky and wriggly and scarred. All the King's women can't put them together again.

XI

Get in on the ground floor

I have tried to show you (*you* meaning practically anybody, male, female, high-school graduate, college undergraduate, college graduate, young people now in dull routine jobs) that advertising writing is your best bet. You are probably thinking, "It's too late now. I am a successful bookkeeper. I should have started to prepare for an advertising career fifteen years ago."

Nonsense, you sound like the thirteen-year-old girl whose grandmother had given her a diary for her birthday. Her reaction? "The diary is lovely. But I should have gotten it years ago. It's awfully late to start a diary now. Everything has happened."

Don't think everything has happened in advertising, either. It hasn't. If you get in now, you will start on the ground floor. After all, advertising in its modern form is less than ninety years old— one of the youngest professions. There are all kinds of products and services that have never been exploited at all. *You* could be among the first to exploit them.

Apples had been falling off trees for centuries, and people had been reclining in orchards watching them fall without getting any message, until one day Newton, reclining in an orchard, watched an apple fall, put two and two together, and got gravity. That's why it's foolish to think everything has been done already. Somebody sitting in your place is going to think up something new—or glance perceptively at something old—if you don't do it first. "Creativeness" often consists of merely turning up what is already there. Did you know that right and left shoes were thought up only a little more than a century ago?

Charles Helser, one of the best merchandising men I have ever known, once saw an immense stock of pewter porringers for babies. They had been lying around for years in a wholesaler's stock room. "Porringers are out of date," the owner of the porringers murmured sadly to Charles in a reminiscent tone as the two of them were passing the porringer mountain one day. "And even if they weren't, what could be more old-fashioned than this Early American design?" Charles looked hard at the porringers and made a deal.

The wholesaler could hardly believe his ears—not that the price was so high (it was rock-bottom) but that a smart merchant would fall for porringers at all. Now, the usual markup that a store tacks on for this kind of promotion is 40 per cent. Charles marked up his porringers over 55 per cent, and Gimbels had a sellout on the first ad! He advertised them not as porringers but as ashtrays. And what do you suppose was his principal selling point? He played up the authentic old-fashioned Early American design.

They say that David Ogilvy tests the creative ability of a prospective employee by having him think up a completely original product and then prepare the advertising and publicity to launch and sell it.

Try to think of fields that are virtually unexploited, where practically nothing has been done. One of these can be your "field day"; the prospects are astronomical.

I have always been fascinated by General Robert E. Wood, the genius of Sears Roebuck. Of all the thousands of retailers of that day, General Wood was the only one who looked into the future with clairvoyance.

Legend has it that about the time of World War I General Wood was the only retailer who understood clearly the immense effect that the low-priced automobile was going to have on America. Before World War I, people riding in cars were heckled with "Get a horse!" Not till the war was almost over did most people realize that the car was here to stay and would eventually be an important means of transportation. But General Wood saw far, far beyond this. He could shut his eyes and see the throughways and the freeways of today with miles and miles of cars inching their way along the roads.

In those days practically everybody worked within walking distance of his home. And practically everybody went to school within walking distance of his home. But General Wood saw that the car would change all this. He saw the suburbs springing up, the developments opening, the shopping centers blossoming.

General Wood saw that people would be working and children would be going to school many miles from their homes. He saw how all this would affect the lives of all people. In other words, General Wood used his head to think out *how* Americans were going to be, *where* they were going to be, what kind of furniture they were going to sit on, what kind of clothes they would put on their backs, where they would want to do their shopping. He thought it all out so well that he gave Sears a giant push ahead—so far ahead that nobody else has ever been able to catch up.

The future—you can color it rosy. As the affluent society becomes more affluent and widespread, you'll find that more and more people have more money, and more time to spend it.

Well, let's take a look into that fabulous future. The population explosion will make people long for privacy. They will no longer want to huddle in little developments with ranch house on top of ranch house. The workweek will shorten to three or four days. The weekend will lengthen to three or four days. So a family will need *two* homes: a close-in, convenient one and a far-off, outdoor one for getting away from polluted air, smog, and noise. This second home will be a real home—two million have been sold already. But almost 200 million families will want one. A beach bungalow on Fire Island, a mountain lodge in the Poconos—you name it, people will want it, and have it with your help. I can see a headline now: GET READY FOR THE SECOND HOME COMING!

Of course this second home will have its own dishwasher. And so will the regular home have a dishwasher. When you think what a small percentage of homes now have dishwashers, it does seem that Americans (despite the fact that their standard of living is the highest that the world has ever known) are still living like peons and peasants. Today when the young bridegroom carries his ecstatic wife over the threshold, the dear girl doesn't realize that she's facing the washing of 85,000 dishes in the next twenty years. How can she feel cherished when her pinkies are buried in dirty dishwater several hours a day? But she won't wash the dishes. She'll rebel. And her husband will rebel too. (Europeans smirk over the fact that there are more male dishwashers in America than in any other country on earth.)

So plan on selling millions of dishwashers and millions of clothes dryers. If I had to choose between indoor plumbing and a dishwasher, I'd take the dishwasher.

And I can't understand why appliance manufacturers haven't put a clothes dryer in every home. The advertising copy can be so convincing.

You know it sounds sacrilegious, but it's true—electric drying is better for fabrics than God's sunshine. Don't have the little woman age before her time. Pamper her. Don't let the honeymoon end too soon. Can't you just picture her, "a prisoner of the gutter" or the basement, or just plain downstairs, as she lugs the wet wash from the washing machine into a rickety basket, and up and out to the garden clothesline? Better to have stayed home with Mama than to face such indignities.

The market is there and it will be there . . . and it's your job to motivate it. Plunge in and sell the desire for electric dishwashers and the desire for electric dryers. You'll have a ball doing it.

Then of course after a family has lived half the week in pure fresh air, it will demand air purifiers and air humidifiers in its city home. These things are now necessary because everyone has become so aware of air pollution. In Grandmother's day, provided Grandmother didn't live in the very shadow of the locomotive roundhouse, whole weeks might go by without one speck of soot alighting on Grandma's row of hollyhocks, on Grandma's starched shirtwaist, on Grandma. The sky was washed and clean, the air was free from contagion and pollution, the west wind carried no heavier cargo than the scent of honeysuckle or perhaps a tiger swallowtail butterfly. Grandma took a bath only on Saturday night —because Grandma didn't get dirty till Saturday night. Comparatively, Grandma's world was squeaky clean. But today is the day of the Diesel, of internal and external combustion, of blast furnaces and turbines, of oscillating and reciprocating and triple-expanding engines, of incinerators and power plants—all of which load the very atmosphere with dirt.

Since the whole country has a "thing" on physical fitness, be prepared to sell everybody all sorts of exercise machines and equipment. And be prepared to sell totally different play equipment for children.

No longer will a sissy little swing and slide and sandbox suffice. It's been proved that American children, whose legs are wonderful, are, because of bikes, flabby from the waist up. While European children are climbing trees, our American children are cruising around on bikes. Be prepared to feature Irish Mails (they are also called Row Cars) and climbing ropes and climbing ladders.

For years F. A. O. Schwarz on New York's Fifth Avenue has been selling these to the upper crust. From now on the bottom crust is going to demand everything that the upper crust has. The physical accent, for adults and children, is on "vigah"—and "vigah" in the cultural pursuits as well as the physical.

There will be a great demand in the music department. Psychiatrists have found that the families who *play* together *stay* together. There should be a great demand for musical instruments. The guitar is very much in fashion now, thanks to the Rolling Stones, the Dave Clark Five and many others. But the vogue may change. Who knows how many instruments will be popular in 1985?

And many Americans are going to travel for the first time in their lives. (Do you realize that over 50 per cent of Americans have not been over 200 miles from home? And over 60 per cent have never been in a hotel or motel?) What will that mean? More cars, car equipment, and really lightweight luggage. And really chic wash-and-wear clothes. ("Love 'em and lave 'em" would be a fine slogan for wash-and-wear clothes.) Air travel will be most important . . . and so will ads on air travel. My imagination somersaults with glee when I think of the millions upon millions that will be spent on advertising. When Doyle Dane Bernbach took over Eastern Airlines advertising, they flew the copywriters assigned to that account (via Eastern, of course) to every stop on Eastern's schedule. Their copywriters returned, in two weeks, knowing intimately every sound, smell, and pulsebeat of air travel. What fun to be in something like that!

And the shoe field is wide-open. A well-dressed man should own a dozen pairs of shoes. Now he owns fewer than two. Women should own many more pairs of shoes than the four they now own. In a child's shoeiest years, he needs ten pairs of new shoes a year; he gets only about three. These facts have never been told to the public. Think of the thrill of being responsible for perfect adult feet rather than the crippled dogs that now waddle, mince, strut, or shuffle.

Where are the customers' yachts? . . . Right there in the marina

Nothing gives so much privacy and quiet as water. So prepare for a gigantic boat boom. For some people, their second home will be a boat. And why not? What a wonderful market for sailboats, yachts, yawls, launches, and whatnots . . . including all their accessories. The future ahead is unlimited. I envy all of you.

And here's another idea—wall freezers.

The average apartment provides a refrigerator that has only one main door. That means that the small freezer inside the refrigerator is of little use. Unless a freezer has its own door, it will not keep ice cream, and will not deep-freeze many things. A smallish built-in wall freezer would be much more valuable to me than a wall oven.

And of course storage problems present a wonderful opportunity for inventive geniuses. The average house has too little storage space. Apartments have practically none.

A good ad comes out like a man fighting bees

I imagine that we will see the return of hot and heavy competition. In recent years I have missed the ferocity we used to have in advertising and promotion. I have a hunch that it will come back. "Sanforized" has started it with "Be suspicious." And many of the carpet companies have become combative. Advertising can be interestingly combative without becoming bitterly denigrating.

Now stretch your mind and speculate about that future we colored rosy a few pages ago. Some philosophers hold that our very affluence will ultimately kill off the "passion for possessions" that enabled Americans to capture more comfort and luxury than any society, civilization or nation—ever. All the rupees of ancient India couldn't buy the comforts of electric living.

But, the argument goes, when everybody has practically everything, possessions will be so taken for granted that we will no longer seek to acquire them. Status symbols will then leap from the *thing* area to the *cultural* area. Even now we are experiencing a cultural explosion.

The most important possession modern man is now acquiring is *time*. More and more leisure hours for play, relaxation, reflection, and thought. You can see it happening all around you. One wants to excel one's friends by becoming a brilliant conversationalist, a great pianist, lecturer, writer, dancer, world traveler or well-informed and active citizen. Of course this transition from things to culture will take time, and will probably not come before the year 2000 A.D.

I think, therefore, we can count on three decades of hot, heavy competition for things—acquisition competition. So, fill the inkwells, sharpen your pens, polish your writing skills, and leap into the thick of it now.

If you start preparing for your advertising career right now, you will also be preparing for the switch from material possessions to mind-perfecting cultural skills which may or may not come about in 2000 A.D. but which will come sooner or later. Your advertising career, with its heaps and heaps of attractive dollars, will give you the edge over your contemporaries. Your writing skills will have been polished, you'll be literate, your English will be flawless, your cultural enrichment (obtained through your preparation for an advertising career) will give you a Golconda of the best and finest that has been thought and written all through the centuries of man's long and audacious climb from ape to angel. And you will have that as long as you live.

Ready for a career in advertising? What are you waiting for?

XII

Thrift was thrust upon me

From my earliest years on the farm, thrift was thrust upon me. That turned out to be good. Thrift was my rabbit's foot. My two famous slogans featured thrift.

Except at Macy's, where I was not responsible for the whole budget, I have always had to struggle to make a too-small advertising budget stretch out to cover a lot of things.

I went back to Wanamaker's in the middle of the thirties at $25,000 a year. Why did I leave Macy's? It was during the Depression. Macy's wanted to cut my salary; and I didn't want my salary cut.

The one advantage I have had in my career is that I have always had some independence. My husband was a successful lawyer. That's what two incomes (instead of just one) do for a family. If I had been the sole support of myself and my two children, I would have had to take the cut in salary, and I'd have lost my chance to make a dramatic success in both Wanamaker's and Gimbels. That's why I think it's so unrealistic for people to say, "A woman can always help her husband most by staying at home."

How did I happen to go to Wanamaker's the second time? Dorothy Shaver, president of Lord & Taylor, had told Wanamaker's that they'd be crazy in the head not to get my magical pen to work to lure crowds into that lovely old deserted building too far downtown.

At the time, I was out on the farm in Wisconsin building a glamorous 100-foot barn with a bubble fountain and salt cup for each of our pure-bred Guernseys and Holsteins—Holsteins for quantity and Guernseys for creamy quality.

Why wasn't I home in the suburbs trying to become a suburban matron? Because after one week's trial, I knew I'd *never* be a contented suburban matron. So Wanamaker's wooed me over the long-distance phone—with all the Waunakee neighbors listening in on the party line.

I was delighted to get back to New York. But I was shocked when I set foot in Wanamaker's. Having recently been in mob-jammed Macy's, I was dismayed at Wanamaker's empty, cavernous aisles. I'd have to fill them up with human bodies.

Now, a man is more concerned with his dignity and achievement, and is always eager to align himself with prestigious going concerns. A woman, who is seldom concerned about such things, is likely to go into a business that is going downhill and help shoot it up as fast and as furiously as possible.

Wanamaker's offered me just such a challenge. I knew I had to change the store from a sleepy old downtown emporium whose advertising consisted in pious pontificating quotes from the Sayings of the Founder, to a crisp, up-to-the-minute store just as lively as its uptown competitors. I also knew that (this is the kind of thing a woman knows which a man doesn't) if you are going to change something, you should change it lickety-split the moment you take over the new job. The average man says, "I am not going to change anything. I'll just sit by and observe for the first six months." By the seventh month he's out!

Because business was off, the Wanamaker advertising budget had been severely reduced. There was little enough money for salaries and media. There was almost nothing for art. And there was absolutely nothing for publicity, crowd-getting events.

Could I do it? Of course. I knew I could sell. And the product was lovely—a fine honorable aristocratic institution, not unlike a gently bred delightful old dowager who had fallen on hard days.

I remembered what a famous fashion expert—I believe it was Edna Woolman Chase of *Vogue*—had said: "The two requisites for being beautifully dressed are 1) taste, and 2) a severely limited budget." "Mediocrity," the fashion expert had said, "is the result of having too much money to spend." Well, my advertising would not be mediocre because of having too much money to spend.

So having been poor as a church mouse in my youth proved to be a blessing now.

I decided that everything we published at Wanamaker's would have to be very very interesting to women. I realized that every ad would have one strike against it. It seemed to me that New York had become bored with Wanamaker's and especially bored with Wanamaker advertising.

What interested people most? I had noticed that almost every new magazine featured "Letters to the Editor." *Time* and *Life* did this right from their very start. Even the stately *New York Times* devoted half a page to letters from readers. Evidently people liked to read other people's letters. I'd have to write ads that provoked letters . . . and then print the letters, and often our answers to the letters.

An analysis of the letters in *Time* magazine and in *Life* proved that readers knew they were actual letters; because the pans as well as the puffs, and the brickbats as well as the bouquets, were always printed. You know that "a little bad always makes the good believable." I know a placement executive who always makes up a slightly derogatory shortcoming so that a prospective employer will believe all the important good things he is saying about an applicant. That's what I did when I went to Wanamaker's. That's what Doyle Dane Bernbach has been doing most effectively for its client, Avis Rent A Car.

How could I get readers to write letters to Wanamaker's? By jolting them. As the Irish say, we'd have to "create a disturbance." We had to be unforgettable.

An obvious way to become relatively unforgettable is to take off your clothes and turn cartwheels the length of Fifth Avenue. But this will earn you other attentions as well.

Plainly, being unforgettable (pleasantly so) is not a matter of a single, stirring, startling, dramatic performance. Instead, pleasant rememberability depends upon the sum of a lot of little things, each as perfect as possible in itself.

A person rises above his fellows as a brick building, made up of a lot of little (unforgettable) individual bricks, rises on the skyline; as a colossal coral reef, made of lots of little (unforgettable) coral skeletons, rises to the surface of the sea.

I realized that I was going to have to be more than just unforgettable in describing articles for sale.

I would have to think up irresistible store events to lure crowds of people in. I was going to have to line up specialists to talk: authors, cooking experts, decorators, skiing instructors, baby nurse experts, children's psychologists, book reviewers, and so on. I'd have to clear out the advertising department, make all the help put on their coats and hats and go down to fill up the emptiness and pretend they were customers, so as to make our publicity events appear more successful than they really were.

In a situation as desperate as this, I'd have to write appealing and powerful ads: ads so irresistible that readers who had not darkened Wanamaker doors in decades would be forced to come in. And I'd have to sneak some money out of the media budget and use it for promotion and publicity.

This was just at the time when the 1939 World's Fair was in the planning stage. All the stores in town were running full pages on the Fair. And there I was, without a cent to make a handsome gesture! That was especially bad, since a Wanamaker director, Grover Whalen, was running the Fair.

But I had an idea and called in *Cue* magazine. I wanted to make Wanamaker's the Information Headquarters for the Fair. I wanted to hire a beautiful female who would know more about the Fair— what to see, where to go, how much it would cost, and so on—than anyone else in the U.S.A. We would feature this know-it-all genius far and wide and everybody would race down to Wanamaker's (and we meant *down* because Wanamaker's at that time was on Eighth Street in New York).

I found a lovely attractive location for this beautiful female— but who would pay her salary? Would *Cue* magazine pay it if we called the girl "Susy-Cue"? *Cue* would. *Cue* did.

And the beautiful Susy, who came out first in a grueling examination on everything about the Fair, became the most-knowledge-able-about-the-Fair person in the whole country. (The following year she married a handsome New York department store advertising director.)

The crowds came. Susy-Cue's office was jammed all the time. Hundreds of people wrote to her from coast to coast, called on her when they got to New York and wrote thank-you letters to her when they got back home.

The cost to Wanamaker's? Practically nothing. We promoted her, not in full pages—just in little "corners" and "ears" which I call p.p. ads (position protectors) tucked in over a big ad to reach to the top of the page. I resolved to use them often.

A position protector took at most 100 lines, maybe fewer, and cost the store at most only $50. Actually they didn't cost anything, because the layout artist just used the regular amount of space and squeezed each merchandise item a little.

Then I asked myself, "Besides letters to the editor, what interests women?"

Food, of course. Recipes. Cookbooks. All through the Depression, cookbooks sold merrily—even gourmet cookbooks, although the readers couldn't possibly afford to buy the costly ingredients needed to make the dishes. Recipes have been credited with building the enormous circulation of the women's service magazines. Obviously, women were mad about food.

When I learned that *The New York Times* (of all papers) published more than 1,300 recipes a year in its daily pages, I knew we couldn't emphasize food too much.

I got my interest in food from the farm too. There was always much talk about food. "Did you notice Aunt Charlotte's pie on Thanksgiving?" asked a critical member of the family. "It was too tidy. Tidy pies are always bad. Her lemon pies are too neat and trim. A good pie should shiver and shake and collapse in a mess on a plate."

> *Can she make a messy pie,*
> *Billy Boy, Billy Boy?*

So our ads for the Wednesday night dinner in Wanamaker's restaurant made a note of this: "Wanamaker's lemon pie trembles as it's placed on the table." People would jam the restaurant and ask for "that lemon pie that trembles." When the public picks up foolish little phrases verbatim in their speech or letters to the store, then you've hit the target!

Several people, including the top brass in the Wanamaker Philadelphia store, criticized me for running too much copy. They said, "Who will read that much copy?" My answer, "Nearly everybody." And I'd pull out letters to prove it.

One time we featured a special Thanksgiving turkey dinner, and we said that if you came early enough you could get the choicest part of the bird (that little tidbit that goes over the fence last) called the "parson's nose" or the "pope's nose." Mr. Shipley, president of Wanamaker's, New York, heard, with his own ears, customers ask, "Are we too late to get the parson's nose?" That silenced my Philadelphia critics for the time being.

We had no competition from other stores in advertising our restaurant. Other stores, with excellent (maybe better) restaurants, would never peep about them. Why? Because their brainy young men, with slide rules and Harvard Business School training, could prove that a store restaurant could not really make a profit and therefore must never be promoted.

It was a good thing that Wanamaker's did not know too much about the highbrow orthodox theory of retailing. Because our trembling pies helped build a booming furniture business. Late night openings always increase furniture business because both wife and husband can be present. Soon our furniture floors were more crowded than any other furniture floors . . . in all New York. People came to eat in our wonderful restaurant and stayed to buy our beautiful furniture. We kept featuring food in our ads. (Pretty soon meeting one's husband every Wednesday night for dinner at Wanamaker's became the *in* thing to do.) Of course we had critical letters on food: "You are crazy to stuff a goose with prunes." And "Whoever heard of such a ridiculous thing as crumbling little pork sausages and big Brazil nuts in turkey stuffing?" And so on.

On holidays we'd offer special dishes for which we'd print the recipes in our little p.p. ads. I remember particularly a St. Patrick's Day feature:

Scallion Champ: Peel and boil eight medium-size potatoes in salted water until tender. Cook six scallions in a pint of milk. Drain potatoes dry. Whip the potatoes. Beat in the hot milk and the scallions and continue beating until smooth. Add pepper and salt and butter.

The biggest flood of food letters came after I had run a boost for our Wednesdays during Lent. Lenten Wednesdays at that time permitted Catholics meat only once a day. Wanamaker's New England clam chowder was the best in town. "The secret of our clam chowder's excellence is the salt pork in it," we advertised.

Protesting letters deluged us. "You know Catholics don't eat meat more than once on Lenten Wednesdays. Take that salt pork out of your chowder."

Another letter said, "I was so delighted that Catholics can put salt pork into clam chowder on an Ember Wednesday. I think I always knew it; but your announcement was almost like an imprimatur or at least a 'nihil obstat' from the Vatican."

I called the Cardinal's residence. And the clergyman who answered was as broadminded as if the Ecumenical Council were in session. He said, "That little bit of salt pork is perfectly fine. Keep it up. New England chowder needs it." (He must have been a Bostonian.) He went on to tell me that theologians call a minuscule flavor (which is not an ingredient really, just a faint tinge of flavor) "*parvitas materiae.*" We came right out with a headline: PARVITAS MATERIAE, assuring people that to eat that little bit (a paucity of material) of salt pork on a Lenten Wednesday was quite all right.

Does all this sound pretty silly? Well, it was just such foolishness—the prune-stuffed goose and the collapsible lemon pie (the messiest in town) and the *parvitas materiae*—that was jamming the store when it was open at night, and building the Wanamaker furniture business into the biggest in town.

We even got the owner of a good nearby restaurant (Billy the Oysterman) to write a protesting letter to us saying that all his customers had started to demand messy pies. We answered his protest in a little p.p. ad at the top of our page.

Whenever our Philadelphia mother store criticized us we'd take a customer count on the furniture floor on Wednesday night. We could prove that Wednesday night openings at Wanamaker's New York store were pulling in lots more customers than the Philadelphia store Wednesday nights. That was all we had to do. We were really making Wanamaker's famous coast to coast.

Then I looked around. What else could I learn from the women's magazines? It was women we wanted most of all. Women gossip more. Women would be more likely to chat among themselves about a p.p. ad that read:

HAVE YOU NOTICED THE CHANGE IN STAID OLD WANAMAKER'S?

We wanted women to say things like this: "I was down at Wanamaker's the other day, first time in years, and I ran into the most fascinating fashion show. The clothes were terrific—just what Wanamaker's used to carry back in the good old days. And the fashion show was different. It featured dance dresses for cocktails and evening. It was a *dancing* fashion show—all the mannequins who wore the fashions danced with Arthur Murray. Maybe you saw the ad. And there were male models who danced with Katharine Murray."

How did I happen to think of the Arthur Murray dancing fashion show? Same old thing. We were strapped for money. Models were expensive.

Arthur Murray had the best dancing school in New York. It occurred to me that instead of hiring models for a fashion show, we could have a tie-in with the dance studio. Our clothes would be modeled by the Murray dance instructors, who looked good as well as danced well. Then Wanamaker's would not have to hire models. In payment we would plug the studio in our ads. Our little p.p. ads were headlined:

WALTZ ME AROUND AGAIN, ARTHUR

This Wanamaker dancing fashion show made the Murray Studio widely known. Later the Murrays gave similar dancing fashion shows all over the United States. The Arthur Murray fame had a meteoric rise which blossomed ultimately into a very successful TV program.

I bequeath to posterity . . .

If I were asked what I believe to be my biggest contributions to retail advertising, I'd have to list the ingenious use of those tiny-space image-sell editorials way up near the top of a page. They were run at the top of an eight-column ad, and we called them "buildups" as well as "position protectors." I hear they are now called "stoperettes." Years ago they were called "ears."

Now, I certainly did not invent "ears"—they have been around a hundred years. They've been used for store hours, telephone numbers, or addresses. But at Wanamaker's, I began to use the space to stop and stir and startle.

Remember, it's not just the size of the space, it's the size of the idea. Every "buildup" had to be specific—not dreary editorializing generalizations on value and dependability and all the other dull abstractions that stores, even today, waste their good money trying to put over.

Incidentally, an unbiased survey showed that these Wanamaker buildups were the most read items in the papers we used except for front-page news!

Sometimes it pays to be smarty-pants.

One of the most famous of our little position-protector ads stated frankly that some people were reading Wanamaker's advertisements just for the sheer fun of reading them. The people were a group of Divinity School students up at Yale. Maybe Divinity students want but little here below—and maybe they were picking up that little at local stores in New Haven. Anyway, the ads had all kinds of repercussions.

No sooner were the morning papers on the street than the Wanamaker top brass phoned from Philadelphia: "Miss Fitz-Gibbon, you are supposed to be selling Wanamaker's—*not* beautiful prose."

Pompous advertising experts around town were caustic: "Now Fitz has really put her foot in it. She actually admits that people read her ads for the writing in them."

Ah, but there were lovely repercussions too. We heard from twenty colleges whose instructors in composition told us that the Wanamaker ads were discussed regularly in their classes. We *were* selling the store, in a silken, insidious way that is the very apogee of salesmanship, to all kinds of people in every state in the Union. Here is our follow-up p.p. editorial:

Our ads are an

"George, will you please bring me 'Bartlett's Quotations' and the French dictionary? I want to read Wanamaker's ad about moth balls."

THERE'S A YALE DIVINITY THAT READS OUR WORDS, ROUGH-HEW THEM HOW WE WILL

On the second day of spring, a Yale Divinity student walked into Wanamaker's advertising department. He turned out to be a delegate from a group of forty. Every morning the members of the group read the John Wanamaker ads. This Divinity representative went on to tell us that whenever we missed being in the morning *Herald Tribune*, the Divinity students were desolated. Wouldn't Wanamaker's please see to it that there was a Wanamaker ad in the *Herald Tribune* every morning?

Then we ended our advertising message by saying that, although the Divinity students enjoyed reading the Wanamaker ads, their emissary admitted they didn't buy much.

Things were going swimmingly at Wanamaker's. Ads were pulling. Departments were jammed. Business, in all departments except fashions, was booming.

education in themselves!

Helen Hokinson's dear lady is quite right. Our advertisements demand admiring study. Not even the bright aphorists of the "New Yorker" staff mold a metaphor with a defter hand. Yet no woman was ever won with fair words alone. We are sure the increasing thousands of women who read, avidly, studiously, our daily contributions to the press, find them much more than an education in versatile verbiage. They find them an education in intelligent shopping, a quick, sure guide to the right thing at the right price.

While Miss · Hokinson's housefrau admires our etymology, she bows also to our entomology. She knows that we know what kind of moth ball (a generic term) will most quickly purge any lepidopterous aggressors. She knows we won't let moths bore her winter woolies. She knows *we* won't bore *her*.

But I had to spend too much time and energy struggling with the heavy hand of the heavy institution, Wanamaker's Philadelphia. The Philadelphia top brass resented my throwing out the "Sayings of the Founder," which had been displayed for decades across the top of every Wanamaker page. They were pontifical, boresome, musty, and fusty. I am certain that old John Wanamaker himself, if he had been around, would have tossed them out. It was he who said, "I am sure I could cut out half my advertising and save money. Trouble is, I don't know which half."

Another problem was the curious holdover from former days of glory that afflicted many of the store's employees. I had been imbued with thrift for so long (early farm years and my twelve years at Macy's) that I couldn't see why any New Yorker would bother coming all the way down to Eighth Street unless there was some saving in money, however little. It made sense to me, because we were certainly out of the high rent area. Many of the Wanamaker buyers agreed and cut their prices slightly. Soon our ads carried a mild "lower price" note. I was congratulating myself on having developed into quite an entrepreneur. But I had a sharp awakening when I happened to overhear a conversation between a customer and a Wanamaker doorman. He was the magnificent be-all and end-all of all doormen—almost seven feet tall and dazzling in his gold buttons and gold omelet shoulders, the epitome of snobbery and dignity. Here is what I overheard a smartly dressed woman saying to the doorman:

"I am delighted with the new Wanamaker's. I just found a wonderful bargain—a man's golf jacket that was priced $8 less than the identical jacket at a famous sports store uptown."

Our magnificent doorman drew himself up in hauteur and said, "Madam, there must be some mistake. This great John Wanamaker store never undersells anybody. Wanamaker prices, here and in Philadelphia, are usually higher than any other store's prices!"

A well-run store is one whose philosophy of retailing is understood by everyone in the place from the president right on down to the doorman. That cohesiveness, that oneness, was never true of Wanamaker's. The Wanamaker store-running philosophy always reminded me of the little dachshund whose head didn't know what his tail was doing; it's older than the hills—I don't know who wrote it:

> *There was a dachshund once so long*
> *He hadn't any notion*
> *How long it took to notify*
> *His tail of his emotion.*

> *And so it was that while his eyes*
> *Were filled with woe and sadness*
> *His little tail went wagging on*
> *Because of previous gladness.*

But what bothered me most was the top brass's tampering with my copy. We had run a successful promotion on Shaker furniture made upstate, in Lebanon, New York. Then we followed it up with Shaker fashions. My copy made it clear that the demure little round white collars and other innocent touches were deceptive. I said that the clothes were really sexy and rich. The phone rang: "Miss Fitz-Gibbon, you must take out both of those offensive adjectives—'sexy' and 'rich.' Our customers are not sexy and rich. They would be insulted with the implication that they *wanted* to be sexy and rich."

"Goodness gracious," I thought to myself. "Here we are in the middle of the Depression fighting for business. Everybody ought to want to be sexy and rich. We must have the wrong kind of customer. Wanamaker customers want to be non-sexy and poor."

I offered to take out the word "sexy." I'm always ready to concede a comma to achieve a paragraph. But that wasn't enough.

Sometimes hard-sell ads sell soft and soft-sell ads sell hard

So when Fred Gimbel called on me to say that Gimbels hard-sell ads were not selling hard and that his shoppers had reported that Wanamaker's soft-sell ads were pulling tremendous response, I lent an attentive ear—especially when he added that he would pay me a percentage on the increased volume of business.

Perhaps Wanamaker's was my biggest achievement. At Macy's, the great thrust forward was due to brilliant merchandising as well as brilliant advertising.

Same thing, in a different way, at Gimbels. But at Gimbels, the brilliant merchandising coups were sporadic. At Macy's, they were a day-in, day-out, everyday affair. At Wanamaker's, it was mostly words, words, words, wonderful words that accomplished the miracle and on a very tight budget.

So in 1940 I cleaned out my desk and moved into Gimbels. Kenneth Collins, who had left Macy's a few years earlier for Gimbels, had just left Gimbels to go to *The New York Times*.

XIII

The Macy miracle and the magical mix

I have never heard a good analysis of the Macy miracle that astonished the whole business world in the twenties and thirties, but I'll give you *my* analysis right here and now. That sounds like the small boy who told his mother that he was drawing a picture of God. She said, "Nobody knows what God looks like." The little boy said, "When I get this picture finished, everybody will know."

How did a big, old, homely discount store suddenly, in the middle twenties, start a dizzying upward climb and, in no time at all, almost while nobody was looking, make itself into the biggest and probably the finest store on earth, the General Motors of all department stores?

It was my luck to be at Macy's during some of those epochal years. And it was Macy's luck that I was there to wrap up this upward soaring in five wonderful words: "It's smart to be thrifty." And four of those wonderful words were monosyllables. Ever since 1928 when I coined the slogan, just one week before my son Peter was born, Macy's has used it.

And it was Macy's luck *and* my luck that the man at the Macy fashion helm at that time was the incredible Eddie Marks.

Eddie Marks was one of the three geniuses I have worked with—Fred Gimbel and Kenneth Collins were the others.

The older I get, the surer I am that genius consists of continued sustained attention: the ability to concentrate totally—complete absorption. Most of us are scatterbrained. We think about too many things. Therefore the attention we pay to any one thing is wandering and unfixed.

Eddie Marks's attention was fixed—fixed on how he could make Macy's the headquarters for the finest merchandise, and at the same time keep up and add to the gigantic volume. Up till then, everybody agreed that a store had to choose between being quality or quantity—it couldn't be both.

My slogan, "It's smart to be thrifty," was a succinct summing up of the startling new philosophy that thrift and elegance were not mutually exclusive. Up to that time, Macy's commanded respect because of its rigorous honesty coupled with its sharpness in knowing how to cut prices and practice storekeeping economies which made it possible to stay in business.

But Macy's had little entrée to manufacturers of top-quality merchandise. Macy buyers had no recognition in the *crème de la crème* resources of Paris, London, and other world centers. Indeed, few Macy buyers could even set foot in the exclusive Seventh Avenue fashion houses.

Eddie Marks set out to change all that, and he used my slogan to help him do it. Inspired by Eddie Marks's concept of a store that could be both quality and quantity, and aided and abetted by my five-word slogan, Macy's entered its incredible golden era. Macy's decided to appeal to the rich—knowing full well that on the heels of the rich pour the unrich: the people who spend all the money.

Of course most of Macy's volume lay in inelegant areas—Bronx Renaissance furniture, work pants, cotton housedresses, muslin sheets, and cast-iron skillets. But, under Eddie Marks, the merchandisers began to sprinkle through every department a smattering of top-quality, even exotic merchandise. The aim of this was to appeal to the urbane, sophisticated customer whom Macy's needed to lure the unsophisticated, not-so-moneyed customer. Increased volume always depends on the unmoneyed customer—there are more of her.

Macy's thought nothing of pointing proudly in an ad to one of its duck presses (even though you could put Macy's duck-press volume in your eye). At Macy's you could even buy exquisite Danish silver, English bone china, shrimp deveiners, or a tiny little hat direct from the Avenue Montaigne in Paris. You couldn't buy very much or very many, of course. But the fact remained that at Macy's you could buy almost anything that entered your head.

Perhaps people are foolish, but a housewife who never in a million years would want a duck press would rather buy (other things being equal) a frying pan at a store that stocked duck presses than at one that didn't. Appearing to "trade up" can be a beautiful way of increasing the movement of more earthy goods.

Macy's did more. Macy's did everything in its power not to offend the taste of Mrs. Astor. True, we did not float rose petals in finger bowls at the lunch counter; the only finger bowls at Macy's were for sale (but even *having* an assortment of finger bowls for sale was something). We didn't employ Diego Rivera to paint frescoes on the walls of the ladies' johns, or spray Chanel No. 5 onto the customers as they came in and out. Macy's, in other words, was less afraid of sins of omission than sins of commission.

The advertising was cleaned up. Layouts no longer assaulted the eye. Type no longer screamed in noisy braggadocio. We began to reason with the reader, quietly and persuasively, instead of beating him over the head with a wagon tongue. Mrs. Morgan would never have hung a Macy ad alongside her Renoir in the morning room;

but at least no Macy ad insulted her intelligence. Macy's also improved the windows, interior display, the signing, and the housekeeping. And it worked! The rich trickled to Macy's. And the unrich—with all the money—thundered after them.

Just about this time Macy's appointed a new furniture buyer. He was a squat, tough, terse Scot who had pushed his way up from the very bottom. He had no taste, no posh ancestry, no background, and not even the slightest knowledge of color or harmony or design or decor or the history of furniture. How did he fit into this new upping policy of Macy's? He didn't. But he had plenty to offer—a powerful personality, probably a genius I.Q., and an incredible gift for getting the most out of people who worked for him. So what did Macy's do?

The story is that Macy's went to the head of the Metropolitan Museum and asked him to find an assistant—someone of impeccable taste and genteel breeding—a refined, fastidious blue blood from a good old family. (As Cleveland Amory says, a good family is one that used to be better.) The blue blood arrived at Macy's exuding frigid hauteur. As Ring Lardner would have said, "She resembled a duchess looking at bedbugs"—haughty and supercilious, but patrician and unimpeachable in taste.

To make a long story short, Mr. A and Miss B built a furniture business that was the amazement of the whole retail world. They combed two continents—he using his horse sense, and she using her thoroughbred sensibilities. They started the Corner Shop and filled it with the finest antiques. They ran a negligible yearly volume in furniture up to more than $13,000,000.

Later the Scot landed the gentry. They married and retired to Arizona, building a fabulous ranch second only to the famous Hearst ranch.

You see, these two proved the Macy contention that what retailing needed was the Renaissance Man (a whole, abundant, cultivated person—a twentieth-century kind of Leonardo da Vinci).

More and more, that sort of person got into the merchandising picture at Macy's.

In this furniture instance, it took two people to make one da Vinci. But ever since, the most successful retailing stores seek out a da Vinci type in one person. That is why my urging you to start to dig deeply into the humanities, to start a learning dinner hour in your own home, is the shrewdest kind of practical advice. Even the haphazard course in the humanities that I got on a dairy farm from 1910 on gave me a giant push. When I was graduated from the University of Wisconsin in 1918, the University offered me a teaching fellowship in English and a chance to stay on for higher degrees. I turned it down because I was tired of being poor. Retailing gave me a surcease from poverty and a good time.

To get back to my "It's smart to be thrifty" slogan: Every good slogan needs someone in a high place to protect and promote it.

Eddie Marks was in a high place; and he protected and promoted it. Protected it from whom? From everybody—including Ken Collins and me. Ken and I would have used it everywhere and on everything. And, eventually, like most advertising people, we would have tired of it and dropped it.

But Eddie ruled that "It's smart to be thrifty" could be used only in ads for Macy's Little Shop, which was born about the same time as the slogan. And Eddie did more. He ruled that every ad that carried the slogan must be hand-set, which meant that instead of the regular machine typesetting by a newspaper, which cost the store nothing, the "It's smart to be thrifty" ads would be set by hand in the shop of a typographer. And Eddie even selected the typographer—the immaculate, impeccable shop of Fred Farrar, who charged more than anyone else. Away back then, Eddie Marks was aware of "graphics."

Most of us in advertising had never even heard the word "graphics," which of course is all over the place today.

All kinds of other changes were going on about this time at

Macy's. There was intellectual ferment and experiment and excitement—such as what Washington, D.C., experienced when Franklin D. Roosevelt brought in his brain trusters from Harvard. It was very much like the days when John F. Kennedy lured the Schlesingers and Sorensens and McGeorge Bundys and Kennans and Hellers to his New Frontier.

Macy's was no longer merely a step on the way from manufacturer to retailer to customer. Macy's became a creator of some of the finest things ever conceived in the mind of merchant. Of course, there were other brilliant minds besides Eddie Marks.

The fabulous triumvirate (Jesse Straus, Percy Straus, and Herbert Straus) was there. They were all over the place and all into everything: rubbing a finger under a counter to find a fleck of dust, combing the advertising proofs to weed out any minute inaccuracy or exaggeration.

Macy Whiz Kids still rule retailing

Oswald Knauth, a former professor of economics at Princeton, also came into the merchandising picture. And dozens of young tough Turks, both male and female. The egghead was in the ascendency. It was smart to be smart. Soon Macy departments were filled with Phi Beta Kappas and Ph.D.'s and even Rhodes scholars. Extraordinary ability sparked every merchandise division. To name just a few: Helen Needham, considered the best decorator in the United States; Joseph Kasper, who revolutionized housewares, china and glass (he later became president of the Associated Merchandising Corporation); Walter Hoving (now chairman of the board of Tiffany), who left his faultless taste on everything he touched; Helen Murphy, who built the greatest underwear departments in existence; the Misses Ruth Katsch and Celia King and Helen Feree, who took females of all ages out of prim dowdy spectator dresses and created a new kind of sportswear dash that has influenced fashion ever since; Robert Magowan, once a buyer of handbags at Macy's, now chairman of the board of the Safeway chain; and Joseph L. Eckhouse of Macy's and Gimbels, now president of the Grand-Way chain. And recently the brilliant Steven Osterweis left his Gimbel post to become president of A.M.C., the nation's leading retail organization.

Jack Straus, who took over from the triumvirate, continued to search the world for top talent. It was he who brought in the famous author of the pay-as-you-go plan, Beardsley Ruml, who became treasurer of Macy's.

In one fell swoop, the new Macy operation killed the "ribbon counter complex" that had kept top talent away from retailing. This new operation compelled the most brilliant college graduates to apply for jobs at Macy's, and it compelled customers to come to Macy's. If the rich wanted the finest modern rugs—the modern movement was just coming in—they *had* to come to Macy's big cash emporium for the very simple reason that they could not find the finest things anywhere else, either here or abroad. Macy designers had designed the rugs themselves and had taken the designs to Sweden, where Macy's experts supervised their production, and of course Macy's had sewed up the entire supply.

Something like this happened in almost every department. One of the brilliant young Macy Whiz Kids of the time was Jed Davidson, who went to France on a buying trip. Jed was a buyer of curtains and draperies. When he returned, Macy's staggered the entire merchandising world with hand-blocked chintzes from France—the quality that hitherto sold for $7 and $8 a yard. Jed now sold them for 79 cents a yard! Davidson's 79-cent chintzes had more freshness and charm than competitive chintzes at ten times the price. Another Davidson coup revitalized the textile business. He came back from the Continent with the sleeve of a costume worn by a Bohemian peasant and a gay apron from the Balkans.

These two imaginative fragments sparked a series of fresh textile designs of which Macy's sold millions of yards. A few years ago Jed Davidson retired after having served as president and chairman of the board at Bloomingdale's.

The hitherto closed doors of quality manufacturers swung open to Macy's now. I am not sure whether Macy's store-wide modern promotion was the first, but Macy's Forward House was certainly the most elegant. In many categories, Macy's began to carry the most high-priced merchandise made: the finest bone china in the world, including many new designs, all of course confined to Macy's.

Macy's was also the first to introduce "Color in the Kitchen"— hitherto no pot or pan came in any color but dreary institutional white.

At the bottom of it all was just this: Macy's never underestimated the taste or intelligence of the American public. Macy's, way back in the middle twenties, began to chart its course on the assumption that the general I.Q. of the United States would go up, not down. "Egghead" was never a term of derision at Macy's. Eggheads flocked to Macy's. There was little flying-by-the-seat-of-the-pants and little buying-by-the-seat-of-the-pants or writing-by-the-seat-of-the-pants. Science entered in—but did not take over completely. There was always room for originality.

Besides the eggheads, Macy's was smart enough to cherish a different type. Bea Rosenberg, the first woman vice-president Macy's ever had, retired a few years ago. She still retains an ebullience and a bounce-back resilience that were most inspiring to us copy-writers over thirty years ago.

Whenever Bea, who was merchandise manager of a good chunk of the soft-goods business (hats, shoes, slippers, accessories, etc.) brought up an item to be advertised, she was bursting with an enthusiasm that was infectious. This same limitless vision was a characteristic of Macy's best merchandisers. They felt that nothing was impossible, that there was no limit to what they could accomplish.

An illustration: One day Bea brought me a bedroom slipper and said, "Fitz, you must write this ad so I'll get orders from all forty-eight states." I said, "Why would a woman in Red Oak, Iowa, need to send all the way to Macy's for a pair of bedroom slippers?" Her answer, "Because nowhere else in the world can she match these slippers in looks or comfort."

So I wrote the ad with a headline saying we expected orders from forty-eight states. Bea bounced up later, triumphant but not satisfied. "We got thousands of orders from forty-six states. But, Fitz, we didn't get a single order from Utah or Nevada. Let's go back in the paper and jog those odd people that live in Utah and Nevada to send in orders."

I wasn't quite sure what I'd say; but that evening I took a pair of the slippers home with me to the suburbs. After dinner, I told the problem to my family—my lawyer husband, my son, Peter, home from Annapolis on holiday, and my high-school-age daughter. I said, "Now just suppose *you* are a woman in Utah or Nevada —what could jolt you into sending for the slippers?" Peter asked, "How bad are her old slippers?" So I said, "Wait and I'll put on my worst old slippers." I did. They were pretty bad. "They are awful," said Peter. "Your feet look like two dead rabbits."

There was my headline: "Come on, Utah and Nevada. You are the only two states who did not order Macy's unbeatable slippers. Throw out your old slippers that look like dead rabbits and get your order in. We may not have any more for another six months." Orders poured in from Utah and Nevada—as well as more orders from the other forty-six states.

It was Bea Rosenberg who bearded the exclusive snobbish designer, Paul Rodier, in his Paris den. Instead of humbly requesting him to sell Macy's, Bea drew out a scissors from her handbag and slashed one of his yard-wide scarves crosswise. As he gazed aghast,

Bea told him what was wrong with his $25 and $30 scarves. "They are big and bulky, and make women look old. You have sold a lot because they are so beautiful women can't resist them. But you aren't selling many to young women and girls." So she threw a big bulky one around her shoulders. Bea was—indeed she still *is*—a good model. She said, "See? It adds years to me." Then she modeled one of the small triangles she had just cut. The great Rodier was astonished and delighted. Rodier quickly adjusted his scarf machinery to Bea's new dimensions. His astonishment and delight grew with the years as the triangular Rodier scarves sold by the millions! And sold for under $5 instead of $25 and $30. *He* made more money. *Macy's* made more money. And women looked younger. Yes, those were the days when one could do anything at Macy's.

I forgot the Queen's tea

Bea Rosenberg had her head in the clouds, never edited anything fresh out of copy; but her feet were firmly on the ground, which was lucky for me one time when I ran an Easter headline. The ad was on women's hats—matrons' hats—and my headline was:

EASTER RIBBONS AND BOWS
AND NOT A QUEEN MARY IN THE LOT!

(In millinery parlance a "Queen Mary" was a dowdy dowager hat.) Luckily, Bea took out that last line before the ad was released. Because Jesse Straus, head of Macy's, who had just been made Ambassador to France, was at that very moment being entertained by Queen Mary at tea in Buckingham Palace!

What has been the most successful advertising in the whole history of American retailing? To my mind, it was that Macy golden era that was sparked and crystallized by my "It's smart to be thrifty" slogan. That was in 1928. From then on, Macy's advertising, under the aegis of Kenneth Collins, changed the Macy appeal from a shrill, hysterical pounding for business to gentle reasoning, couched in simple, sophisticated, the-way-people-talk words. Never again did a Macy fashion ad say "Dame Fashion dictates, and Milady acquiesces."

Spending a couple of days in your local library reading the files of *The New York Times* for that era would be a good investment in time for anyone wishing to break into the retail advertising business.

Macy's new relaxed easy sell was keyed to appeal to the "best brains." The best-brained, the highly educated, the better-heeled, in any community, are but a tiny minority. But this tiny minority —the "thought leaders," the "upper crust," have an incalculably large influence on the bottom crust and the vast filling in between the top and the bottom crusts. Appealing to the better-off sophisticated upper crust won't lose you the bottom crust. Quite the contrary. Walter Lippmann, in his *Newsweek* column (November 23, 1964), analyzed the reasons for the continued growth of the Democratic party. This piece provides a good illustration of the wisdom of the Macy change in advertising and merchandising from 1928 on.

Since Mr. Lippmann is a better putter-down of words than I am, I'll quote him:

STRENGTH FROM EGGHEADS. Because the Republican leadership has been so wrong on the great problems of American public life—on the issues of war and peace, on the issues of economic progress and social welfare —it has repelled the best brains of the oncoming generation. The Democrats, on the contrary, under Wilson, under Franklin Roosevelt, and under Kennedy, have sought out and wooed and provided attractive careers for the talented.

It is no accident that the Democratic Party has been overwhelmingly stronger than the Republican in the colleges, among scientists and scholars and artists, among the great intellectual communities in the cities. The Democratic Party wanted the eggheads, not because they have many votes, but because they have influence and ideas, and from the eggheads the Democratic Party has drawn enormous strength. From these eggheads, which Roosevelt, Kennedy and Johnson gathered around them, came the ideas and the programs around which were built the Democratic majorities.

The highly educated, the specialists, and the experts are in numbers a tiny minority. But their influence on the formation of public opinion, even more on the invention and making of policy, is incalculable. Thus, modern fiscal policy has produced the good times which have made President Johnson virtually unbeatable. The germ of the ideas for that policy was fertilized in the brains of theorists, one a Swede [Gunnar Myrdal] and the other an Englishman [John M. Keynes]. The present generation of American economists has been applying and developing this discovery and is in the process of proving by experiment that it works.

ALIENATION OF INTELLECTUALS. This commanding position in the field of ideas has in the past half-century given the Democrats a virtual monopoly of constructive proposals in public affairs. That is why there is a certain truth in the Goldwater complaint that the liberal and progressive Republicans are me-tooists. The Democrats have pre-empted almost all the attractive proposals because they have included so much of the intellectual community which is capable of devising attractive proposals.

Ever since Wilson and Roosevelt, the central Republican leadership has been alienated from the intellectual community, and in the years when it backed McCarthy, it in effect declared war on the intellectual community. The Republican Party will not, I believe, restore itself as long as it cuts itself off from the bright young men who carry in their heads the seed corn of the future. The Republicans will have to find a way to end their alienation from the best brains of the nation.

Mr. Lippmann's analysis of politics should make every store or industry head sit up and wonder if his advertising is aimed high enough. Usually the client thinks, "Oh, that's way above people's heads." Chances are it isn't high enough . . . it's under people's heads.

That explains why there are so few Republicans today. And that explains why Macy's is the biggest and finest store in the world. It's smart to be smart. And Macy's and the Democrats were smart to know it's smart to be smart. My own politics? I'm a liberal, of course. And a Democrat, naturally.

Macy's took the worry out of being close

The words "close" and "penurious" have always had a bad connotation. Americans don't relish being regarded as tightwads or skinflints. They don't admire Scrooges or Hetty Greens. My slogan stressed the fact that thrift was the fashion—not just a grubby habit of watching every penny that one acquired from one's poverty-stricken progenitors.

Right from the beginning I stressed the snobbishness of the slogan. What we were saying was this: It's patrician to spend one's money thriftily. It's only the slobs who are wastrels and throw their money around. Don't be a slob. If you want to show your posh ancestry, do as the rich have always done—spend your money carefully, thriftily. We stressed the point that people who have always had money are careful not to spend one cent more than necessary. In other words the "old money" people—the ones who have always had it—are on Macy's side. It's the new money, the *nouveaux riches*, who throw their money around.

Now, every ad didn't spell out this snob appeal in every detail . . . but it was always there. That's why the version of my slogan which Macy's is now running on radio—"It's smart to be thrifty at Macy's"—isn't the story at all. For instance, English royalty, the house of Windsor, has always been notoriously thrifty. *Burke's Peerage* in England and the Social Register in the United States are filled with the names of people who have a genuine respect for money. That's why they have so much of it.

Macy's should get back to my five wonderful words. "It's smart to be thrifty" is an observation on life. It has a universality that explains why, from the very first, people have used it in ordinary conversation.

Of course, I had luck because the time was ripe for the slogan. And of course, the words in the slogan, important as they were, were less effective than the miraculous merchandising that was going on simultaneously at Macy's. Those were good times for a department-store buyer to flourish. Buyers were encouraged to have wild ideas, to go ahead and take a chance on wild ideas, to go ahead and attempt to do what had never been done before. No matter how outrageous, how fantastic, how crazy your idea— out with it.

That's where I learned to run a creative copy department where it was safe to make mistakes of over-imagination, over-originality. There's an old saying—"You can never get enough without an excess."

But the irresistible drama at Macy's was what I have always called the "magical mix." While the rich were up on the seventh floor selecting the costliest handmade modern rugs in the world, at that very moment there would be a line for blocks outside of Macy's where thousands were queued up to get Macy bargains in the almost daily Macy-Gimbel price battle. When Mrs. Well-off went downstairs to climb into her chauffeured limousine, she saw signs naming the featured bargain of the moment, which might be, as it was once, "70 spools of Coats & Clark's O.N.T. thread for 1¢." Yes, seventy spools of thread for one cent. And Mrs. Well-off knew that that was the thread used in her own sewing room. Already she felt better about the eight hundred dollars she had just spent on the modern rug. She just knew in her bones that the rug had been a good thrifty buy too!

Or Macy's Little Shop might be selling a $300 woman's suit at $282 (6 per cent less) at the same time people were lined up to get sixty cakes of soap for one penny! Or $2 Modern Library volumes for 8 cents each!

Who could beat a combination like that? Practically nobody. Of course, Gimbels was also giving away bargains at about the same fantastic prices. But they seemed less dramatic; because Gimbels carried little glamour merchandise in the high elegant areas.

Later, of course, Fred Gimbel got drama with the William Randolph Hearst collection and with the fabulous Marcus & Co. jewel galleries that moved in, bag and baggage, from upper Fifth Avenue—and the Todhunter wrought-iron business from exclusive East 57th Street.

It was Mr. Todhunter who gave me the idea of searching through old nineteenth-century Dublin to find hand-wrought iron medallions to use in iron grillwork in porches on our farmhouse. Now I don't want to give the impression that the farmhouse is all that East 57th Street elegant. It isn't. It's just a farmhouse. But it's more elegant than it would have been if I had never worked at Macy's and Gimbels.

As I mull over my advertising past, Thomas Hardy's words keep coming back to me: "We're fools to play at games for which there are no prizes."

Retailing still offers prizes all over the place. I envy you young and airy people who are going to start a career in a store.

A miracle, says Webster, is "an event or effect in the physical world . . . deviating from the known laws of nature or transcending our knowledge of these laws."

The Macy upward leap transcended the laws of nature. It had never happened before. It may never happen again. The "magical mix" did it. Think of it! At the very minute the aristocracy was selecting an antique armoire at $2,000 in the Corner Shop, *wham!* the aristocracy *and* the squatocracy were both grabbing up a bottle of aspirin at 90 per cent off the regular price down in the drug department!

XIV

Ten o'clock and not a blow shtruck

Those are the words of an old Irishwoman in the days of the Easter "troubles" in Ireland in 1916. She was disgusted with any surcease in the heavy, hearty fighting. Those words expressed my feelings when I got to Wanamaker's. I missed the sizzling Gimbel-Macy feud. I asked myself, How can I start a feud with someone? With whom? It would be exciting to start a Wanamaker-Macy feud.

Everybody loves a lover, but . . .

As Elsa Maxwell once said, "There are three surefire conversational subjects for a party: sex, love, and who hates whom. And the surest-fire is the last one—who hates whom."

I realized that the ancient Macy-Gimbel feud (always a delight to the public and of inestimable value to Gimbels and to Macy's too) was what I needed. Where and how could I get conventional aristocratic old Wanamaker's into a feud with bright up-on-its-toes Macy's? An opportunity popped up accidentally.

Wanamaker's buyer of men's underwear showed me some men's shorts. They were a special purchase from a fine old maker. I asked, "But can you sell many? After all, Macy's has the men's underwear business right in the hollow of its hand." I recalled that when I was at Macy's, our ads on men's banjo-seat shorts were always sensationally successful. "Besides," I said, "banjo-seat shorts have been such a success. Are these banjo-seat shorts?"

"No," he said indignantly, "they are not, for a very good reason. Men aren't built like banjos."

Goody! I had it! Something to start a feud with. Our headline said, "Wanamaker's men's shorts are *not* banjo-seat shorts, because men are not built like banjos."

The paper was scarcely on the street, when violent objections came from Macy's, which had enormous investments in banjo seats. Now we had a feud! I'd keep it up.

But we were served with an injunction that forbade us ever again to mention the word "banjo." And Wanamaker's conservative legal department in Philadelphia called and warned me to obey the injunction.

"Well," I said sadly to my staff, "the feud is petering out."

"I know what we could do," said a copywriter, a former editor of the Harvard *Lampoon*. "We won't print the word banjo—we'll just draw a picture of a banjo in place of the word."

The art director sketched a layout—six full columns—and we showed a man in his underwear lazily strumming on a banjo:

I'VE COME FROM ALABAMA WITH A ———— ON MY KNEE
. . . NOT ON MY SEAT

That did it! The town howled with glee. The feud was hot and heavy. The president of L'Aiglon dresses was so delighted that he bought several hundred copies of the ad and sent them to people all over the country.

People thought I was mad at Macy's. Even Macy thought I was mad at Macy's. I wasn't. I was grateful to Macy's for giving me a feud.

By the time I moved from Wanamaker's to Gimbels I was disappointed to find everything sweetness and light between Macy's and Gimbels.

I needed a feud that could be fanned into a campaign with continuity. I found such a feud in the shortage of merchandise after World War II. I started with stockings. Every store was out of nylons except Gimbels.

This shortage of merchandise—refrigerators, washing machines, nylons, Scotch whiskey, and all electrical appliances—was true of almost every big store in America, except one: Gimbels, New York. This was due to the astute unorthodox genius of Fred Gimbel. Stores all over the country began running ads, offering sharply limited amounts of scarce merchandise such as this:

"Blank's will have nylons next Thursday."

"Blank's will have refrigerators next week."

Ads all over the country seemed to be talking about what stores would have at some future date. Nobody actually had the stuff except Gimbels.

This precipitated my famous campaign, probably the best in my whole career—Gimbels HAS. We would taunt competitors with their limited offerings, their feeble promises. They didn't seem to *have* anything. They just *would have*—or *hoped that they would have*—a week from Monday. So I refueled the feud. "Gimbel HAS . . . not sometime in the future but tomorrow—Gimbels HAS all the things you can't find elsewhere. Come now. Gimbels HAS right now. [The word HAS was drawn by hand so that it could be enormous—usually half the depth of a full-size newspaper page.] There are no limits on what you can buy. We have nylons when nobody else has them. And Scotch whiskey . . . and so on, ad infinitum."

We headlined one of these early ads:

DOES MAISIE TELL GIMBELS?

The ad went on to say that Maisie was symbolic of the working girl—the secretary—the typist—the teacher—the nurse—who was desperate for nylon stockings and couldn't find them anywhere and had told Gimbels that she simply had to have nylons and not at some vague time in the dim by-and-by. Maisie told Gimbels she had to have nylons now—not tomorrow. And Gimbels was about the only store in the U.S.A. that had scarce, wanted merchandise —nylons, Scotch, major kitchen appliances, furniture, power lawn mowers, soap, and so on. How did Gimbels happen to have gigantic stocks of the scarce, wanted things? Gimbels guessed right. Most big stores guessed wrong. They guessed that the war would be over quickly, and so of course didn't want to tie up a lot of money and warehouses with huge stocks.

Fred Gimbel guessed otherwise. He guessed that the war would be long and that merchandise would be hard to get. Fred, of course, was right as rain. His brother, Bernard Gimbel, agreed with him and went out and bought or leased warehouses to hold the stuff. (As I remember, the talented Hammer brothers, Dr. Armand Hammer and Victor Hammer, who had helped Fred Gimbel get the William Randolph Hearst collection, were of great assistance in securing scarce merchandise during World War II.) We tried to walk that delicate tightrope where we crowed about having things, yet tried to avoid too much swaggering and gloating.

I suppose that guessing right is the ultimate proof of high intelligence.

No wonder Gimbels was the fastest-growing store in the whole world! No wonder the public inferred that if Gimbels was its best bet to find an assortment of fine sofas it probably was its best bet to find practically everything else.

And so it went—hot and heavy, or cool and cozy. After we had played it to the hilt on the shortages, peace again descended. But occasionally in the midst of peace and quiet, a lovely red-hot price war would bob up.

In 1951, perhaps as a result of bulging inventories, a beautiful battle burst forth. Toastmasters were slashed from $23 to $14, Sunbeam Mixmasters from $46 to $26, men's Haspel summer suits from $32 to $19, best-selling novels from $4.50 to $1.94.

Usually women shoppers experienced such euphoria as they realized how much they had saved on loss leaders that they spent freely on anything and everything else. At such times the storewide volume at both Macy's and Gimbels jumped 50 per cent.

When we weren't feuding, we were making up. Every now and then Macy's and Gimbels *would* make up. And that was fun too. When Macy's flower show opened, Gimbels ran an ad urging everyone to go. The whole town murmured something about the miracle of 34th Street. Here is the ad:

DOES GIMBELS TELL MACY'S?
NO, GIMBELS TELLS THE WORLD!

Gimbels isn't just telling Macy's (Macy's knows it already). Gimbels *is* telling the world (that remote corner of the world which hasn't heard) that the most glorious department store flower show in all the world is happening in miracle-crazy 34th Street at Macy's (just a block from Gimbels' door). NOBODY BUT NOBODY sold Gimbels these raves. When we first saw Macy's ads, we raised heavy, competitive eyebrow over jaundiced competitive eye. At the stroke of 9:45 Monday, Gimbels' big brass marched to Macy's with confident, competitive step. Have we seen Gimbels' big wheels since? Not on your life. Our Mr. E was last reported *up to his neck in anemones,* our Mr. M was swooping low over a spray of lily-of-the-valley, our Miss F was *languishing in the hydrangeas.* Even our great Mr. Gimbel himself was transfigured in the *tuberous begonias.* Gimbels tells Macy's that Macy's Flower Show is the greatest miracle to hit 34th Street since 34th Street and miracles (and Gimbels and Macy's) were invented. *Gimbels tells New York* that the competitive spirit (for the moment) can go hang. Gimbels tells the world that it's just plain silly if it doesn't get to Macy's for the greatest flower show 34th Street has ever known!

After the "Gimbels HAS" campaign, I was confronted with a problem. I needed money to finance a big institutional campaign announcing the passing of plain old Gimbels and the birth of beautiful new Gimbels which had just been rebuilt and redecorated by the famous Raymond Loewy to the tune of a few million dollars.

I had another matter that needed institutional advertising. And I had no money with which to do it. Gimbels had just been named *The* Brand Name Department Store of the nation. This was a great honor. It meant that, of all big stores in the whole of the U.S.A., Gimbels had been selected because it stocked—and kept stocked and promoted—more famous brand articles than any other store. It also meant that Gimbels was the most discussed department store in the nation.

I'd have to do two things in the one campaign. I could even do a third—needle Macy's because it preferred to feature its own brands rather than the nationally famous brands.

I got an idea which maybe would not be proper now; but it was then. I'd mention a couple of famous brands in each ad, and get the brands to pay for the whole campaign. *Would they?* They were delighted to, because Gimbel advertising all through the forties was the most admired, most talked-about department-store advertising in the country. "There are more Gimbel ads on presidents' desk spindles than any other ads," I was told repeatedly.

This campaign featured the million-dollar face-lift by Raymond Loewy of plain old Gimbels *plus* the fact that Gimbels had won the honor of being selected *The* Brand Name Department Store of the year. *And*, the beautiful part of it all was that the campaign didn't take one red cent out of my advertising budget. It was a delight to write, and a delight for the public to read.

Gimbel merchandise managers had never liked the plain-old-Gimbels theme. I loved it, because I have always believed that any advertising claim should be made believable by the facts. And the facts screamed aloud: Before Raymond Loewy did over the store not only did Gimbels look plain . . . Gimbels looked terrible! With the admission of that obvious truth, it was easy to build up our reputation as bargain headquarters. We capitalized on our inelegant decor by saying that we couldn't afford to run a beautiful store, that we couldn't afford to spray elevators with Chanel No. 5. Since Gimbels looked bad and smelled bad, it was easy to see at a glance that we were telling the unvarnished truth.

In publicizing our proud boast that plain old Gimbels had been chosen "Brand Name Department Store of the Year," we headlined our little top-of-the-page editorial with this:

GIMBELS CAN EAT THE DUNMOW FLITCH, CAN YOU?

What's the Dunmow flitch? It's a side of bacon, the same as you ate for breakfast this morning. But Dunmow bacon can't be had as easily as Smithfield or Swift's. There's a catch. Our copy explained the old thirteenth-century custom in Dunmow, Essex, England. *You can't get a smitch of the flitch unless you're happily married.* You have to swear on the stones at the Dunmow church door that for twelve months and a day you have never had a wish, even a little tiny wish, to be single again.

We went on to say that Gimbels was married to the finest old aristocratic brands in America, that we never ogled strange brands on the street, never squabbled with a fine old brand, never supplanted it with some common new upstart. We said, "Through thin and thick we always stick with America's best"; That's why you'd find the finest assortment of Carter's underwear for babies, men's B.V.D.'s, Arrow shirts, and so on at *the* brand name department store—Gimbels.

We were flooded with grateful notes from readers. "Thanks to Gimbels I was able to identify the Dunmow flitch in my college entrance exams," said one. Another said, "I had never known the word 'flitch.' Now I dazzle Schrafft's short-order man when I order 'a rasher (not a flitch) of bacon and two eggs sunny side up.' "

Another little top-of-the-page editorial met with the same success when we explained the "Buridan's ass" problem which engaged much scholarly debate among ancient schoolmen in the Middle Ages. We explained:

> *Buridan's ass was a little donkey*
> *who couldn't bray yea*
> *and couldn't bray nay.*

The copy explained the problem:

If you place a hungry donkey equidistant from two bundles of hay, would he be able to decide which he should eat? Or would he be unable to decide and die of starvation?

Again we were flooded with little appreciative notes from readers. People love to acquire bits of erudition—if they can do it painlessly.

> *Customers said "Oh pshaw"*
> *to Gregor Mendel's law.*

One reason Wanamaker ads in the thirties became required reading in some of the best composition courses in leading colleges (see the *New Yorker* cartoon in this book) was our adroit working in of some bit of knowledge, sometimes simple and primerish, sometimes highbrow and esoteric. New Yorkers realized that even if they didn't want the item advertised they could usually pick up a tidbit free. Once at Wanamaker's we ran an ad for baby layettes. In it we quoted Gregor Mendel. *We* said that *Mendel* said that two blue-eyed parents couldn't have a brown-eyed child. A dozen indignant letters arrived.

I remember one of the briefer ones: "You don't know what you're talking about. My eyes are blue. My wife's eyes are blue. The baby's eyes are brown. How do you account for that?"

We didn't publish a smarty-pants answer. However, scientific research has *recently* revealed that about once in a million times two blue-eyed parents *can* produce a brown-eyed child. Think of the answer we could have run:

"Dear Sir: You are one in a million. . . ."

To return to feuding. Of course there never was any personal malice toward Macy's. I've always been grateful to Macy's because it gave me my first big chance at the right time. My Wanamaker and later Gimbels needling of Macy's amused the public, didn't hurt Macy's, and was fun to do.

One Christmas we all—Gimbels, Saks 34th, and Macy's—decorated Herald Square and Greeley Square together and turned it into the town's Christmas crossroads, celebrated in this poem by Gimbels.

CHRISTMAS CROSSROADS

Peace is upon us, and Christmas is nigh,
The dove is on hand and the goose will hang high—
Gimbels and Macy's and Herald Square Saks
Have kissed and made up—and have buried the axe.

Macy's told Gimbels and Saks lent an ear;
"Let's all get together for Christmas this year;
It's smart to be Yuley. Let's tinsel a tree,
Nobody, but nobody, will match it, you'll see."

Those old feudin' pistols are high on the shelf,
It's hard to believe it so see for yourself,
How Gimbels and Macy's and Saks–34
Have trimmed their façades to resemble ONE *store.*

Instead of our usual businesslike square
A gay Christmas Crossroads is going to be there
With skyscraping sugar canes, huge trees, and holly
To make sure Christmas shopping is ever so jolly.

Bundle up Peter, grab Susie, bring Pop
You'll find Christmas Crossroads the best place to shop.
Yes, Macy's and Gimbels and Saks are all set
For the happiest, PEACEFULEST *Christmastide yet!*

And whose big boy are you?

There are all sorts of Gimbel-Macy stories. Legend has it that one day Jesse Straus, then president of Macy's, was on a tour of the New York store when he came across a young man playing with the electric trains. The young man was wearing a stock boy's jacket. "Are you a stock boy?" inquired Jesse with a frown, after watching for some time. "Yes, sir," replied the stock boy. "What department are you stock boy in?" persisted Mr. Straus. "Blankets, sir," came the reply. "And how much money do you make?" "Eighteen dollars a week." Jesse pulled out his wallet and counted out the stock boy's salary for the week, plus two weeks' notice. "You're fired," said Jesse as he gave the young man the money. "I should have told you," blurted the young man as soon as he was well out of Jesse's reach, "I'm a stock boy at Gimbels!"

XV

From Grace Church to Greeley Square

When, in 1940, I moved to Gimbels, Fred Gimbel assured me that Gimbel customers not only wanted to be sexy and rich, but *were* sexy and rich.

It just so happened that 1941 was the year of Gimbels' centennial. So, again, I had to talk about the Founder. This time the Founder was Adam Gimbel, who founded the Gimbel business out in Vincennes, Indiana, in 1841.

Here was our institutional angle, which we ran for our Milwaukee and New York stores:

ADAM GIMBEL WAS A MAN WITH AN IDEA

"Fairness and equality to all" was his motto. City dweller, frontiersman or Indian—it made no difference to Adam. He started the first one-price store in America. Nobody had ever heard of charging an Ojibwa the same price for a plug of tobaccy as you charged a farmer over Wabash way! Everybody robbed the Indian. Everybody *but* Adam Gimbel. Pioneers and Indians liked his one-price policy. Gimbels caught on.

Switching from Wanamaker's to Gimbels was pure delight. At Gimbels I didn't have to run any solemn, pompous ads. One of

our best centennial ads was a page in *Harper's Magazine* with
the headline:

CENTENARY—SCHMENTENARY

The ad was written by one of my Gimbel Phi Beta Kappa cubs,
Riva Fine Korda, and later brought me much centennial business
from stores when I had opened my own shop. She is now a vice-president of Ogilvy & Mather. Riva proves the wisdom of my old rule
"Always hire people smarter than yourself." You have probably
been delighted with Riva's copy on "Schweppervescence" and other
Ogilvy accounts.

Despite our occasional differences on copy, Wanamaker's hated
to see me go. Suddenly they loved every word of mine. They made
me promise not to take a single writer with me. They wanted the
whole copy department left intact. I promised. I could hardly do
otherwise. If one is certain, as I have been for a long time, that
anybody, but anybody, can be taught to write advertising, it's
palpably silly to go into a new job and throw people out.

I kept my word about not luring anyone away. But most of the
writers resigned anyway. And one day I found them sitting around
the Gimbel offices all ready to write copy. I didn't *take* them. They
insisted on coming. So, as soon as possible, I put them to work. And
presently Gimbels became the great launching pad for advertising
aspirants, just as Wanamaker's had been before.

I have always had the reputation for being a hard-to-work-for
perfectionist. Yet everybody has always wanted to work for me.

Right smack after we'd finished up the centennial campaign
where we pointed out the fact that it was Adam Gimbel (not
Marshall Field or John Wanamaker) who really instituted the
one-price, no-haggling policy in retailing, I began to put to use
what I had learned at Wanamaker's. Theoretically, Wanamaker
customers would be very different from Gimbel customers. But
surprise, surprise! They weren't! Gimbel customers were just the

same as Wanamaker customers. And both were pretty much the
same as Macy customers. And all of them very much like the
solid-gold Marshall Field customers.

What a mountain of research money has been wasted by manufacturers and retailers trying to prove their old pet cliché "Our
customers are different."

This is certainly a higgledy-piggledy book. I no sooner state
something than I remember an exception—the exception that
proves the rule.

Sometimes people *are* different. Such as the time, in my own
business, when I was writing ads for the Denver Dry Goods Company. The president of the Denver Dry Goods Company objected
to our ad on its new Teen Consultant in its newly opened Teen
Shop.

Our copy stressed the fact that teen-agers would take fashion
advice from their teen peers—and they would be delighted to
take advice from the Denver's Teen Consultant. But teen-agers
don't want clothes advice from their mothers. Our headline was:

SHE'S A YOUNG THING AND CAN'T BELIEVE HER MOTHER

"Can't believe their own mothers?" said the president of the Denver
Dry Goods Company. "All the women in Denver would rise in
wrath if we ran that!"

I said, "No, they won't." And I added, "If you get any un-
favorable reaction, you needn't pay for the ad."

The ad ran. A couple of Denver mothers were mad as wet hens.

Even so, Mr. J, the president, gallantly insisted on paying for
the ad.

In 1940, Gimbels was at the lowest point in its history—lowest
in looks, merchandising, advertising, and general acceptance. It
had sunk way down.

My first ads admitted all this. We came right out and said how down-at-the-heel we were. Here is some of the copy about plain old Gimbels:

> Great-grandma never worried about whether
> there was a monogram on her nightie or a
> rose petal in her finger bowl.

The copy went on:

> By the time she had milked her seven cows,
> separated the cream, scalded and put back
> together the separator, taken the skimmed
> milk down on the stoneboat to the two
> litters of pigs, you can bet your last piece
> of cornbread that she wasn't worrying about
> the monogram on her nightie or the rose
> petal in her finger bowl.

Then the copy went on to tie in Gimbels' simple sensible thrift ideas. We got scores of letters asking what in Tophet was a stoneboat. But we got one letter which differed with us on the use of a stoneboat. Here is the letter:

Dear Plain Old Gimbels:

Just what was Plain Old Great-grandma figurin' on doin' with the plain old skim milk after she had taken it down on the stoneboat? A stoneboat is a plain old sledge or drag, used for transporting plain old rocks (stone). Its usual function was to haul plain old stone off the field onto the plain old fence row, or wherever the Plain Old Farmer wanted it. To put it plainly, NOBODY, BUT NOBODY, but Plain Old Gimbels' Plain Old Great-grandma would ever take skim milk on a stoneboat, unless she or your Plain Old Copywriter was nuts. What was this, a funny farm?

Cheerfully yours,

Plain Old X

Of course we published this gem along with several others that poked fun at our plain-old-Gimbels theme.

Several months later we received a letter saying we were right, and our critic was wrong. Here is the letter, which we published too. This letter was from Wisconsin's erudite and articulate merchant, Jack B. Yost:

Dear Miss Fitz-Gibbon:

Tell Mr. Plain Old X that down in Missouri, about the end of the "Mauve Decade" they "did so" slide the skim milk to the sty on a stoneboat. Who had any money for wheels? Plain Old Great-grandma couldn't lift those heavy cans into a high cart! She could wheel 'em onto a stoneboat, however—which is but five inches off the ground. And the load slid along fairly easily over the black gumbo.

Trouble with these modern X's is that they won't touch anything which "Uncle Whiskers" hasn't subsidized. And no give-away bureaucrat would know a stoneboat if he saw it.

The public liked Jack Yost's letter too.

One of the bonuses for running fresh, rememberable advertising is that industry pours money into your hands.

For instance, Red Cross shoes used Gimbels' advertising department as its own creative agency.

Oh, Red Cross had its own agency; but an agency just doesn't understand selling shoes the way a retail advertising department does. So we would get a full page on Red Cross shoes paid for in a paper like *The New York Times* or *Daily News* or *Journal-American*.

I remember getting the money for a full page from Red Cross merely because we roughed out a page with this headline: THERE ARE 26 BONES IN THE HUMAN FOOT. Then Red Cross sent the ad out to hundreds of its stores all over the country as an inspiration.

That little bit of research, finding the number of bones in the foot, was an inspiration when I later named Genesco's famous child's shoe "Number 26."

Certainly, there was nothing startling about counting the bones in the human foot. I've been telling you all along that you don't have to be brilliant to turn out a brilliant ad.

Another time we got thousands of dollars when we used the same idea in an ad for a corset company. Our headline in the full-page ad was:

THERE ARE 210 BONES IN THE HUMAN BODY
AND *ALL* OF THEM ARE CURVED

All we needed was to look at a simple primer of physiology to do that one. But didn't we have to pretest the headline? No, I knew in my own 210 curved bones that that headline would interest the average woman. Obviously, a woman would know we were telling the truth. Subconsciously she might think: "Other stores may have girdles for people with 210 straight bones—I'd better go to Gimbels where they have girdles for curved bones."

Right off the bat I took a shine to the brothers Gimbel—Bernard and Fred. They were both sophisticates, but they had the simplicity, directness and candor of Middle West farmers. They came from Indiana. Although they were descendants of Adam Gimbel, I knew that I would not have to quote heavy pompous moralistic maxims across the top of every page. No more sayings of the founding father . . . although the Gimbel founder was as distinguished as the Wanamaker founder.

When Bernard Gimbel was eighty, he looked sixty, and thought fifty. He had the advantage of a couple of extra hours of living and learning every day because he flourished on a minimum of sleep. No wonder his interests were so wide and so varied: merchandising, sports, the theater, finance, politics, economics, anthropology and all local civic problems. You name it, Bernard was interested. His all-consuming interest was New York City, which he believed to be the most fascinating city in the world. He was also an expert on Francis Bacon, and knew by heart almost everything Bacon ever wrote.

Bernard was immensely popular with my copywriters. He used to drop in to their offices to chat. He would pick up a piece of copy that had run the day before: "That's the way to put it! Who wrote this? Why can't everybody write like you people? After all, if a guy is drowning, he doesn't yell, 'Assistance, Assistance.' He yells, 'Help, Help.' Keep up your good work. Everybody is reading Gimbel ads."

Going to Gimbels was a little like going to Wanamaker's. Both stores had apparently lost the interest of the public. Both stores had lost much of their volume. Many advertising experts believe that my job at Gimbels was my best. I think that my Wanamaker achievement was best, because there I had less merchandising skill to support my words. And the merchandise, of course, is always more important than the words that describe it.

At Macy's the merchandising was sensational—especially after Macy's had been hit by grace in the late nineteen-twenties. From then on, Gimbels' merchandising coups were brilliant but sporadic. There wasn't the consistent pursuit of excellence that the brain trust of intellectuals at Macy's had provided.

Bernard Gimbel's philosophy of running a store resembled Pope John XXIII's philosophy of running the church: "See everything. Overlook a lot. Correct a little." Indeed, Bernard resembled John in many traits—warmth, good rustic common sense, a liking and understanding of everybody everywhere . . . the ability to put himself in other people's shoes and see things their way. And Bernard, like John, was a talented listener. As he said, "You can't learn anything when you are talking. You can learn only when you are listening."

Both Bernard and Fred possessed that great gift—the ability to recognize the obvious. So did Eddie Marks.

And so did Winston Churchill. All through the thirties, Churchill warned England, almost daily, to beware the rising Nazi threat and rearm. England couldn't see any threat at all, did not wish to rearm, and called Churchill a crackpot.

Eddie Marks's ability to recognize the obvious was demonstrated when he turned thumbs down on what I considered one of my best campaigns—a salute to "Rue de la Seventh," a salute to American designers.

Eddie admitted that it was a sound idea; but he said Macy's at that time didn't have the fashion prestige. He thought that Macy sponsorship would hurt—not help—American designing.

A couple of years later Lord & Taylor came out with the same idea and won permanent prestige and glory. I was furious. But Eddie Marks was right. He was enough of a realist to recognize Macy's few weaknesses as well as its many strengths.

I shudder to think of all the money that has been spent on pompous promotions of abstractions:

The utilities love abstractions. "More power for progress." Get any picture of progress? And that awful, pious pronouncement that Curtis ran in every medium a few years ago: "The Curtis Commitment."

When anyone announces his credo or commitment, I die of boredom. Funny that big industry is so far removed from ordinary people that it thinks statements like "We welcome the challenge of this great era" and "We are dedicated to the comfort and happiness of our great and growing public" have any appeal. Who reads or believes or cares? Nobody. Because muddy, murky abstractions can't paint pictures in the mind.

Why is gossip interesting? Because it is concrete, personal.

A dissertation on "Faithlessness in Marriage" would be dull. But "Who Ran Away with Whom," with names and dates and places, would be fascinating.

Yes, the best way to promote a store is to make up a page of items (as Bergdorf-Goodman of New York does). Then across part of the top of the page drop one or two institutional messages such as those to be found in a Wallachs ad by Les Pearl or an old Wanamaker or Gimbel ad by Bernice Fitz-Gibbon—or by one of her trainees, who were for the most part better than Fitz.

Rosser Reeves, in his brilliant book *Reality in Advertising*, says that a copywriter must not seek to please his own ego—that a campaign should not be the individual expression of a writer's ego. True, I suppose. But there is a lot of ego in most good advertising campaigns.

And, speaking of Rosser Reeves's books, which should be read by every aspiring copywriter, retail or national, where did Mr. Reeves get that terrible title?

A title, like a headline, should paint a picture in the reader's mind. What kind of picture does "reality" paint? No kind of picture. It's abstractions instead of concretes that result in bad slogans.

"You'll be worry-free if you buy G-E." Too glib. Unbelievable. And I can't summon up a picture of worry-freeness.

Even in ordinary conversation, learn to particularize—not generalize. My six-year-old grandson, whom I quoted earlier, was right when he said, "Don't say *grapes*—say Thompson's Seedless."

Bernard Gimbel was more customer-conscious than anyone I have ever known. He really believed what every store head professes: "The customer is boss." He and I got along just fine. I had learned early in life that it's smart to give in to a boss or a husband on the little things: "You can make a man change his whole way of life; but you can't get him to change his bootmaker." Bernard wanted the store name and the store hours displayed clearly at the top of every ad. The big store name and big store hours were his bootmaker. I have always liked to use that prime spot for a sireny enticement that would lure the reader into the body of the ad where he would be convinced that it was silly not to plunk down his money for an article that would benefit him so enormously. I finally learned to do both.

In a department store the most important classification is soft goods, fashion. Gimbel fashion, like Wanamaker fashion, seemed to be at the bottom of the heap.

Back in 1940 when Fred Gimbel took over with his new team— new merchandise managers, a new general manager, and a new advertising head, me—the store had really only one successful soft-goods department, Mary Kohn's housedress department. Mary Kohn sold carloads of bungalow aprons and cheap housedresses— and that was the extent of Gimbels fashion business. Paris didn't exist for Gimbels. So important is a fashion reputation in a big department store that, like James Barrie's description of charm: "If you have it, you don't need to have anything else; and if you don't have it, it doesn't much matter what else you have."

As at Wanamaker's, Paris was not in the Gimbel picture. But Paris is always important. Even in a volume store, fashion and Paris are important. A good reputation in fashion makes it easy for a store to sell, at a profitable price, everything else from a yard of linoleum to an automobile tire or a spool of thread.

How successful were Fred Gimbel and his new team? From no soft-goods business except carloads of bungalow aprons and cheap housedresses in eight short years (after that Fred Gimbel bowed out of the picture to spend his time in travel) Gimbels became the fastest-growing retail business in the world. We more than quadrupled the volume. Gimbels was selling more copies of Paris imports than any other store in the United States. We zoomed up from nothing at all to beating all our betters.

That's the magic of retailing and retail advertising in New York, where, if you catch the imagination of the public, miracles can happen. Our fashion director, Elizabeth Appenzeller (Appy, we *beyond the Alps lies Appy*

*"Beyond the Alps lies Italy," said Hannibal—"and Appy, too,"
says Gimbels. Appy, to be formal, is Elizabeth Appenzellar,
Gimbels top fashion expert.   Naturally, Appy's in Italy.
Where would she be during the Florence couturier openings
—sitting home in Horace Greeley's lap? Not Appy. She sat
in the Grand Central ballroom, saw Gabriellasport's
coat with the umbrella in the pocket. She clapped for
Veneziani's silver diaper pins, La Boutique's suit of
straw. She cabled back "Maraviglioso!" (Watch for
Gimbels line-for-line copies of Italian spring originals). When this goes to press, Appy will be literally
over the Alps—in a plane bound for Paris. She'll
trot from Dior to Desses, from Fath to Lanvin,
from Balmain to Balenciaga.   Then a wave at
Spain. Then a wave at Appenzell, Switzerland
(for sentimental reasons).   Then home—with
trunks of fabulous imports—for Gimbels to
copy line-for-line—for you to buy for only
a fraction of the time, the energy and, of
course, the money that the originals cost.*

called her), came from Saks Fifth Avenue. Soon Appy became the
best-known American buyer all over the Continent. Fashion editors
wrote her up in exclusive magazines. French couturiers applauded
her. I was delighted that Gimbels finally had a peg on which to
hang fashion stories. So we featured Appy far and wide. When she
was scouring Italy for beautiful hand-knits, we photographed her,
naturally, on the Appian Way.

What made success so swift at Gimbels? How did it happen that
members of the Social Register, in town and out, flocked to Gimbel
fashion shows at the Plaza, where Appy presented the latest Paris
originals alongside the faithful line-for-line Gimbel copies? Of

course we mentioned the fact on the runway, as well as in the ads, that although the two garments looked identical, one cost (landed) $2,500 and the beautiful Gimbel copy cost $49! All of a sudden it became the "in" thing to say, "This copy of a Grès cost me only $49. I picked it up at Gimbels in Appy's Specialty Corner."

What happened to Appy? Retailing, which opens so many delightful doors, opened a particularly delightful one to her. On one of her crossings to the Paris openings, she met an Englishman, Frederick Parsons. She married him and is now the decorative chatelaine on a 2,000-acre farm in Sussex. Whenever we get to England, we retailers make a beeline to Sussex; we sit in Appy's rose garden, sniff the roses, and gaze out dreamily at the glittering Channel a couple of miles away.

Fred Gimbel's policy on advertising was laissez-faire. What helped this policy? His flexibility. His recognition of what would appeal to the public and entice them into Gimbels, like millions of dollars' worth of ball-point pens that could write under water! People didn't stop to think that they might never need to write under water. Everybody fell for the sorcery of our ads. They barged in by the thousands and plunked down $12.95 for each pen.

Then Fred Gimbel made a tieup with Ed Goldstein of Marcus & Co. I believe Fred was the first retailer to take over the liquidation of jewels from private estates. All of a sudden it was possible (at Gimbels, of all places!) to buy an ancient brooch set with emeralds and diamonds. And they were some of the finest diamonds in all the world.

"The rich are different from us," F. Scott Fitzgerald once remarked to Ernest Hemingway. "Yes," said Hemingway, "they have more money."

The very smart are different from you and me. Yes, they have more brains. When they concentrate, they concentrate totally. When they are preoccupied with something, they are wholly absorbed. (Einstein once said that early in life he had read every word that had ever been written about physics.) Any copywriter who proceeded in that way could produce unbeatable advertising. He wouldn't need to chew his pencil or rack his brain hoping for a brilliant inspiration to come out of the blue.

This sounds egghead—*is* egghead.

Fred Gimbel was a scholarly intellectual pragmatist. It seems to me that is the ideal merchant or advertising expert. Eggheadedness: scholarship, intellectualism. And, of course, pragmatism. The test should always be: will it work? Fred Gimbel would have been surprised at being called a scholarly academician, but that's what he was: "a scholarly academician with a lot of horse sense."

Meet me among the Matisses, Maggie

Haydn once wrote an artful symphony. It has been called the "Surprise" because of the loud chord, supported by a drum tap, which bursts into the calm and quiet of the slow dreamy move-ment. A copywriting department is much like that. Just when there's too much calm and quiet about to settle like a pall, a buyer shows up with a bulletproof vest than can now be had in misses' sizes or a new kind of mattress with a built-in bedboard.

Just such a startle was sprung on me soon after I arrived at Gimbels, when Fred Gimbel asked me if I thought plain old un-fancy Gimbels could sell millions of dollars' worth of the most fabu-lous art treasures in the world, which were sitting in a New York warehouse. They had been assembled over many years by the lord of San Simeon—William Randolph Hearst.

I was sure we could. I've always been sure that anything good will sell. First, however, we made a test with a collection of ex-quisite old Japanese bronzes; then a collection of hand-embroidered brocades of museum quality. Both events were wildly successful. The ads appeared on Sunday. By 9:30 A.M. Monday, half New

York came roaring in to grab up everything. Scarcely a smitch was left.

Now we were ready for the Hearst treasure trove: priceless antiques in paintings, furniture, china, glass, jewelry, religious art, statuary, porcelains, sculptures, coats of mail, carved altars, stained-glass windows, paneling, staircases from old castles, and even an ancient Cistercian monastery moved stone by stone from Spain to the Hearst warehouses in New York.

I have been given credit by speakers and in newspaper and magazine articles for being brilliant enough to pull off a merchandising coup of this caliber.

Of course, I had nothing to do with *getting* the Hearst collection in the first place. Once a retail advertising director has the eyes of New York riveted on her or him, the advertising director is given the credit for everything good that the store does, and for most of the bad. I am sure many writers in advertising agencies labor long and hard and get no personal credit, because they are obscured by that tent of anonymity that settles over an agency. I kept denying that I had anything to do with securing this plum—probably the most beautiful and legendary collection ever sold in New York. But the story still persists.

As I remember, this is what happened: The Hearst heirs wanted to liquidate this costly collection. It was first offered to Macy's, then to Lord & Taylor. But no deal was closed. So the brilliant Fred Gimbel went after it. At first, the owners turned him down; but when Fred's fresh and flexible mind evolved the plan of displaying part of the collection in the immaculate and exquisite windows of America's highest-fashion store, Saks Fifth Avenue, an agreement was reached. (Saks Fifth Avenue is part of the Gimbel chain.)

I had nothing to do with getting the merchandise—the lovely stuff was dropped in my lap. But I had a lot to do with selling it. And sell it we certainly did! People from every state in the Union, and from every country in Europe, poured in and bought like mad.

Handling the Hearst collection was perhaps the most exciting promotion of my fourteen years at Gimbels. Why didn't the collection go to New York's most famous art dealers? Probably because of the century-old Gimbel reputation of careful dependable dealing. It was Adam—who, along with America's other legendary merchants, John Wanamaker and Marshall Field—established the fixed, fair-price policy backed up with truthful description of the article.

Every Hearst item sold carried a tag with a history of the item and proper authentication.

Fred Gimbel with his wonderful let-the-advertising-alone policy let me sell the Hearst stuff with our customary spontaneity. I am convinced that the sensational success of the whole project was largely due to the casual, informal way we talked about priceless treasures. Instead of stiff, pompous announcements, reeking with reverence and awe, we proceeded to sell items as naturally as if they were run-of-the-mill Gimbel bargains. Igor Stravinsky once deplored teaching people to have respect for music. He said they should be taught to love music, not respect it. Our copy showed more love than awe-stricken respect.

Like most country people, I am impressed with quality—but not too impressed. I believe that customers were convinced by our candid admission that plain old Gimbels was just out of its depth, that plain old Gimbels wasn't cultured enough to appreciate these lovely things. They thought to themselves, "Since Gimbels can't possibly appreciate these irreplaceable marvels, let's hurry down and snap 'em up before Gimbels wakes up to their worth." Well, Fred Gimbel knew their worth right down to a mill.

I don't have the opening announcement of the Hearst sale. But I do have this lovely headline that ran in the Sunday *New York Times*: THE GIMBEL PAGES IN TODAY'S NEW YORK TIMES ARE FULL OF BARGAINS RANGING FROM SEERSUCKER (ONE YARD FOR 89¢) UP TO AN ORIGINAL RENOIR (ABOUT 2 YARDS)—$240,000. The charm of this headline was the obvious fact that we did not let the having of a Renoir throw us.

We didn't have any Sargents in our art collection, so that fact inspired "No time for Sargents"; and of course we couldn't resist "Hearst on its own petard."

I tried, but never really succeeded in getting our elevator operators to announce: "Fifth floor—children's clothes, garden hose, and Van Goghs."

Moral: Don't be too impressed—with either top brass or top merchandise.

Before we ran the big Hearst announcement in February 1941, we tried several other little sallies into high-priced luxury promotions to see what Gimbel could sell and for how much. Like the time we offered a collection of "ancestor portraits" for $400 and $600 and $800: Our headline was:

HAVE YOU ALWAYS LONGED FOR AN ANCESTOR?

Then we listed the upper-crust names of the subjects painted—like Peabody and Rutherford, Brittingham, and Willingham and Cadwallader and Ogilvie. Our copy went on to say that maybe one of these precious portraits is *your* ancestor. The response was simply smashing. Hundreds of New Yorkers parted with $600 or $800 for the thrill of hanging an ancestor—or at least somebody with the same name—over the family fireplace.

The portraits were excellent, because many of the itinerant painters who wandered through early America were fine painters.

Yes, if Gimbels could sell ancestors, then Gimbels could sell anything. And what was most interesting was that these Gimbel ancestor portraits sold to regular Gimbel customers. Often the $800 portrait went right on an old charge account whose owner had hitherto bought only sheets and mattresses and mundane necessities from us. And usually the Ogilvie portrait was charged to an Ogilvie. And the Rutherford to a Rutherford. And so on.

While our ads for the Hearst collection didn't genuflect in awe, we didn't clown or cut up. It was straightforward sensible selling.

While *I* was taking the cold marble rhetoric and awed museum hush *out* of the advertising, Charles Helser, the merchandise manager who had been put in charge of the Hearst collection which filled the whole fifth floor at Gimbels, was busy putting hush and dignity and formality *into* his fifth-floor personnel, selling, display and accounting.

Charley, the same fellow who sold the mountain of porringers that I told you about earlier, was new at Gimbels. He didn't care for the easy informal relaxed attitude of the Gimbels sales force. He was a martinet and tried to introduce formality, decorum and even a little pomposity. But the sales force remained pretty easygoing and undisciplined.

The New Yorker, in "Talk of the Town," reported the experience of a customer who was examining some tiny silver spoons with human figures on the handles. She asked, "Are these apostle spoons?" "Yes indeedy," answered the friendly salesgirl, "these spoons were used by the twelve apostles."

The *New Yorker* stories and cartoons stemming from the magazine's apparent delight in the incongruity of the priceless treasures being at plain old Gimbels at all, carried the sale along with its monthly (sometimes weekly) stories of what sold and what didn't, and why and how much.

Probably the *New Yorker* stories accomplished as much or more than the advertising did. But I don't really believe that. I always give the credit to advertising.

Preparing the advertising taught me a lot. It taught me that when the merchandise was good enough, the mere catalogue listing of it was more effective than stringing along flattering adjectives. We didn't pause to praise. We dealt in nouns—pictorial nouns. Like our ad on a Cellini cup wrought in gold and set with emeralds and rubies: What more needed to be said? It would have been an impertinence to use a single adjective telling how good the gold or how dazzling the emeralds and rubies.

Every day on the way to my office, I would escalate up to the fifth floor. The whole floor was a lure: A 1556 silver tankard for which Hearst had paid $30,000. A rock crystal chandelier which we tagged with a bargain price of $3,000. (They say that Hearst always went out and bought things whenever he was worried.) Of course the paintings were the most thrilling—Gainsboroughs, Bouchers, Murillos.

As I remember, practically everything sold. Everything except the biggest bargain of all—that Spanish monastery, built in 1141, which Hearst had bought in 1927. He had it dismantled, stone by stone, and shipped to his New York storehouse in fourteen thousand crates.

Gimbels marked it $50,000. The dismantling, shipping and storing had cost $500,000! We almost sold it to a Spanish millionaire, a dashing octogenarian with a square-cut gray beard. He was going to take it back to Spain and have it erected on its original site, Sacramenia, a little town in Segovia Province.

But then he remembered William Randolph Hearst and the Spanish-American War. And there was no sale.

We finally marked it "as is" and reduced it to $19,000.

The $19,000 price was a bargain and the monastery was sold several times. Each time the sale collapsed because of the cost of moving it.

Eventually, Gimbels and the Hammer Galleries dropped the Hearst collection and we lost track of the monastery. One day, years later, the phone rang. It was Fred Gimbel saying he had just stumbled on it in Florida: "It's a tourist attraction right here in North Miami Beach. Just one block west of U.S. 1."

"If you're so hell-bent on buying something that belongs to Mr. Hearst, you can get a Journal-American for three cents."

"My wife snapped it up at a Hearst sale."

"Are we still in the Hearst collection?"

Good ould Gimbels loves good ould Ireland

I particularly wanted to put on an Irish Fair at Gimbels in order to flatter the millions in greater New York who were wholly or partly of Irish descent.

I knew that most New York stores infuriated the Irish by displaying pipes and shillelaghs tied with green ribbon on St. Patrick's Day.

Being a fourth-generation Irisher myself (Limerick County) I knew that Ireland had been the center of culture and learning for hundreds of years when Britain and the Continent were overrun with ignorant savages. I thought that the best way to tell New York that was by a big Irish Fair and Exhibit.

I knew Ireland was full of beautiful things—ancient and contemporary. But who would pay for transporting the stuff from Ireland to Gimbels?

American Airlines said it would fly everything at no expense to Gimbels. American Airlines did, paid the insurance and all expenses, including flying me to Ireland to find the stuff. Of course, we featured American Airlines in all our windows and publicity.

We got free publicity in national media as well as full pages in all New York and Dublin papers. Our Irish Exhibit was loved and talked about on the radio—everywhere.

When American Airlines saw how the Irish piled into the store by the thousands, it suggested that we run a contest to find Miss Ireland, who would be flown to Ireland for two weeks, all expenses paid, and then flown to London for a film test. All girls between eighteen and twenty-five who had lived within fifty miles of Gimbels for one year, were eligible. They had to be a little bit Irish—only one-fifteenth, which we figured out was one great-grandparent from the Ould Sod. All they had to do was send in a photograph.

We had a big celebration in the store. Bernard Gimbel got his friend Morton Downey (now called the world's oldest choirboy) to sing "Galway Bay." Our publicity ran this way:

Some people think all Americans are millionaires, or movie queens or Indians who like baseball and comic books. They think that all Americans eat hot dogs and ice cream cones, and never stop hurrying from morn till night, except at the opera, where they sleep.

Some people think all Irishmen are crosses between Mr. Gallagher and Mr. Sheehan, and the corner cop who warbles "Danny Boy" and wields a shillelagh, who woos you with "blarney" in a Barry Fitzgerald brogue, eats Mulligan stew six days out of seven, and names all of his children Pat & Mike.

If Ireland is to you more than a potpourri of banal symbols . . . because Erin is your land or your father's . . . if you have starch in your backbone and a soul that sings . . . don't miss

GIMBELS   AMERICAN AIRLINES
SALUTE TO IRELAND

Largest display of Irish wares—antique and contemporary . . . handmade and manufactured . . . ever shown in this hemisphere!

See priceless specimens of Carrickmacross, Limerick, and Youghal lace . . . the largest collection of handmade lace ever shown in New York.

See a replica of the fabulous "Cross of Cong" on loan from the National Museum of Dublin . . . a 12th-century art treasure.

See soft subtle tweeds . . . big bulky tweeds . . . hand-loomed in Ireland of native wool, signed by the individual weavers.

IT'S SMART TO BE IRISH

good ould Gimbels loves good ould Ireland.
Don't miss Gimbels-American Airlines Irish
Exhibit . . . see 27 windows full of Irish
treasures unveiled at 11 am Monday.

There's more to Ireland than shamrock, shillelaghs, and Mulligan stew. *Did you know* that when the Huns were romping around Central Europe, the scholars all fled to Ireland, seat of learning, to hear themselves think? *Did you know* at one time ⅓ of the Irish population were poets? *Did you know* that the Irish write the best English? *Did you know* the average Irishman's vocabulary is 4,000 words—his English counterpart's vocabulary a measly 500 words? (That's true . . . we have it from Padraic Colum.) What's more, Handel said he would rather have *Eileen Aroon* to his credit than all the music he ever wrote. You probably know that hundreds of ancient relics have been preserved in the germ-free soil of Ireland's bogs.

But did you know that a wooden firkin, perhaps 2,000 years old, was found—with butter inside as fresh as the lump in your freezer? *Did you know* that Guinness stout is provided free to nursing mothers of Dublin? *Did you know* that the Countess of Cork (described by Sir Walter Raleigh in his "History of the World") lived to the ripe age of 140 and that she came to her untimely end scrambling up a tree after nuts?

Did you know that Dublin Airport, the most modern in the world, was dreamed up by Desmond FitzGerald? *Did you know* that you won't find a single corn on a single Aran Islander's toe? You'll love our bainin (pronounced bawneen) jackets, crios (belts) and pampooties (woven hide sandals).

See a gold-plated ewer and basin set with moonstones . . . just one among many samples of Irish genius in elaborate metalwork.

See "bainin" jackets, "crios" and "pampooties" (belts and hide sandals) hand-woven and worn by the Aran Islands fisherfolk.

See Dun Emer carpets, Horn gloves and sun-colored Wicklow pottery, beehives and combs of Irish honey from Michael Rowan.

See a replica of the exquisite Ardagh chalice and the Shrine of St. Patrick's bell, on loan from the National Museum . . .

See a real Irish farmer's pony trap made by McSweeney of Cork . . . every stick, stitch, and nail native Irish except the rubber tires.

See present-day silver from the world-famous house of West & Son . . . 19th-century antique silver crafted by Matthew West.

See jewel-like stained-glass windows and rich ecclesiastical vestments encrusted with precious gold and silk hand-embroidery.

See a harp that's been in the Connaught family of O'Hara for half a dozen generations . . . there are only 9 ancient Gaelic harps in existence.

In a short time all New Yorkers (and many from out of state) were convinced that the Irish were of royal and aristocratic lineage. Every time I have been to Ireland since, I find appreciative Irish people still talking about that wonderful Irish exhibit at Gimbels, New York.

While a successful advertising head always gets plenty of personal publicity, it sometimes gets out of hand. For instance, this little story trickled back from Dublin: Many of the Irish were saying, "Did you know that the Gimbels have all left Gimbels and the big store has been taken over by one of our own—Bernice Fitz-Gibbon?"

Fortunately Bernard Gimbel had a good sense of humor.

Anna Mary Robertson Moses

I am a grandmother six times over. Which has nothing to do with advertising. The only reason for mentioning it is that it leads nicely into my favorite grandmother story.

In the same year that we were publicizing Gimbels' 100th birthday and emphasizing the Gimbel image of ye olde, simple, unfancy, plain-talking, plain-selling department store, another problem suddenly faced me. I needed a headline for a big Thanksgiving spread (newspaper spread, that is).

Now, anybody knows that when you think of Thanksgiving you think of Grandmother and a table loaded with turkey and creamed onions and potatoes both mashed and sweet. What's more, you think of sleigh bells jingling and horses breathing white frosty smoke, and before you know it, you're saying, "Over the river and through the woods to Grandfather's house we'll go." Grandfather, grandfather . . . grandmother: a pattern began to form in my mind. A grandmother—that's what I needed. And don't think I didn't find one.

I had heard—from Louis J. Caldor, who came to my office one fine day—of a remarkable grandmother (almost eighty) who'd just taken up painting. Where other grandmothers were whipping up afghans, she was whipping up paintings of tight, tidy fields with blobs of pink apple trees in childlike rows or farmyards studded with lopsided barns and tipsy-tilted evergreens. My informer had spied her oil paintings in the corner window of a drugstore in Hoosick Falls, New York. Even surrounded with shaving cream and glycerine soap, her paintings looked mighty good. He made inquiries. Yes, they were the works of a resident of nearby Eagle Bridge: Anna Mary Robertson Moses—Grandma Moses for short.

He had visions of something bigger (and more lucrative) for Grandma than a drugstore window. He approached me at just the right time. There I was, looking for a grandmother. He had one. We invited Grandma Moses to come to Gimbels, paintings and all, and we would put on an honest-to-goodness showing—her first big one, I'm sure. From there on, everything worked like a copywriter's dream.

Grandma epitomized the kind of image I was striving to create for Gimbels. Grandma and Gimbels were both chock-full of the best of the old American traits: plainness, unfanciness, rusticity. Neither Grandma nor Gimbels put on airs. Both were fanatically thrifty. And both passed on the fruits of that fantastic thriftiness to the general public—Grandma, with her enchanting pictures of country life modestly priced at $5 and up (and not very up); and

Gimbels, who passed on the fruits of its hardheaded, hard-hitting shrewd merchandising by putting low, low prices on all kinds of unbeatable bargains.

We advertised Gimbels and Grandma to the hilt. Our full-page ads were headed "Over the river and through the woods to Grandmother's house we go," with pictures of platters and carving knives and cranberry jelly from our Epicure Shop. We editorialized at the top of our pages and invited the women of New York to come and meet Grandma. New York must be a grandmotherless town. Women of all shapes and sizes and ages poured in to meet Grandma. Mind you, that was twenty-five years ago. No one knew Grandma as an artist—she was just a grandma.

Grandma arrived—white-haired, blue-eyed, pink-cheeked—armed with pictures and a big box of homemade Grandma Moses' grape preserves. I was pretty busy. I turned her over to two copywriter cubs, Dorothy Kennedy and Eleanor Milligan. They ooh'd and ah'd and clucked over this little visitor to the big city.

"Hardly got here," she told them. "I was painting the kitchen right up to the minute I left Eagle Bridge."

We hung her paintings in an auditorium, an abandoned lunchroom. Somehow the feat of painting *them* wasn't half so remarkable to any of us as the fact that she had painted the kitchen walls. We loved her.

The paintings? Well . . . not many sold. After all, they cost from $5 to $25.

One picture was even a few dollars more. "It's bigger, you see," Grandma explained. "I had to use more paint. And paint, you know, costs money."

I called in Dorothy Kennedy and Eleanor Milligan. "Are you going to buy one of these?" I asked Kennedy.

"Heavens, no," said Dorothy. She was enamored of the French Renaissance at the time and had no use for art unless there was a unicorn visible.

"How about you?" I asked Eleanor. She was in the clutches of a Victorian mania at the time. "Doesn't go with Belter," she said, and then trotted off to a Third Avenue shop to buy a couple more milk-glass hands.

"Me too," I thought. After all—$25.

I decided to buy the preserves. Back to Eagle Bridge went the pictures. And I had wild grape preserves on my croissant.

On my desk, as I put this on paper, is a magazine with its center spread devoted to a reproduction of Grandma Moses' *Winter Scene* from a private collection, shown by the Farnsworth Museum in Rockland, Maine, in its exhibit entitled "Paintings to Live With."

Now why, just why, didn't I stock up on Grandma's pictures instead of her preserves? I imagine that $250 invested then would have netted me about $150,000. The grape preserves disappeared quickly.

All this goes to prove, dear reader, that you can be completely brainless in one direction, and still be a success in another. I just thank heaven I wasn't looking for a grandfather and Picasso had arrived.

One day I woke up to find myself famous

In department store copywriting, a person may rocket to fame practically overnight. This is because in retail advertising departments there is no anonymity.

In an advertising agency, there are so many fingers in the pie that it is hard to pin down the writer of any particular piece. Then there is such a stretch of time after the agency ad is written and its appearance in a publication—usually a magazine—that it's hard to determine who had the idea in the first place and just who put the words on paper.

Department store writers, whose work appears mainly in newspapers, work much more quickly—there's usually no more than two weeks between the time the ad is planned and its appearance in the paper.

I have known young cubs who have been in the department less than six months to produce such fresh startling headline and editorial copy that people all over New York were asking, "Who wrote that terrific ad for Wanamaker's that ran in the *Herald Tribune*?"

Even though the policy of an advertising department is always to say, "It was the work of the department—we do not give out individuals' names," by nightfall scores of people would know it was actually little Mary Ellen McGillicuddy who wrote it.

And the fame lingers long after nightfall when you have come up with that elusive little jewel that immediately captures the public's fancy and becomes a household word. I found myself in that happy circumstance after coining the "nobody but nobody" slogan for Gimbels.

The "nobody but nobody" slogan came about this way: I was on my way to the ancestral acres in Wisconsin one July day back in 1945, when Fred Gimbel came into my office.

"You're not going away now—not *now* when we're in the middle of this price war?"

Well, we were always in the middle of something; and I *had* planned on taking the Northwest plane to Milwaukee in about three hours.

I sought to reassure him. "I'll leave a headline that can be run across every page till I get back. I'll be back in a week."

I thought to myself, "My goose is cooked, I'll never make the plane."

Of course, I knew what the gist of the headline had to be. It had to say, in no uncertain terms, that no other store had lower prices.

I couldn't say, "No store sells for less," because the newspapers had censorship rules and would not permit the word *store* to be used in that way. "No one" was feeble. "Nobody" was the right word. "Nobody" was a good full-bodied word with a fine dactylic rhythm. "Nobody undersells Gimbels"—that was a little bald and bleak; and besides I needed more words in order to make the eight-column headline the proper size.

I sat there muttering "nobody, nobody" when suddenly I remembered the last few lines of a poem by A. A. Milne, "The King's Breakfast." You remember the King asked for very little. All he wanted was "some butter for the Royal slice of bread": He first asked the Queen and the Queen asked the Dairymaid, and the Dairymaid asked the Alderney, who was too sleepy to stand up to be milked and suggested that "many people nowadays like marmalade instead." Whereupon the Dairymaid returned to the Queen and said, "Marmalade is tasty, if it's very thickly spread."

The last lines slid back into my memory and I found myself muttering:

> *"Nobody," he said,*
> *As he kissed her*
> *Tenderly,*
> *"Nobody," he said,*
> *As he slid down*
> *The banisters,*
> *"Nobody,*
> *My darling,*
> *Could call me*
> *A fussy man—*
> *BUT*
> I do like a little bit of butter to my bread!"

"Nobody, nobody, nobody" was emphatic, but a couple of characters too long. "Nobody but nobody" was just right.

I called in the layout man, who lettered in the line, and I grabbed my hat and ran for the plane, hoping that the words would do what a good ad should do: cut across the readers' complacency, stop them, stir them. The words did. They cut. They stopped. They stirred.

On one of Winston Churchill's visits to New York, Bernard Baruch gave a dinner for him. In the middle of the dinner, Churchill put down his knife and fork, turned to the assembled guests, and—apropos of nothing at all—asked, "Is it true that nobody, but nobody, undersells Gimbels?"

That slogan "Nobody but nobody undersells Gimbels" is still being used. The twisted semantics, the nutty repetition, caught on like wildfire.

The first part of the slogan became a bit of Americana overnight. Solemn pieces analyzing it appeared in trade magazines. Psychologists analyzed it too. There were switches on it: "no place, but no place," "no man, but no man," "nowhere, but nowhere."

And it came about because of a refrain in a Milne verse which I had accidentally memorized when reading the Milne verses to my children! Memorizing a memory gem! What could be squarer? A good advertising writer is always a little bit square.

Advertising has been the butt of consistent carping and sniping for its part in commercializing Christmas.

I can remember my grandmother's saying, "Christmas isn't the same any more—it's too commercialized. If only my grandchildren could have a good old Christmas—the kind of Christmas we had in the good old days, *that* would be a Christmas they'd never forget!"

I liked Christmas as it was. So one day I asked her, "What was so good about the good old Christmas? What were your presents? What did you get?"

Her answer: "Oh it was all so lovely! Presents? Each one of us always got warm mittens and an orange in the toe of our stockings."

"Huh," I thought to myself, "mittens and an orange! That would certainly be a Christmas we'd never forget!"

If all Christmas commercializing stopped I believe that everybody would be brought up short as I was. A noncommercial Christmas would be a "warm mittens and orange" Christmas. And who really wants that? I am sure that almost everybody would miss those last months when all the stores are fragrant with mammoth wreaths of pine and shining holly, and mistletoe decorates the tall columns. The piny perfume of the north woods mixes with the essence of jasmine and carnation and rose in the Perfume Section; and over this floats the delectable citrony aroma from the Food Shop, where mountains of fruitcakes and plum puddings and roast geese with crackling skin and roast young pigs with apples in their mouths are on display.

All these lovely smells float up the escalators and help give the entire store a feeling of warm good will and hearty hospitality. The average store is Christmasier than Washington Irving and Clement Moore and Charles Dickens all rolled up together. And I, for one, love it.

Gimbels chimney Christmas window was the best in town . . . and cost the least

Months before Christmas, promotional directors and display managers go into a harried huddle trying to decide on a unique, charming idea for an automated Christmas display to pull in children and their parents. Usually a whole bank of windows is taken for an enchanting automated telling of some lovely old fairy tale—like "Cinderella" or "Jack and the Beanstalk" or "Hansel and Gretel." If the display is beautifully done with exquisite costumes and realistic figures, the whole thing runs into money—generally *big* money because automation and sound are expensive.

Many years ago at Gimbels I was racking my brains to think of something that would be imaginative, appealing, and inexpensive. So I asked myself, "What would *I* want to see at Christmas if *I* were a child under six? What would capture my imagination and be a complete delight?" The answer came through clear as a bell. I'd want to see Santa come down a chimney.

It was so obvious that I wondered why no one had thought of it before. Of course, I'd want to see Santa Claus come down a chimney. Even a five-year-old realizes that it's utterly absurd for a jelly-belly Santa to go down the average suburban chimney. How can he do it? It's like a camel going through the eye of a needle. Every child has seen hundreds of *pictures*. But a picture is only a picture. He's never seen the real thing. Gimbels would have to show him.

So we took Gimbels' immense corner window and built the rooftop of a typical Colonial-type suburban house with a red brick chimney. On the rooftop was a big sleigh spilling over with toys and gifts—and drawing the sleigh were eight prancing reindeer. The two leading reindeer (Dasher and Dancer) were half outside Gimbels' front windowpane. All very realistic. All very stop-and-startle. Then every fifteen minutes all day long there was a great commotion of Christmas bells and Ho-ho-ho's and Ha-ha-ha's, and a big burly apple-cheeked *real* Santa Claus appeared on the roof. He sang our theme song, which was the old "Jingle Bells" tune with several verses about Gimbels.

Santa Claus not only appeared and sang but he talked to the children—singling out this one and that one—telling them all the latest North Pole gossip. He told them all about Mrs. Claus and the elves who work on the gifts and how Blitzen caught his left antler in the Northern Lights and how Comet is a hot-rodder and streaks all around the Arctic at 150 miles an hour, and so on. He also talked with bluff heartiness about Gimbels' Toy Department, and how he had to rush up there after he went down the chimney. Then he *went down the chimney*! (By collapsing his collapsible stomach.)

Chimney Christmas on a shoestring

Well, chimney Christmas! That window got more attention than any other Christmas window in town. Hordes of bug-eyed children stood out in front. It is an understatement to say that they were fascinated and enchanted. They were literally glued to the spot. When a mother would finally manage to get hold of her child's hand she would say, "C'mon, Sara Jane, let's look at Macy's window." But Sara Jane wasn't budging. She *knew* Santa Claus wasn't at Macy's. How could he be at Macy's when obviously he was at Gimbels?

Here was an absurdly simple and very inexpensive idea. Sometimes the simple obvious thing is the best. And it is always wise to work with props that can be used year after year with just a little painting and refurbishing.

We repeated the idea without change every year, always with the same overwhelming success. I think Gimbels is still using it, which would give it one of the longest runs on Broadway—over twenty years.

I had a pretty long run myself on Broadway—fourteen years. In 1954 I left Gimbels to open my own agency on the corner of 56th Street and Fifth Avenue.

How did Gimbels do after I left? Gimbels did all right. Under the brilliant aegis of Bruce Gimbel and his New York store head, Bernard Zientz, Gimbels has been cracking all previous records in volume and profits. And a member of the Gimbel chain, Saks Fifth Avenue, has been hitting fantastic heights. Little wonder. The man that heads Saks Fifth is Adam Gimbel, conceded to be the greatest fashion expert on the face of the earth. The dazzling runner-up must be Stanley Marcus of Dallas.

XVI

How to tell the nuts from the dolts

I was a perfect boss. Because I provided a climate where it was safe to make mistakes. Don't start any kind of writing career in any environment where it is not safe to make mistakes. Some advertising managers and copy chiefs and account executives are so scared of top brass that they discourage departures from the norm. They frown on any wild excesses of originality. Not me.

I welcome wildness. There are always plenty of people around to tame things down. Taming is easy. If you must choose between a nut boss and a dolt boss—take the nut.

I remember one such nut. He was offered a job as advertising manager in a stodgy Milwaukee concern at three times his Macy salary. The morning he reported for work he called a meeting of the writers and told them, "I'll never last here—but it will take them a few months to catch on to me; then they'll fire me. And during those months, if you people play ball with me, you can build up the most sensational sample books in the Middle West."

They did. The advertising was shocking, sensational, and it sold goods.

Those copywriters were lucky to get a chance to work for a nut
(even for a few short weeks) where everything fresh and original
and sound they wrote got into print, and was published. What happened to the nut ad manager? He was out in four months. But
he's been soaring higher and higher ever since. And so has every
one of the writers, but not in Milwaukee.

If you want your ads to be read, look for the boss who encourages
copywriters to be fresh and original—I don't mean cockeyed and
impractical.

At Macy's I found such a person—Mr. Eddie Marks, Vice-president and Merchandise Manager of all fashion. He never killed a
good headline. He fostered "freshness" and "difference" even
though he was not directly connected with the advertising department. When our timid advertising manager was about to kill my
headline—HOW DO YOU KEEP IT UP NIGHT AFTER NIGHT?—on a
Macy coup, the first strapless evening gown, Eddie OK'd it and put
it through.

Later our timid ad manager left Macy's and the incomparable
Ken Collins moved in. Kenneth Collins was the best thing that ever
happened to retail advertising. In the middle twenties, before Collins, stores were still running three kinds of copy:

1. Simpering fashionese that babbled on about Dame Fashion dictating and Milady acquiescing (the customer was always
   Milady).
2. Noisy rock 'em and sock 'em hard sell.
3. Pompous institutionals signed at the bottom "from the office of
   the President" with the date. They always contained the deadly
   words, *rewarding* and *challenge* and *dedicated*.

Did Macy's run stuff like this? Macy's did. What was the matter
with Macy copywriters—couldn't they write better stuff? They
could. They did. But they couldn't get it printed. They couldn't
even get it in type. And then came Collins. And with him that
glorious golden era A.C. (after Collins) when his wit and warmth

and naturalness changed retail advertising into civilized communication.

Kenneth Collins was born in Minnesota, was a Signal Corps pilot
in World War I, got his B.A. from the University of Washington
(where he was Phi Beta Kappa), his M.A. from the University of
Idaho, turned down a Rhodes scholarship to become an Austin
scholar at Harvard, where he taught in the English department.

This sounds egghead and doesn't sum up Collins at all. He was
not sum-uppable. He was out of his time and century. He was *the*
Renaissance Man, the whole man, the abundant man, popping up
in the twentieth century. He was a topnotch taxonomist and knew
a hepatica from a trillium and a lady's slipper from a Jacob's-
ladder. He was ornithologist, psychologist, Episcopal preacher,
Harvard teacher, etymologist, entomologist, plane pilot. He could
fly through the air with the greatest of ease; but he also knew
plants, ants, bugs, slugs, retailing, sea sailing, and sweet peas. He
was an astronomer of parts, a bibliophile, a numismatist, a colum-
nist.

He even knew whole books of Chaucer by heart. He had talents
so vast and so myriad that he could quote Ovid and Euclid, and
always knew where to put the period. He was at home with Kierke-
gaard, and was such a fabulous raconteur that his listeners always
laughed hard. Who understood Zen? Ken.

He was the hero of Macy's Golden Story because he always gave
other people the credit and the glory. Collins provided the perfect
climate in which to make mistakes. Collins' death in 1962 was an
irreparable loss to all advertising.

At Gimbels, I was lucky enough to work with the perfect pragmatist, Fred Gimbel. The perfect boss or client is one who doesn't
look at the ads until he reads them in the paper or magazine or sees
them on TV.

My most sensational ad was my famous manure ad which I ran

for Gimbels. It has been criticized for being wild and shocking. Critics said that it was not soundly merchandised, and that I ran it only for shock effect. Not true. The whole idea of the ad was flawlessly thought out and from a merchandise standpoint was sound as an apple.

One December day in the forties, Fred Gimbel walked into my office and said, "Fitz, why don't you think up some gift that a lot of people who 'have everything' would like to get, but for some reason never get? There must be something that no store has ever thought of promoting."

I thought and thought. I lived in the suburbs where the women as well as the men were passionately devoted to gardening. I had heard many of them deplore the fact that it was practically impossible to find natural cow manure—in fact one woman said, "That's what I want for Christmas: cow manure."

I had been brought up on the belief that one cannot grow roses without horse manure. I decided to forget the roses, since horse manure would be harder to find than cow manure.

So that was my ad.

I called in the staff. Most of them were shocked at the idea. Especially shocked was Bob, the office manager. He said that we shouldn't run a manure ad at all, for two reasons. "One, we won't be able to sell enough cow manure by the ton to pay for the space of the ad, and two, even if we sell enough to pay for the ad, hundreds of pious customers would be so horrified that they would close out their charge accounts."

I was teetering on the fence as to whether or not to run it, when Rufus Bastian, our art director, came up with an irresistible layout. He said, "The ad will look very Christmasy because most manure piles are just the shape of a Christmas tree, and at the very top of the tree instead of a star we will put a rooster, because there is always a cock on a dunghill." His ad, almost a full page, looked so very Christmasy that it was scary.

Rufus had lettered in a headline that I found irresistible:

NO BOSSY BUT NO BOSSY HAS FINER MANURE
THAN GIMBELS

That decided me to run it. And, as I rationalized, a good headline should cause a disturbance, and since manure is the most wanted and unreceived gift, the whole promotion is perfect.

We sent it out on release. It appeared the next morning in the New York *Herald Tribune*—the most gardeny of all the New York newspapers.

The Gimbels Garden Department buyer thought I was dotty to run the ad. But the minute the telephone board opened that morning, we had an avalanche of orders.

A successful ad is supposed to sell ten times the cost of the ad space in the first two days. This was accomplished in the first forty minutes. For once it was true—that brag of the copywriter: "The ad sold tons of the product." The Garden Department buyer was in a tizzy getting in more manure from the pastures of New Jersey. Long-distance calls and telegrams poured in.

Most of the copy was written by Leslie Forester, but all members of the staff contributed little bits to ham it up: We won't gift-wrap —all sales final—and so on.

This ad appeared in that very fascinating book *100 Top Copy Writers and Their Favorite Ads,* edited by Perry Schofield and published by Printers Ink Books, 205 East 42nd Street, New York City. I was told that the head of Young & Rubicam pronounced the manure ad the best ad of the year.

Did our pious customers threaten to close out their charge accounts? They certainly did—scores of them. Did that upset Fred Gimbel? Not a bit. He said, "Best ad that ever ran. I would much rather have people furious at Gimbels than indifferent to Gimbels."

Then I had a bright idea that would take Gimbel *and* me off the

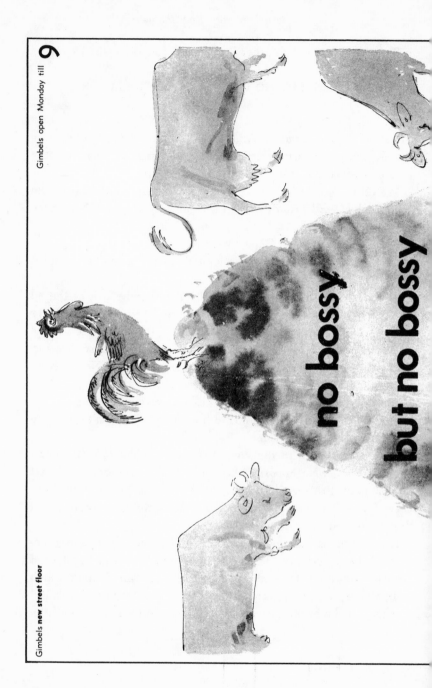

no bossy

but no bossy

than Gimbels

You can take Gimbels out of the farm . . . but you can't take the farm out of Gimbels. In all the land there is not a street floor more chic, more radiant than **Gimbels new street floor.** And on this new street floor you won't find a more beautiful, more "bloomy" shop than **Gimbels new Flower Shop.** But even though our walls are elegantly pink and elegantly green, we're still realists at heart. There's always been something earthy . . . something from the soil . . . about Gimbels. And we can't forget that it's things like **manure** and **compost** and **mulch** at make our **flowers** so breath-takingly beautiful. Why then, should ~ne be startled to find us discussing the merits of organic nutri- ᐧ the same breath with modern decor and indirect lighting? ᐧ ridiculous, say we. We think it's a bright-eyed idea to give someone manure for Christmas. Tickle the earth, say we, and she'll laugh a harvest. And that's the very reason we've made contact with our bovine friends in Westchester, Long Island, and New Jersey. We'll ship a magnificent 1-ton batch of Daisy's finest to your door (or to the rear door or the barn) for $19 (within 20 miles of Gimbels). Or, if you prefer organic and chemical mix- ture, we'll ship same in 50-pound bags for a paltry 2.79. But out of the stable now . . . and back to **Gimbels Flower Shop,** that

patch of good green earth in the heart of our **new street floor.** Here's the spot where smart young wives pick up the roses for the table each morning . . . where the newly-married commuter dashes in for a bunch of "mums" a minute before the Long Island leaves for Locust Valley . . . We can't begin to list the infinite variety of our flowers and plants. But for the opening gun of our new street floor, we're dipping prices on just about everything with the "bloom on." Come in today . . . pick up a dozen **white, yellow, or bronze chrysanthemums.** They're regularly $12 a dozen. Today, **they are $9.** Buy a bunch of yellow, white, or bronze **pompons.** They're regularly $2 and 2.50 a bunch. Today, you **pay only 1.50.** Long-stemmed **roses** that usually sell for $6 to $9 a dozen are going for **2 dozen for $6.** And so on down the list . . . from assorted cut flowers to **Boston ivy** to **Chinese evergreens** to **Holland tulip, daffodil,** and **hyacinth** bulbs. And in a few weeks our **poinsettias** will be bursting forth in all their Christmas glory. All this because we have a brand new street floor. All this because we're so much in love with cows. And if we've convinced you on a manure present for Christmas . . . by all means we think you had better order now. Let's not put a rush on our productive friends in the country.

gift-wrap your package? Hardly. This is just atmosphere. We're phone, no C.O.D.'s. All sales final. Come in to our new Raymond Loewy-designed street floor hook. I called my most erudite friend, Anne Fremantle, an English-woman who taught Creative Writing at Fordham, and who wrote for a great many Catholic magazines.

Here is part of a piece she wrote:

One of the major New York department stores has been advising its clients to give a load of manure this Christmas.

The perfect Christmas gift, their ads read, for a gardener. They don't promise to gift-wrap it, of course.

This certainly does seem the ideal gift for any gardener. . . . What with sanitation, artificial fertilisers and cremation, mulch, compost and manure itself grow rarer and dearer every year. . . .

But it's not only for gardeners that manure is a good gift. It's the first good sign in a signally cheerless fall, that a big store has come out for manure in a big way. The ad itself might be regarded as a gift. For it is a healthy reminder of birth and of growth, as well as our latter end, for the first two, on the highest authority, depend on the last. There's no grass greener than churchyard grass, and the best way to make a rose tree grow is to bury a dead dog at its roots.

How much better and sweeter a gift is good manure, than a dress with a plunging neckline, or a padded bra. How good to see manure advertised, instead of falsies, breatholators, alcohol, and the various other gee-gaws and gadgets with which our lives are complicated. How much nearer to the manger were the ox and the ass, and their manure, than is a TV set that makes our children prouder than their fellows. For if we are so lucky as to receive manure, we must cultivate our garden, and must spend, as Mr. Kipling pointed out, more than half our time upon our knees very properly and enjoyably working out the primal curse. Whereas, if given a TV set, we will waste our time watching circuses, nibbling probably, not bread, but cake. How Shakespeare who saw great Caesar dead and turned to clay, stopping a hole to keep the draught away, would rejoice in this reminder of the quintessence of our dust, and manure brings to mind too, the command from Sinai to Moses to raise an altar, not of gold or silver or wood, but of earth. For from this manure, this earth, this dust, that lies on Helen's eyes, is what we are, and what we shall be. . . .

Mrs. Fremantle's words turned the tide. She had long had tremendous prestige among Catholics, and soon Gimbels and I became famous for having run the only page of the season that was really in keeping with the Christmas message from the stable.

I sent a nice note, and enclosed the Fremantle article, to each of the pious Altar Society critics. Most of them were mollified, and said that of course they would not close out their charge accounts; and many said that they enjoyed Gimbels ads because they were never bored by them.

I was still new on the job at Gimbels, and while I never believe in buttering up the big boss, neither do I believe in irritating him —at least for the first few months. The big boss was Bernard Gimbel.

You can imagine my astonishment when he dropped into my office one afternoon and said, "Fitz, I'm afraid you pulled a boner in yesterday's *Times*—the horse ad. The Poor Richard Club in Philadelphia is thoroughly shocked."

He was referring to an ad headlined THE HORSE WITH THE HANSOM BEHIND, written with the what-the-hell abandon which I think is a requisite for all good writing, whether it's an ad or a piece for the *Saturday Review*. Of course we used "hansom" as a noun, not as an adjective, and we spelled it "hansom." It was a perfectly decent headline.

True, we devoted much of the space to a picture of the south end of a horse. But our copy went on to plug the plain-old-Gimbels story. Our copy explained that back at the turn of the century, when elegant hansoms and broughams and four-in-hands were sweeping up to marquees along Fifth Avenue, no such vehicle ever pulled up to Gimbels. Plain old Gimbels never got the horse with the hansom behind. Gimbels got only the horse with the buggy behind. Here's the copy:

THE HORSE WITH THE HANSOM BEHIND

That's the horse that *didn't* come to Gimbels even back in the days when hansoms and cabbies flourished. Plain old Gimbels never got the carriage trade. The well-heeled set, that put on airs and lived like nabobs, liked to do their shopping in an elegant plush establishment. Gimbels never was elegant, ain't elegant now and (we suppose) never will be elegant. For 101 years Gimbels has had the horse-and-buggy trade—the millions of solid, solvent, substantial Americans who have always let down hems, saved candle ends, counted pennies, checked prices, and demanded every copper's worth of value whether they were spending a buck or a sawbuck. 101 years of dealing with these thrift experts have taught us that thrift consists of buying only what you need when you need it. This *New York Times* carries 3 pages of Gimbel bargains ranging from seersucker at 69¢ (one yard) to a Van Dyck at $79,000 (about 3 yards). But don't buy either or anything else unless you need it. We're glad we didn't get the horse with the hansom behind—we prefer the horse with the buggy behind.

Speaking of cows and horses, the farm barnyard has always provided me with good copy. Like this ad we once ran at Gimbels:

A 2-QUART COW CAN'T PRODUCE
A 4-GALLON DAUGHTER

Blood will tell. We got the piquant aphorism from our bucolic-type grandpa out in the Middle West. The more we look around the truer it seems—and we don't mean just down on the farm. A 2-quart cow can't have a 4-gallon calf. If Gimbels were a dainty little shoppe, Gimbels couldn't produce hairy-chested bargains. Leave it to the big store with the big frame (like Gimbels) and a mammoth buying power (like Gimbels) to come up with a real whopper of a bargain. Put the four huge Gimbel stores together, and nobody in creation beats us. Propagating fat rosy bargains just comes naturally to Gimbels. We do it every day. We've been doing it for 108 years. Ain't we plumb tuckered? Shucks, son, we were just winding up—now watch our speed!

The horse with the hansom behind...

That's the horse that _didn't_ come to Gimbels even back in the days when hansoms and cabbies flourished. Plain old Gimbels never got the carriage trade. The well-heeled set that put on airs and lived like nabobs, liked to do their shopping in an elegant lush plush establishment. Gimbels never was elegant, ain't elegant now and (we suspect) never will be elegant. For 101 years Gimbels has had the horse and buggy trade— the millions of solid, solvent, substantial Americans who have always let down hems, saved candle ends, counted pennies, checked prices, and demanded every copper's worth of value whether they were spending a buck or a sawbuck. 101 years of dealing with these thrift experts have taught us that thrift consists of buying only what you need when you need it. This New York Times carries 3 pages of Gimbels bargains ranging from seersucker at 69c (one yard) to a Van Dyck at $79,000 (about 3 yards). But don't buy either or anything else unless you need it. We're glad we didn't get the horse with the hansom behind—we prefer the horse with the buggy behind.

a 2-quart cow can't produce
a 4-gallon daughter

That is to say, blood will tell. We got the piquant aphorism from our bucolic-type grandpa out in the Middle West. The more we look around, the truer the truism seems—and we don't mean just down on the farm. A 2-quart cow can't have a 4-gallon calf— you said it. If Gimbels were a dainty little shoppe, Gimbels couldn't produce hairy-chested bargains. Leave it to a big store with a big frame (like Gimbels) and a mammoth buying power (like our'n) to come up with a real whopper of a bargain. Put the 4 huge Gimbels stores together, and nobody in creation beats us. Propagating fat rosy bargains just comes naturally to Gimbels. We do it every day. We've been doing it for 108 years. Ain't we plumb tuckered? Is it time to go moo in some grassy pasture? Shucks, son, we were just winding up—now watch our speed!

When that ad was reproduced in a trade journal, people said, "Even if Fitz became advertising head of Bergdorf-Goodman, she'd drag in the barnyard."

Of course I would. Because I long ago observed that everybody is the same. If anything, the upper crust is plainer and blunter than the bottom crust. Putting on airs is plebeian—the lower the social stratum, the more hoity-toity. Humans are pretty much alike. Superficially, one couldn't find two stores more unlike than Wanamaker's and Gimbels. Wanamaker's—dignified, pompous, aristocratic, backed by a century of icy hauteur. Gimbels—big and bargainy, always battling for business, shouting at the top of its voice.

But my operation—advertising—was pretty much the same at both stores. And we got pretty much the same response from the public.

I had learned that Wanamaker customers loved little nuggets of knowledge buried in the advertising editorials. I have always believed that an ad should contain a little bonus for the reader—a little reward for his courtesy in reading the ad.

Once I ran a Wanamaker ad on 18th-century furniture. I had worked out a little scheme of my own to help me keep the Georgian furniture designers in correct chronological order.

Chippendale came first, then Hepplewhite, then Adam, then Sheraton. So the ad said, "The abbreviation for Charles—C.H.A.S. —will help you remember the correct order."

Twenty years later at Gimbels, I repeated the same little nugget. (It's all right for me to plagiarize myself.) I said "C.H.A.S. (the abbreviation for Charles) will help you remember the proper order of the Georgian designers." Scores of thank-you notes from Gimbel customers arrived—almost word-for-word replicas of the thank-you notes from Wanamaker customers.

I did the same thing with a Christmas idea. Our research at Wanamaker's revealed the fact that our modern Santa Claus is a creation of America—not a creation of the Continent, as had generally been believed.

I had been toying with words for a Christmas slogan and came up with "American Christmas and a Happy New Year." We went on to explain: Yes, Santa Claus, with his jelly-belly jollity, was an American creation—from the brains of Washington Irving and Clement Moore, author of "The Night Before Christmas." This roly-poly American Santa was and is completely different from the mean old skinny St. Nicholas of the Continent, who carried a long stick in his bag to discipline naughty children.

Twenty years later, I repeated this at Gimbels. It was perfect for Gimbels. The Gimbel store is on 32nd Street. The home of Clement Moore, where he wrote "The Night Before Christmas," was not many blocks away in Chelsea.

XVII

Let the corpus stay home

Fred Gimbel lured me away from Wanamaker's in 1940. The lure? Money. Also the fact that Gimbels was a bigger operation, a bigger opportunity. I was to get a percentage of the increase in profit plus a minimum guarantee of $60,000. In 1941 or thereabouts, my Gimbel income was about $90,000.

Fred Gimbel, who had just taken over the Gimbel store, had been personally checking on the responses to the Wanamaker ads. He was impressed by the fact that my new different kind of copy for Wanamaker's did such an astonishingly good job of selling. He contrasted the hearty Wanamaker response with the feeble response that Gimbel ads were bringing in. The Gimbel ads were of the hard-sell rock 'em and sock 'em school. The Wanamaker ads with their softer sell (actually I prefer sound-sell to soft-sell) were selling hard. And people all over town were talking about the Wanamaker advertising.

Fred Gimbel had brought into Gimbels a whole new team of merchandisers who were quite upset when he hired me. They didn't want a female in a top position. They urged Fred to take on a certain smart fellow who was a genius with figures. Fred's answer was "I know Fitz won't be good at figures. I am sure she can't even brandish a slide rule. But I don't need a fancy figurer. Because no matter how expertly the fancy figurer figures, he still cannot buy linage any cheaper. So when I pay a lot of money I should get somebody who can personally do part of the advertising job—someone who can either get tons of publicity, or draw pictures, or make layouts, or write irresistible copy."

I first impressed Fred by cutting out waste. In New York, the newspapers charge the stores for changes and corrections in copy and art after the ad has once been set up. The Gimbel correction bill was high. I cut it to absolutely nothing. We never remade a cut.

The copywriter was obliged to get the buyer's OKs on type-written copy. Not a syllable went to paper or magazine that hadn't been OK'd by everybody concerned, including the buyer and his merchandise manager. Occasionally an emergency price change would have to be made at the last minute, but that came within the minimal allowance for which there was no charge.

When Fred Gimbel saw month after month that there was not a penny of waste, he decided that I was a penny-pinching genius. And he gave me a free hand.

How thrifty were we? We saved on everything, even the apostrophes. We changed *Gimbel's* to *Gimbels*.

How smart were we? We hired only Phi Beta Kappas . . . and then used them for secretaries, receptionists, messengers, production trainees.

I think I can safely say that at Gimbels we hired more brains for less money than did anyone else in town.

Over sixty-three years ago Sir Ernest Shackleton, the famed polar explorer, placed this ad in a London newspaper:

Men wanted for hazardous journey. Small wages, bitter cold, long months of complete darkness. Constant danger, safe return doubtful. Honor and recognition in case of success.

Maybe the great success of the Peace Corps is partly due to a similar appeal to young people. I quote *The New York Times Magazine:*

Similarly, Peace Corps publicity describing the low pay (11 cents an hour), long hours (16 per day) and rough working conditions (you're right there with an army of bloodthirsty mosquitoes) seems to be an inducement rather than a deterrent to applicants. This does not mean that college students are ready to go to work for a pittance, but it does indicate an interest in more than just material rewards.

At Gimbels, we offered hard work, stern training, challenge and opportunity, and, ultimately, some pretty handsome cash rewards. But first, training and work. We wanted hustlers and scramblers, the type that takes on tough problems for fun.

There are many people like that, and they don't have to have college degrees. College degrees do not guarantee brilliance. I once hired a girl of sixteen who had never been near a college. Her name was Caroline Kauffman. She turned out to be the best secretary I ever had.

It is true, however, that college does provide some kind of rough sorting system for brains.

It was on the latter theory that we adopted our recruiting policy. Gimbels copy had become so famous that we were overwhelmed with applications from copywriters. When we needed a replacement, it was a big job to thumb through the bulging files. Then I thought of a shortcut solution.

"Let's burn the whole file," I said, "and place a small ad in *The New York Times* saying we'll hire nobody but Phi Beta Kappas. After that we'll pool the names we didn't hire, and draw from that pool when we need someone."

We did, and we didn't. That is, we did place the ad, and after that we didn't hire anyone but Phi Beta Kappas.

Our first ad was minuscule, only 2 columns on 60 lines, and it pulled enormously. From then on we ran a similar version—twice a year—near the end of each semester. Each time, the response brought us the flower of Princeton, Harvard, Yale, Smith, and Vassar. It's a funny thing, but a fact, the *higher and harder you make your standards, the more eager people are to break their necks to meet them.* The harder it was to get in, the wilder the Phi Beta Kappas were to work for us.

What did we pay them? Very little—less than we paid anyone else. How did we start them out? As leg cubs in the proofroom. There's no grubbier job. It meant running your legs off with inky proofs, getting dirtier and tireder than any janitor could get. But our lofty requirements surrounded the job with such glamour that the merest hint of a vacancy filled up the corridors with top brains.

Running the menial errands was really not such a bad way to start. Our trainees saw the operation from the ground up, and they learned early the importance of such mundane mechanical details as that little matter of getting it right before it got into metal.

If the Phi Betes were real hustlers they also seized the opportunity to learn something from the copy sheets and proofs which they held in their hands as they trotted back and forth.

After a while, if they showed promise, we promoted them to slavey. A slavey was a cub who worked for a top-notch writer who once, months or years before, had been just a Phi Beta Kappa running errands.

The system worked, and not only for us. It worked for the slaveys, too. I'm proud to say that many an ex-cub has come around afterward to tell me that he got his real education, the working one, in his slavey days at Gimbels.

The slavey trainees also knew that if their future looked dim— if there wasn't any opening at Gimbels for them to grow into—I would tell them so, and would move heaven and earth to get them jobs in other stores at higher salaries than they were getting with me.

And so they came charging in, these youngsters who were all

rarin' to go. Did they all make it? Practically all did. Those who failed to climb as high as their brains entitled them to go failed for other reasons. They were not really failures. Those Phi Beta Kappas with no imagination or flair we shoved off on publicity, or merchandising, or sign painting or routine conventional sale ads— anywhere to get them out of our way. The other kind, the ones with imagination and flair, we prized and treasured.

We kept them the only way you can keep creative, clever, unusual people. The system can be succinctly stated: *Raise 'em and praise 'em.* While serving as slaveys they got a bare minimum of money, less than other stores were paying, lots of opportunity and as much praise as they earned. When they became top writers, with slaveys of their own, we paid them a good deal more than any competitive stores were offering.

Another important policy was that of giving each group head a free hand to run his own division. He could grant time off to his trainees whenever he wanted. He could let his assistants come in at noon, or keep them late. We really didn't care.

Our position was simple. We wanted top-notch work, on schedule, and we weren't concerned about how that small miracle was achieved. Our motto was, If the spirit is willing, let the corpus stay home.

To put it another way, the *job* was to be covered all the time. The *chair seats* did not have to be covered all the time.

I have never understood why it's so all-fired important that everybody in a store be physically present a rigid number of hours daily. Of course I am speaking of advertising—not selling departments.

Before I could get what I wanted for the advertising department at Gimbels, I had to rack my brains for a solution. I wanted all the copywriters to have something just as attractive as money: *time off.* Of course, the rules of the store forbade this. The rule read: "Two weeks off with pay after the employee has been with the store for a full year." I wanted to give each copywriter about eight weeks' vacation no matter when he started—four weeks in the summer and three or four weeks in the winter.

It was Fred Gimbel's connivance that enabled me to give the copywriters elastic daily hours and seven or eight weeks' yearly vacation. I'd rather have an advertising writer in the advertising department six hours a day but thinking about his ads fourteen hours a day than have his physical presence in the department a conventional eight hours a day and his thinking for only those eight hours. A good advertising person is so involved that he thinks about the promotion of his products practically all the time. This extra thought and concern and devotion on the part of the copywriter can make a store unbeatable. And we did turn out unbeatable ads.

When I approached Fred Gimbel about these elastic hours he said, "That's fine. Just mark them all present in the attendance book."

"But," I said, "my convent upbringing won't let me juggle the records." Actual tampering with records seemed like a mortal sin to me! He said, "All right. Bring the records to me and I'll juggle them. I'll mark them in when they are out." What a boss!

No wonder Gimbels was beating every other store in America. Little wonder that we were the fastest-growing store in the whole nation.

But all the money I could squeeze out of the budget plus plenty of time off wasn't enough. There was a third requirement (and let every copy head and store president note this). Great talent requires one thing more: It wants to work with people as talented as itself. One expensive razzle-dazzle writer on your staff is not enough. Good writers want to work in a climate where they will get the competition and inspiration of other writers as good as they.

Isn't the desire to please the boss enough? No.

Of course the writers wanted the approval of me—Fitz. But Mama's approval (I was called the Mother Superior of retail advertising) or Daddy's approval (Ken Collins was called the Father Confessor of retail advertising) was not enough. Like teen-agers, copywriters want the admiration of their peers. One electric eel isn't enough. You need an ocean of electric eels to spark one another. Edith Sitwell once said, "I am an electric eel in a pool full of catfish." See what I mean when I say you should seek out the nut boss—not a dolt one?

Soon everybody wanted to work at Gimbels, because:

1. You worked with brilliant people.
2. You got six or eight weeks' vacation.
3. You had elastic hours—you could always make a train or a long weekend. (But you had to be in early—anyone who arrived at 9 A.M. was late.)
4. You could get a good store discount on your purchases. I tried to persuade buyers and merchandise managers that it's wrong to try to make a profit on the help; they should make their profit on the public.

No writer like a writer's writer or Fitz-Gibbon's Gresham Law

Just as bad money tends to drive out good money, so mediocre writers tend to drive out good ones. The pondful of electric eels should all be swimming round showing off to one another. Do I mean writers should be writing for one another? I certainly do. I have always believed that there is no writer like a writer's writer, and there's no artist like an artist's artist. When you work with the top craftsmen in your own field in mind, you are bound to extend yourself and do your very best. Yes, a writer's writer, and a lawyer's lawyer, and a physicist's physicist are the best of all possible writers, lawyers, and physicists. The better the writing, the clearer the message—hence a writers' writer writes in good, clear, communicative, selling English.

I suppose that I really should sum up all the above with some pithy statement as to my philosophy of personnel management. Let me put it this way: What I was trying to do at Gimbels was to run a creative department the way Campbell's makes soup.

You know the Campbell slogan: "To make the best begin with the best—then cook with extra care."

As I have said, I am the perfect boss. I am lazy. I love to delegate. I don't grab the glamour stuff to do myself. I don't grab anything I can avoid doing. I'll work harder to teach someone else how to write than to do it myself.

My beginning cubs never got bored twiddling their thumbs in the mail room—which I understand is quite usual in an agency.

My grandfather—so I was told—used to say, "One boy's a boy, two boys half a boy, three boys no boy at all." So pile work on your creative workers. The busier they are, the happier. Relieve them of all dull repetitive grubby detail such as pasting up the ad book, typing copies of things.

Just as every homemaker knows, it's easier to grow many houseplants than one plant. Each "gives off" something to the others. The houseplants, I suppose, create the perfect climate by giving off moisture. The copy people create the proper climate by lighting little fires under one another. And the advertising director has the comforting assurance of a "sequence of bloom." As soon as somebody leaves, someone else (at least partly trained) moves up.

You will endear yourself to a writer by getting his best (or what he considers his best) stuff into type so that he can paste it into his sample book even if it never actually runs. They say that the best stuff written in advertising agencies never gets into metal type. It is perfectly all right to fill a sample book with typewritten stuff; but it does look a bit more impressive in proof.

At Wanamaker's someone did a charming ad on a girl's first bra. She was pictured tearing across the page in shapely profile, yelling, "Look, Ma, no concavities." A good pun: a good spoof on the toothpaste commercial, "Look, Ma, no cavities." Wanamaker's would never let me run it. But I got it in proof. And the writer was delighted. I have always believed that the reason I had hundreds of applicants from every state in the Union, and every province in Canada, and from most countries in Europe, while other stores had no applicants at all, was because I got proofs pulled of the writers' favorite ads. Wasn't this wasteful—after all I have said about thrift? Not for the store. Because each paper permitted a store to change or kill copy if the amount was minimal. I always stayed within the minimal allowance.

I told you earlier to try to get your first job in an advertising department where it is safe to make mistakes. It's also smart to get yourself born into a family where it is safe to make mistakes, and to get yourself placed in a school where it is safe to make mistakes. What kind of mistakes? Mistakes of over-creativity—in other words, find a climate where over-exuberance, over-ebullience, over-freshness, over-originality, are never slapped down. Which means a place where a parent or teacher or business boss is more interested in bringing out individuality in speech and writing than in maintaining conventional safe discipline. There are many copy departments in both retail stores and advertising agencies where any departure from the norm, any burst of wildness, is frowned upon, because it might upset the client.

I was fortunate in having a teacher-farmer father who encouraged wildness. He felt that there were always enough tamers-down around. He equated docility with dullness. He didn't want a house full of docile, respectful children. He wanted kids that exploded with different ideas—cockeyed ideas, unconventional thoughts clothed in an unconventional way. So, don't slap down the spontaneous wildness of your child or writing cub.

Creating this kind of freedom in a writing job calls for the kind of courage the average boss does not possess. He is usually in awe of the boss over him. That is why so much national advertising is just a mouthing of pompous platitudes that will please the vanity of the client. Which in advertising writing is most unwise. The beginning cub, the account executive, the copy chief will all go faster and farther if they throw caution to the winds and spill out their spontaneous wild ideas—which generally are much sounder than fuddy-duddy dignified copy. All this proves that spontaneity and disarming candor can sell more products than conventional prating. The agency which most exemplifies this sort of thing is, of course, the incomparable Doyle Dane Bernbach. When I think of DDB, of course I am thinking of those marvelous Volkswagen and Avis Rent A Car ads. Far and beyond the genuine soundness of these campaigns is the genius salesmanship that sold the clients on running this copy. I am sure that DDB clients never change a word . . . not a word, not a dot, not a comma.

My best campaigns have always been along these lines—but, good saleswoman that I am, I have never been able to sell store presidents as completely as DDB sells its clients.

XVIII

"Slogan" stems from a Gaelic battle cry

Is a slogan desirable? I think so. Good ads, with no slogans or basic themes, are like a lot of loose cultured pearls. Pearls need to be strung. Otherwise they slip away, roll under the rug, disappear. A slogan is a string to hold pearls.

The word "slogan" comes from the old Gaelic word *sluagh-ghairm*, and means "the war cry, or gathering word, of a High-land clan in Scotland; hence, any rallying or battle cry."

I have always maintained that the best advertising comes out slogging.

Most slogans are a waste of money. They are vague and fuzzy and full of empty brag—unbelievable generalizations. This brings us back to good writing. The specific is always more interesting and more believable than a generalization. Most supermarket slogans are dull, unbelievable generalizations: "A bonus in every basket." (Wall Street words like "bonus" and "dividend" and "franchise," all beloved by men, are not woman-words—they just don't register with women.) And silly little rhymes are bad, and so is the follow-ing contrived balanced antithesis: "You don't *pay* more—you just *get* more." It's empty and meaningless. It doesn't convince anybody of anything.

A slogan must not give the impression of being a glib facile arrangement of alliterative words or balanced antitheses. Anything too mannered or contrived doesn't have the ring of truth. For years I have been unimpressed with "You have a friend at Chase Manhattan" because I didn't believe it. Later the slogan was beefed up and made more believable in radio and TV commercials by tying it up with a vivid slice-of-life illustration—showing how Walter Johnson saved $89 by getting his mortgage through Chase Manhattan. These slice-of-life proofs were well done and believable. Walter Johnson didn't save thousands of dollars—he saved just $89. That sounded possible and probable. Promises that are temperate are always more believable. The *Wall Street Journal* circulation ads have always been completely believable with their testimonial headlines: "How John Smith increased his income from $5200 to $8500 a year. Subscribing to the *Wall Street Journal* didn't make Mr. Smith a millionaire overnight; but it did help him up the ladder . . . one rung at a time."

I'd put most slogans under one of these three classifications:

1. No-good-at-all slogans

"A bonus in every basket"
"You don't *pay* more—you just *get* more"
"Where the customer comes first"
"Serving you with power for progress"
"Where better meals begin"

Take this last one, now being used by Bohack's, a supermarket chain in New York City and Long Island. Imagine a woman saying to her husband, "Since we're having your boss and his wife to dinner tomorrow, I want to give a better dinner, and since Bohack's

is where better meals begin, I'll have to drive down to Bohack's."
Is it likely that she'd say that? Or think that? Of course not. But
I know a slogan that Bohack's could use that would be honest and
that would pull in thousands of new customers. Here it is—free to
Bohack's:

BOHACK'S—THE ONLY PLACE IN NEW YORK THAT
CARRIES THE FRESHEST EGGS STAMPED AA

That's true, and it's concrete. Good copy across the Bohack page of
listings could say: "We assume that you are not like the optimistic
English curate 'who rejoiced when even *parts* of his egg were
good.' We assume you want *all* the parts of your eggs fresh. AA
means the egg is refrigerated quickly after the hens drop it, and it
is refrigerated every moment of its trip from a New Jersey farm
to New York City, and from there till you pick it up at Bohack's.
If you paid twice the Bohack price (and some people do), you
couldn't get eggs any fresher than Bohack's."

The Bohack employees that I have discussed this with were completely unaware of the fact that their AA eggs were the best.

Another poor slogan, unworthy of *The New York Times*, the
best newspaper in the world: "If you're without it, you aren't with
it." It seems to me that that slang expression, being "with it,"
popped up about twenty years ago. But it didn't catch on. Recently
it has been revived. It doesn't fit in with the personality of the
good gray solid *New York Times*. "With it" and "without it" is
just a glib bit of smarty-pants, and not very smart smarty-pants.
The former *Times* slogan was much better: "It's much more interesting, and you will be too."

2. So-so slogans

Many slogans are just plain dull. They are neither good nor bad.
Take these, for instance:

"Northeast Airlines treats you like a guest—not like a passenger."

"Reach for the Campbell's—it's right on the shelf."

"With Goodman's . . . what could be bad?" Everything could
be bad. It's foolish to use a rhetorical question when the answer can
be just the opposite of what you want.

"Remember . . . Milton Bradley makes the best games in the
world." I don't believe it—not a word of it. What ever happened
to Parker?

3. Good slogans

Many clever slogans are excellent, such as these:

"It's Cott to be good."

"Next to myself I like B.V.D. best."

"Don't stir without Noilly Prat" and Noilly Prat's latest: "The
couth vermouth."

Occasionally rhyme is good, especially if it carries with it a little
sentiment, like: "Nothin' says lovin' like something from the oven"
(Pillsbury).

This one is also good: "When you serve the coffee don't forget
the cream—the Bristol Sherry Cream."

And then there is Gerber's: "Babies are our business . . . our
only business." It makes one feel that Gerber is capable of taking
over when Dr. Spock passes on.

"When it rains it pours" (Morton salt).

"Does she or doesn't she?" (Clairol).

The Bigelow Carpet people had a wonderful slogan. Besides pushing the Bigelow image way up, it was a wry comment on life in the Madison Avenue jungle of big-industry competition: "A title on the door rates a Bigelow on the floor." Those eleven words spoke volumes. True, it's a jingle—a rhyming couplet. Usually a rhyming couplet is too glib, too facile, to carry much conviction—such as this soap slogan: "Don't wait to be told to get Palm Olive Gold."

Of course, there was one eminently successful rhyming-couplet campaign. The Burma-Shave product was practically created by the little doggerel verses in a series of white-on-red signs, which were planted in the weeds on the roadsides of all states except four. Massachusetts roads were too twisty. The roads of the other three states were too sparsely traveled. Two or three decades ago, at least one passenger in every car worked hard to re-create a Burma-Shave jingle. Imagine that gold mine: somebody in every car working to promote Burma-Shave.

Speaking of Bigelow's good old slogan, it now seems to be replaced by a meaningless rhyme that says nothing and carries little believability: "Those who know buy Bigelow."

I once created a good slogan for the Carpet Institute, which said something: "Carpet covers a multitude of dins." The Carpet Institute didn't buy it—but it made a solid selling point. Quietness is going to be very precious in this crowded raucous world of the future.

To get back to Burma-Shave: When the fabulous Gertrude Stein made her first trip back to the United States, she was impressed by only two things—Woolworth's and the Burma-Shave campaign. Her favorite was:

> *My job is keeping faces clean.*
> *Nobody knows the stubble I've seen.*

I was fond of that and also this one:

Ben met Anna, made a hit,
Neglected beard, Ben-Anna split.

Burma-Shave also stressed careful driving:

Drinking drivers, nothing worse,
They put the quart before the hearse.

Ah well, advertising was simpler two or three decades ago. And so was storekeeping. But who would swap today's provocative challenges for them?

Here are the old rules that govern the writing of a good slogan:

1. It should contain five to seven words.

2. It should have a swinging rhythm.

3. It should contain the name of some word that will identify the name of the product.

4. A good slogan is not too self-serving. It should promote a universal truth so that people will use the slogan even though they're not talking about the product for which it was created. In that way the slogan creeps into casual everyday conversation.

The best advertising, Milton Biow always used to say, is advertising that shows up sharply the difference between its product and all other products. He cited Phineas T. Barnum who understood this and pushed his famous elephant, Jumbo, up above all other elephants. Barnum never told the exact height or weight of Jumbo. He featured him as "eight inches taller than any other elephant on earth." That was enough. Does that mean that good advertising to some degree denigrates its competitors? Of course it does. Breck shampoo does just that when it says that all shampoos, except Breck's, are detergents. The word "detergent" means harshness to most women—so the Breck appeal is sound.

The old Ohrbach slogan was sound. It may well have helped crystallize the whole Ohrbach retailing philosophy, which has been carried on by Doyle Dane Bernbach and has produced some of the best retail copy ever written. The original slogan said, "A business in millions—a profit in pennies." To my way of thinking, the best slogan is a sentence with a subject and a predicate. Such as "It's smart to be thrifty" and "Nobody but nobody undersells Gimbels." Both come out slogging. The Gimbel one is sloggier. The Macy one says much the same thing, but it is a subtler, more philosophical, more thoughtful comment on what is the fashion among the best people in the handling of their money.

People have asked why I or Gimbels didn't object when my "nobody but nobody" slogan was picked up all over the world—as it was. For my part, I'm delighted. That's what a good slogan does: It creeps into the vernacular.

"Nobody but nobody" bobbed up in a full-page magazine ad recently in a salute by *Harper's Bazaar* to its sister competitor, *Vogue:*

> *Vogue, dear Vogue,*
> *Nobody, but nobody,*
> *But Harper's Bazaar*
> *Knows how really good you are.*

How to stumble on a million-dollar slogan

Most slogans come only after a regularly rented brain (it's almost hopeless to try to sell a slogan if you are on the outside) has spent weeks or months or even years steeping in a toothpaste or detergent or crankcase.

Slogans grow out of an atmosphere—but they often seem to be sheer accidents. My "It's smart to be thrifty" slogan was born as a result of my being stopped by a red light on my way back from lunch one day in 1928. An elegant long-nosed limousine was drawn up to the Broadway entrance of Macy's. Someone said, "That's the John D. Rockefeller, Jr., car—it's often parked there."

So, I thought to myself, things have come to a pretty pass when Mrs. John D. Rockefeller, Jr., escalates up and down through the milling Macy mobs to save six cents on a dollar. How different from the days when the gay moneyed blades used to light their pipes with five-pound notes!

When you come to think about it, today it is the *fashion* to be frugal. Saving money isn't grubby or gritty any more. Saving money has become the chic thing to do. Yes, *it's the fashion to be frugal.* That would be a good slogan for Macy's.

But *frugal, frugal,* I thought. Who says *frugal? Thrifty* is the word. My grandmother used to call her geraniums "thrifty." *Frugal* sounds too penny-pinching, but *thrifty* has a fine fat flourishing sound. *It's the fashion to be thrifty.*

Fashion, fashion—fashion sounds so temporary, and Macy's plans on being in business a long long time. But everybody wants to be smart. *"It's smart to be thrifty."* That's it! The perfect slogan for Macy's!

By this time Macy's elevator had reached the thirteenth floor. I dashed out and rushed toward the office of the vice-president in charge of advertising, Kenneth Collins, yelling, "It's come! It's here! I have it!"

Ken Collins dashed out wildly shouting, "Somebody come! Somebody do something! Fitz's baby is here!" I was eight and three-fourths months pregnant at the time.

Never rewrite a hit

Often when the originator of a slogan moves out and someone else moves in, the successor tries to improve on his predecessor's hit. Don't. It won't be an improvement.

I am flattered, not indignant, when somebody steals or borrows one of my slogans. What I don't like is murdering or maiming my slogan, as Macy's is doing right now. I don't like Macy's print version: "It's smart to be thrifty. It's smart to be sure." The fine dactylic rhythm has been lost—the five magic words have been doubled to ten. And the easy casual throw-away brevity, which permitted the slogan to bob up in ordinary conversation, has been lost. From its very start people said "It's smart to be thrifty" in casual talk. But who will say casually "It's smart to be thrifty. It's smart to be sure"? Nobody, but nobody, will. Besides, the word "sure" has been nailed down by, and belongs to, Westinghouse. Just as "nobody" belongs to Gimbels. And "incredible" belongs to Alexander's.

If I dislike Macy's *print* version I dislike the radio version even more: "M—A—C—Y. It's smart to be thrifty at Macy's."

That ruins the meaning completely. The original said that it was smart to be thrifty everywhere on the globe—not merely at Macy's. The implication was that the really upper-clahss people were always thrifty. It further implied that the riffraff—those born on the wrong side of the tracks—were likely to be extravagant wastrels, slobs and squares. It was really a very snobbish, exclusive aristocratic slogan. The public comprehended all this immediately. One just knew in one's bones that Buckingham Palace and the Rockefeller mansion wouldn't dream of wasting one penny.

All of this snobbish exclusiveness, present in the original version, is lost in the radio version, which just becomes a haranguing, nagging exhortation to save your pennies, instead of a reminder that thrift is the chic thing.

Incidentally, one of my former cubs at Macy's, many decades ago, went on to coin the Ohrbach slogan: "A business in millions—a profit in pennies." She free-lanced it for a big agency. She desperately needed fame and money. She got neither. See why I urge you to start in a store? In an agency you get little credit. Everything is covered with a veil of anonymity. In a store you get instant recognition.

Mary Filius, one of my Phi Beta Kappa trainees at Gimbels, fresh out of Smith College, was plucked by an agency. (We kept many of the most talented, but we couldn't keep them all.) Mary worked on the Maidenform account, and her delightful idea, "I dreamed I ———— in my Maidenform bra," has served as the backbone of Maidenform advertising for many decades.

The Fragrance Foundation came to me a few years ago for a slogan. I gave them a charming one. My mistake was that I held back a terrific one, because I knew it wouldn't have the courage to use it. This is what I gave: "There she goes, sweet as a rose." The copy went on to say that everybody smells of something or other—either her own personal body smell or the smell of the soap she uses—be it Fels Naphtha or Dial or whatever. Running through the whole copy was the implied query: "Madam, since you are going to smell of something, wouldn't you rather smell like a rose?"

The problem with perfume is that women possess many bottles but never open them. They (the bottles) just sit on dressing tables and the perfumes deteriorate. The bottles are generally gifts. Women should be urged to carry perfume in their handbags and put it on frequently, as they put on lipstick. They should keep bottles in their desk drawers. Here is the slogan I should have given: "It's more important that a girl smell good than spell good." Now, that was an inspired slogan that would have stimulated all kinds of publicity on radio, interviews or TV panel discussions. Men, of course, would support the "smell good" side. But undoubtedly people like President Mary Bunting of Radcliffe would opt for the "spell good." Anyway . . . it didn't sell.

A very poor slogan, I believe, is "New York is a Summer Festival." Now, who talks like that? Is that idiom? It's certainly not American idiom.

Can you picture John out in Iowa saying to his brother-in-law, "Let's take two cars and all the kids—it'll be more fun to go to New York than to the Caribbean this year, because I've heard that New York is a summer festival"?

Years ago I offered a better one to the Visitors' Bureau, but it was not considered dignified: "You'll be nuts about New York." This was to be followed with a development of all the different facets of New York's glamour—music, theater, art galleries, baseball, and so on.

For several years I was an outside consultant for Chevrolet. During that time, I thought of a slogan that General Motors never used: "No body but no body like a Fisher body"—which *I* would have used if *I* had run the Fisher Body account.

But my best slogan of all was done for the conservative old thread firm, Coats & Clark. The aim of the campaign was to get all the girls sewing, so that they would use C&C thread and needles and zippers. My slogan was "It's sexy to sew." And it was based on solid rock. Here was the argument.

The quickest way to a man's heart used to be through his stomach. But now it's through the bobbin. Sewing is the only female art that hasn't been filched by the male. Men have invaded the kitchen and the supermarket and the nursery and the broom closet. Much to the worriment of Margaret Mead and other anthropologists, men are cooking, cleaning, changing diapers.

But the men haven't clomped into the sewing room yet. You don't find them sitting around evenings in the soft glow of lamplight with a darning egg in their paws. They don't cluster together at parties discussing plackets and pleats and gussets and gores. They don't pour out their wardrobe problems upon Gus the bartender.

I pointed out to Coats & Clark that sewing is more than a feminine art. It is a feminine wile—one of the wiliest wiles left in this shifting world.

Fashions in people, like fashions in clothes and furniture, come and go. Right now it's smart to be a femaley female. The femininier, the better. The girlier, the better. Look around you. The girls are letting their hair grow. They're getting themselves fitted into curvier girdles. They're having babies—fast and furiously. America's femaler females are sewing more than at any other time in our history. Women know in their bones that it's fittin' and proper and feminine to sew. They also know that sewing impresses a man silly. A man thinks any girl with a thimble is automatically sweet, pretty, clever, industrious, thrifty, will be a perfect life companion and a perfect mother of his children. There's something utterly, innately, irresistibly feminine about sewing; psychologists come right out and say girls who sew are femaler females. If you want to reduce a man to blithering helplessness, you should cry on his shoulder or sew on his button. ("If you'd reduce him to nuttin', just sew on his button.") Sewing restores the delicate male-female balance. In the twinkling of a needle's eye, a man is Joe Piltdown with a caveman's club. Mentally, he's got the gal by the hair of her head. Actually, she's got him in the palm of her hand. Yes, needlework is still the woman's bailiwick.

I used these and many more selling points on Coats & Clark. But I couldn't get them to use the slogan "It's sexy to sew."

Coats & Clark has never had the courage to come out with a razzle-dazzle campaign promoting the fact that "men always get itches for girls who sew stitches." If I had had the selling genius of a Doyle Dane Bernbach, "It's sexy to sew" would be on billboards from coast to coast. Ah, well, you can't sell 'em all.

Coats & Clark shuddered at the word "sexy." They were wrong. "It's sexy to sew" has a direct, fresh, childlike innocence. It's as innocent as a morning in May. It's completely unlike the faintly prurient perfume and cosmetics campaigns that are running today in our best magazines—*they* are *charged* with suggestiveness.

Here's another good slogan I've never used: "There's nothing like shoes for the blues." The shoe people ought to get a positive plug into all their advertising for *new* shoes. The theme, or slant, should run like the Mississippi River, spang through the middle of shoe advertising to both men and women: *"There's nothing like shoes for the blues.* How long has it been since you treated yourself to the boost that a new pair of shoes can give you? (How old are the oldest shoes in your closet? What is the average age of the shoes in your wardrobe? How many pairs of shoes do you own?) It will lift up your spirits."

The hat people have always promoted the lift that a new hat gives: "If you feel low and depressed, go buy a new hat." Well, as a matter of fact, you can't even see the hat on your head. There's *no* lift in the world like the lift of a new pair of shoes. Say so. You can go into a shoe shop feeling like a stick-in-the-mud and come out feeling like a fleet-of-foot god or goddess. You can even look down and *see* your shoes. There's no self-therapy better than a new pair of shoes. *There's nothing like shoes for the blues.*

The A&P campaign featuring the slogan "Who cares? *We* care" is being called the two-handkerchief commercial. It is tender—too tender. The guy who delivers it on the radio is all choked up with tears. He almost breaks down and sobs as he thinks that good old A&P doesn't make a dime on seven dollars' worth of food—"eight or nine cents, maybe, but not a dime." That "not a dime" bit seems sort of tricky after all that sentiment. But one thing about the A&P campaign is excellent. It isn't just empty words. The big superchain follows it up with a promise that if the A&P runs out of a special, the manager will give any customer a rain check so she may buy it the following week. That is smart . . . much smarter than bandying about meaningless things like "A bonus in every basket."

All the banks are dripping and spilling over with friendliness. But does any one of them really come up with a special service for the customers they insist they love so much? Never. If I were a bank,

I'd loot a leaf from A&P and offer something definite to my customers, such as selling postage stamps. It's a time-consuming chore to buy a stamp—at least in large cities.

Some of the very old slogans are the very best:

"I'd walk a mile for a Camel."

"Say it with flowers."

And never, but never, forget that

"It pays to advertise."

XIX

Men do so *belong in advertising*

I'd like to make one thing clear. I'm not a feminist. I'm not *for* females any more than I am *for* cows and *against* horses. I've never claimed that women should take over the advertising business. Men do *so* have a place in advertising—a place, but not the whole hog. There's dire dark discrimination against letting the female copywriter stand in the highest advertising places of this world. This is not a Fitz-Gibbon theory—it's a proved fact. Just check the top brass in the largest advertising agencies and you'll see that men are firmly in command. As, of course, they are in banking, publishing, law, and medicine.

Girls are brighter than boys up through age five, then the boys catch up. But they never outdistance girls. Unlike the missionaries who went to the South Seas to do good and ended up doing well, women in business have done good, but they have not done well for themselves. They don't hold the top jobs. They don't draw the biggest money. The assistant to the Secretary of Labor for women's affairs took American women to task for not even seeking key jobs. One out of every eleven men who work earns $10,000 or more a year. Only one out of every one hundred and sixty-six women who work earns $10,000 or more. In other words, your chances of earning $10,000 or more are fifteen times as good if you are a man.

Most advertising departments are overmanned and under-girled. Oh, there are always some females around. "They're necessary," said one agency head. "For instance, one of our women writers suggested giving a lily-of-the-valley scent to our insect repellent. Only a woman could have thought of that." Women can do lots more than make an insect repellent smell like lilacs. Here is some solid advice to agency heads as well as to store presidents: *If you want more legal tender, hire more of the female gender.* We females haven't progressed much beyond the peasant woman of Mexico who walks with the bundle on the head while the lord and master rides the burro a gentle distance behind.

You've heard, of course, of the American consul to Burma who, during his tenure, regretted the lowly status of women in that far-off Asian land. He left Burma, but revisited it several years later. To his surprise, women now walked well in advance of the men whom they had previously followed. "My, what a change. Your women seem to have acquired a new status," he said to his Burmese friend. "They now walk in front of the man." "Yes," replied the Burmese, "just in case there are any land mines around."

The anti-female pill is a hard one to swallow; but there's no need to be bitter about it. For a woman it's a bit of a struggle all the way, but once you've proved what you can do, you'll be accepted royally. You'll be a star in your own right, with star acclaim, star billing and star pay. I found this out when I went to Gimbels. As I walked into the top advertising job, some merchandising men walked out: "A woman—God forbid!"

Why, at this point—two thirds of the way through the twentieth century—are women still working for peanuts? What's holding them back? Are they mentally inferior? Do men conspire to keep them down? Do women dread the lonely isolation of a really lofty position? Does their subconscious tell them that a lady's name should appear in print only three times—when she's born, when she marries, and when she dies? Are women content to bask in the boss's reflected glory just as they have been content to bask in their husbands' reflected glory for thousands of years? Is it true that women don't want to work for a woman boss?

The answer to most of these questions is a good loud *no*. A miss is as good as a male. Women are equal to men in all native qualifications of intelligence, imagination, originality, industriousness, and what have you. I said equal—not identical. Woodchucks think woodchuck thoughts. Whippoorwills think whippoorwill thoughts. Women think woman thoughts. Which is just the way Nature, in her compensatory planning, wants it. But there isn't a shred of evidence to prove that woman-thinking isn't every bit as good for big business as man-thinking.

Women today, even women "leaders," are not struggling to be lords of all they survey, first fiddles, biggest frogs in the pond, or cocks of the walk. Today's women are very feminine females. They want to raise hordes of children, wear Chanel- or Pucci-inspired clothes, run a charming home, put an orange glaze on a spitted Long Island duckling, *besides* having a career outside the home because they enjoy it or need the money.

Could it be that women are *afraid* of the top? Could it be that women have actually fallen for that hoary hoax, perpetuated over the years by presidents and chairmen of the board, that it's *harder* at the top?

It's easier at the top. Despite what the men say, the higher up, the lighter the load, and you're loaded besides. Take a department store, for instance. The head of stock has a better time than a salesgirl. An assistant buyer has a better time than a head of stock; a buyer better than an assistant buyer; an assistant merchandise manager better than a buyer; a merchandise manager better than an assistant merchandise manager; a vice-president better than a merchandise manager; a president better than a vice-president; and a chairman of the board better than a president. The higher up you are, the more fun, the more money, the longer vacation, the less worry.

Take that assistant buyer down the line. Maybe she's in petticoats and Dior turns thumbs down on petticoats. Her whole world falls apart, her figures disintegrate, her bonus never gets its head above sea level. This means little to her merchandise manager, whose petticoat slack is being taken up elsewhere in his division by a run on bustles, and it means less and less up the line. To put it another way—if there's grouse shooting in Scotland, who gets to shoot?

Once upon a time women shied away from the physical setup of the office. What woman would want to be the boss when the boss's office was full of cigar smoke and spittoons? The old gray lair ain't what it used to be. The office these days has the equivalent—in spirit, if not in fact—of rubber-tile floors, limed pearwood woodwork, Jens Risom desks, Charles Eames chairs, big-leafed schefflera in painted pots, chartreuse or beige typewriters, an orchestral arrangement of *My Fair Lady* piped in over the sound system, and the miniature office Frigidaire filled with ice cubes for the client coming at four.

The sun has set on the day of the dusty rolltop desk, the bookkeeper's high stool, the green celluloid eyeshade, and the concept of the office as a place where drudges are herded to eke out their livelihood in an atmosphere as convivial as that of a Renaissance crypt.

Much of this is because women have, in the half century or so that they have been working, accomplished a revolution in the office. And decorative changes are merely a manifestation of a half century of women's influence on the business world. Women's impact on the office goes much farther than putting a rose in a Baccarat vase atop a robin's-egg-blue filing cabinet.

There's an old chestnut that girls don't like to work for a woman boss. It's not true. Decades ago, when the American dream was to marry the boss, a young woman unfortunate enough to have to earn a living would naturally want to work for someone she could marry. So she would take her starched, shirtwaisted self into the dusty, musty moil of the coal dealer's office merely because he was an eligible widower.

Today's girl still wants marriage—but not necessarily to the boss. What she wants, first and foremost, is a social arena. She doesn't want to stay at home. It's lonely. In an agrarian economy, home was not lonely. Today it is—and that is the basic reason why the domestic servant has just about vanished from the scene. The working girl wants people—lots of people of both sexes. The office is now the major social arena of the community—and women have made it so.

The working girl wants the camaraderie and chitchat and town tattle of a big, gay, busy office. She wants to slip out for a Coke or a cigarette with the girls. She wants to shoot the breeze with the boys at the coffee break; she wants to bat an eyelash at the new account executive at the water cooler.

She likes working for a woman boss because she is aware, consciously or unconsciously, that this sociological revolution that has taken place in the office is the work of women who just naturally can't abide stuffiness or formality or pompousness. (A woman is incapable of thinking up a phrase like "yours of the 18th instant." I actually heard a chairman of the board of a large mail-order business, when asked "How long will it take?" come up with the jawbreaker: "It depends on the celerity with which we can assimilate the work-load"—instead of saying "two weeks." Right then I sold my stock and bought Sears Roebuck—a wise switch.) Everybody everywhere is looking for love. And love is just lapping round an office.

And today's girl wants to get ahead. She's on pleasure and profit bent—with the accent on pleasure. The office is better than the movies. At the movies you can only *look* at another life. In the office you can *live* another life. The woman boss has not only infused the old barren treadmill with warmth; she has brought in classlessness. Women are much more democratic than men—much less snobbish. (I recall that at Gimbels I was the only executive to give an annual *vertical* Christmas party including everyone from the chairman of the board down to the scrubwoman in the ladies' room. All the men executives gave *horizontal* parties for their peers alone.)

The office is in the control of the desk set—the women—and this is good. Offices, with their present female-engendered informality, turn out more work per head than they ever did. I can't prove it, but I'll bet that Bob Cratchit, nose to the grindstone in monastic misery, couldn't begin to match the efficiency of one girl today.

If it is women who have changed the complexion and the sinew and the marrow of the office—which it is—why aren't there more women heads of things—like Elsie Murphy, who used to be head of Stroock Fabrics, or Catherine O'Brien, now chairman of the board of Stanley Home Products? Or Dorothy Shaver, who ran Lord & Taylor for so many years? Why aren't there more women bosses scattered all the way up and down the office superstructure?

I have wondered myself for years. Now I know. But I must admit that it was a man who tipped me off. (And *that* certainly means something or other.) It was Don Gibbs, well-known writer and sharp observer of the contemporary scene, who laid bare the nub of the matter. Said Don, "Women have not caught on to the fact that big business is infatuated with figures. Women don't realize that the common denominator in all talk is figures and the lingo that goes with them. Until the ladies learn the lingo, they can't even talk with top brass—and if you can't talk with top brass, you can't get far."

Mr. Gibbs is right. I know that I would have gone much higher if I had long ago learned to lisp in numbers. I can remember way back thirty-five years ago when this whole figure furor began to trickle in from the Harvard Business School, the Wharton School of Finance, and Pace Institute. I was at Macy's then; and all executives were compelled to attend the monthly executive luncheon where economists and financiers harangued us for an hour on carloadings and soybean futures and bulk-line costs. You could hear a decimal point drop. Every man was spellbound. I, along with the rest of the girls, had an automatic shutoff in my ear for figures and spent the hour thinking up copy slants, headlines and slogans.

Like the Duchess in *Alice in Wonderland*, I just couldn't abide figures. I might be president of the Macy chain now if I had minded my interquartiles and modes and medians and weighted aggregate indices way back when the whole thing was building up.

Yes, being figure-minded is important. I heard that Mildred Custin, the razzle-dazzle president of Bonwit Teller, has always been a wizard at figures as well as a wizard at fashion.

And I hear that the razzle-dazzle Mildred Finger of Bergdorf Goodman was a Phi Beta Kappa math major.

Most American men are frustrated CPA's (men who aren't presidents or vice-presidents or CPA's). Anyone who thinks that the real appeal of baseball is watching a grown man throw a ball to first base before another grown man arrives there is naïve.

Why is baseball the national game? Because the average man likes to go to the ball game? Definitely not. Think of any fanatical baseball fan (male) that you know. He quotes the batting averages of every player in his favorite club. He talks glibly of RBI's and earned-run averages. He knows the record for the most two-base hits in a game by a pitcher or most errors in a game by a shortstop. But does he really know baseball? No. But he talks figures so glibly everybody *thinks* he's a baseball expert.

Listen, will you, to the man who owns a few shares of stock. He can quote you every eighth of a point gained or lost by the list of leading stocks in the *Times*. He talks about railroads easing off and oils firming up. Yet he wouldn't know firmed-up oil if he stepped in it. All his mumbo-jumbo about rediscount rate, equity financing, and utility flotation he gets right from the financial page, just as he gets the won and lost baseball percentages from the sports page.

American men like nothing better for breakfast, lunch, and dinner than baked statistics.

To prove that what I am talking about is gospel truth, I invite anyone to take the "club car test." Walk into the club car of any good train, sit down and listen. The group you are eavesdropping upon may include an oyster-cannery president, a garment-hanger manufacturer, a hair-dryer sales manager, a detergent vice-president, and a roach-killer chairman of the board. No matter how diversified the group, no matter how many esoteric and peculiar-unto-themselves businesses are represented, the talk's all the same. Everybody not only understands everybody else, but actually thinks like everybody else. And you get the impression that at top level it doesn't make any difference what business you're in because business is just business.

If a man has three bright daughters and one dull son, the son gets the company. Why can't companies be handed down from father to daughter? I think that if the daughters knew Dun & Bradstreet as well as they know the frug and the watusi, if they thought in terms of millions instead of cotillions, they'd have a few more businesses in their own names—provided, of course, they bent the old man's ear with figures, figures, figures.

The number of women on boards of directors is scandalously low—too low for the good of the country's corporations. Perhaps it's the high cost of plumbing that keeps corporations from adding females to their boards. The problems of two johns, you know.

Spout figures, sweet maid, and let who will be clever. A few figures dropped in the right place will do a girl as much good as ten years of hard work. The less she makes herself understood, the more effective she will be. Who'll dare call her bluff when she's holding forth on contingent liability, marginal utility, multiple regression, or the confidence interval of the conditional mean?

The situation's not going to change, girls, so if you can't lick 'em, join 'em. Don't let the men keep score at the bridge table; grab that pad. Don't play for a tenth of a cent a point. That's too easy to figure out. Play for an eleventh of a cent and you'll end up with a lot of lovely decimals to rattle off, as in "If we make this slam, I'll be 87.83 cents ahead." Or if you notice that unsweetened pineapple juice is two cans for 25 cents at the A&P and it was two for 27 cents yesterday, don't say it's two cents cheaper, say "Unsweetened-wise, the pineapple-juice picture has eased off 7.41 per cent."

In business, it isn't what you know, it's how you say it. If she wants a title on the door and a Bigelow on the floor, the woman should:

1. be presented with an abacus at six, a slide rule at ten, and a subscription to *Fortune*, the *Harvard Business Review* and the *Wall Street Journal* at sweet sixteen;
2. take a night course in economics, not to give her insight into the Malthusian law but to give her terms such as Gossen's law of satiety to sling authoritatively;
3. bone up on the basic percentages of business. For instance, pick up the annual reports of some big corporations and memorize a few figures. They'll make a devastating impression when quoted casually and with timing: "I don't know, P.J. I think our personnel costs are pretty low at 23⅜ per cent. General Motors, you know, is bucking a 27 per cent nick for salaries and benefits";
4. learn immediately the meaning of the phrase "standard deviation of conditional probability distribution." This will put you ahead of most men in the conditional probability distribution department;

5. *never underestimate the power of a weighty memorandum.* Men
   complain about the quantity of paper that passes across their
   desks, but this is an executive pose. And if your name is Mary
   Alice Johnson, sign yourself "M. A. Johnson." Don't ask why.
   So, learn the jargon. Flash the slide rule. Talk wisely on the
payment of capital investment based on increasing productivity
per man hour of labor—that's still the big subject. Maybe you still
won't rise to the presidency of the corporation. Maybe the men
just don't want us up there. Like the old vaudeville lampoon act,
maybe as you are about to step into the presidency, the chairman
of the board will throw you out on your ear, saying, "She ain't done
nothin', but it's snowin' and out she goes!"

Of course women's lack of interest in fancy figuring is not the
only reason they have not risen to the top in advertising—a field
they are eminently fitted for. President Bunting of Radcliffe said
that women haven't done better in their career-climbing because
they are not, like boys, brought up in a spirit of expectation. Boys
expect to do something when they grow up. When adults talk to
little boys, they say, "What are you going to *be* when you grow
up?" Boys grasp the idea early that they are supposed to *be* something. It doesn't occur to any of them to say, "I just want to be a
daddy and have a lot of babies." But adults expect a little girl to
say she just wants to be a mommy and have a lot of babies. Little
girls grow up in a state of *unexpectation*—they just plan on getting
married and begetting.

That's not enough. Not any more. In these times of lightened
housework and lengthened lives there is an obligation for a female
to do something—there is an obligation to use a good brain.

Well, the girls had better wake up. Because it looks as if practically all women are headed for decades of working outside the
home whether they want to or not. The experts who know these
things say that a married woman can expect to work twenty-five
years. And an unmarried woman can expect to work forty years.
Those are the facts. And you can't fight facts. Fewer than one

woman out of ten will never work outside the home. And you are not likely to be that one woman. If working for twenty-five to forty years is inevitable, you may as well relax and enjoy it. And the only sure way to enjoy it is to prepare yourself for a job that is fun and pays well.

When the top men in advertising have been asked what they thought of women in advertising, they always say lovely things like: "Women are wonderful—much smarter than men. We men hold them down, because we aren't bright enough to compete fairly with them." Curiously enough, several ad-women I interviewed agreed with the men that the women were smarter. Both men and women were impressed by "women's intuition."

Then I interviewed *me*. I disagree with the men and the women. Women aren't brighter than men. Men aren't brighter than women. No sex—but no sex—is superior to any other sex. And that intuition stuff is malarkey. I have found that this sixth sense is generally claimed by females who show little indication of possessing the other five.

I think that women copywriters *appear* brighter than men because more of them come out of a retailing background. In a retail advertising department the gestation-creation period (see, I too can do double-jointed adjectives, just like the agency copywriters) is very short. If one has to write an ad on a Teddy bear or an étagère or a wash-and-wear, one looks at the thing, thinks about it, writes it up, gets a layout made, gets the type marked, sends it to the paper, and seventy-two hours later it's out on the street.

Although the title of this chapter is "Men do *so* have a place in advertising," most of it has been about women. My point was— strange as it may seem—many people feel that women are always better advertising writers than men, because women purchase most of the things advertised. I don't agree. Since neither sex is brighter than the other, no sex, but no sex, is better in advertising writing than the other.

And I do not agree with store heads who often feel that only females should write store ads. I usually had more males than females in copy. You may be thinking "You wouldn't have a man writing fashions." I would. And did. Writing is writing. If you can write a good ad about one thing, you can write a good ad about anything. That's why it's silly for an employer to go looking for a copywriter with rug experience or one with food experience. If you can write pickles, you can write petticoats.

One day at Gimbels when we were on our usual lookout for top brains, a tall lad, an Alabaman, walked in. He had just been graduated from Notre Dame—no experience. We took him on, gave him the lowliest job—cub writer for the Gimbels leased departments. Leased departments are not the store's own departments; they are run by companies who just rent the space. Charlie's job was to write the copy for automobile tires, garden accessories, and so on. He was intelligent, industrious, dependable.

Then, out of the blue, our fashion writer was lured to a big advertising agency at double her Gimbels salary. (The agencies have always acted like vultures, ready to pounce on any cub I had trained.) Mean trick, but understandable. Since I am basically a teacher, I'm always pleased that so many young people moved out and up. Sometimes they came back. I always took them back if I possibly could. Since a fashion copy job is pretty complicated with lots of detail, I thought dependable Charles should take over fashion. He was horrified. We talked him into it. Charles Kleibacher (that was his name) dug in and put his finely honed mind on fashion. You undoubtedly have heard of him. Today he's conceded to be one of the top American designers—right up there next to Norman Norell, maybe *alongside* of Norell. Charles's dreamy seductive dresses have made him "bias king" of the world. His fame is international. His 1965 showings brought rave reviews. His dresses retail for $500 up and on into the thousands. Charles's especial contribution to designing is his seductive silhouette that follows the feminine figure but is alluringly loose-ish around the waistline. As Kleibacher has pointed out, "The natural waistline is not a sudden pinching—it's a gradual slenderness." As a good retail copywriter, Charles had learned to observe.

See the opportunities in retail advertising? *See* how many doors retail advertising opens?

Of course men have a place in advertising. But they ought to give the girls a fairer shake. After all, advertising is selling *things*. And it's the girls who are *thing*-minded. Girls ought to be able to earn top money so they can buy all these things. Men aren't really thing-minded. They don't need as much money as girls do. Girls yearn for things. Men want to be important. Men hanker after prestige, recognition, power. Back in 1779 Alexander Hamilton said, "I wish to exalt my station." That's good. Let the men be exalted—let them be president and chairman of the board. And double the girls' salaries. They'll be satisfied to take the cash and let the credit go.

Another of my merchandising triumphs was a doll promotion that proves that women are necessary in the creation of a product as well as in the advertising. It happened when I had my own business.

The product in this instance was a doll, an unusual doll, a doll that got sick and then got well. All the men (the toy buyers of the nation) turned thumbs down on the doll. Any female would have known that it would have proved irresistible to little girls. Every male throughout the nation thought the doll shudderingly bad.

Since most department-store toy buyers are men, this meant that the manufacturer of the doll was stuck with a warehouseful of them. It was October and the doll firm came to me and asked me to do a campaign quickly. I said I would. And I did, quick as a wink. First I took the doll home with me. My granddaughter and all her little friends up and down the road were crazy about it.

They all said that that doll would be all they'd want for Christmas.

The doll was named "Marybel, the doll who gets sick and then gets well." Incidentally, Marybel came in a beautiful box complete with adhesive tape, Band-Aids, bandage roll, crutches, a plaster leg cast, a plaster arm cast, a roll of measles, and a roll of chicken pox. These last (every measle and every pox) could be pasted on the little sufferer when she came down with the disease, and taken off when she recovered. The doll also had to wear dark glasses during the measles period.

It was this preoccupation with disease that revolted all the men toy buyers who predicted that the doll would turn all little girls into hypochondriacs. Stuff and nonsense.

We ran a full page ad in *The New York Times*, which, of course, has a large national circulation.

We heard later that every toy buyer in the country was called on the carpet and chided for not having stocked Marybel. The orders rolled in. The warehouse was emptied. The reason our copy on the doll emptied the warehouse was that I understood, as any woman would have understood, that all little girls love disaster. They were delighted with the thought of sickness striking their little doll families. They were enchanted with the thought that they'd have to work and worry and hover over their little doll invalids till they recovered. After all, sickness *does* strike. Realism, as well as romanticism, is good for advertising. Women are good in both. We ran the ad only once: because the manufacturer was in a dither between then and Christmas trying to fill the mountain of new orders.

And women not only know what little girls like; they also know what is good for breakfast. Eastern Air Lines, eager to improve its reputation for good food, has just announced that it would serve a 9 A.M. breakfast of eggs Benedict. Apparently the agency does not have a woman on the account. Any woman would know that nothing could be more repulsive to a queasy stomach or a hangover from the night before than facing Hollandaise at 9 A.M.! Eggs, of course. Ham and eggs. Even steak and eggs. But never eggs Benedict for breakfast. Yes, men do so have a place in advertising. And women could have a bigger place and a higher place than they now have.

Since men work to be important, to be powerful, and impressive, and successful, and women work for gain rather than for glory— here would be a fair division of the spoils.

Let men be the presidents and chairmen of the boards.

Reward the women with money.

That would result in less money for the men and more money for the women, who, having a passion for possessing, would go out and spend the money for more things.

The sales of all these extra things will redound to the glory of the men, who will be well rewarded by the increased volume of their businesses and the increased importance of themselves.

XX

Talleyrand was right about war

"War is much too serious a thing to be left to military men," said Talleyrand. "And merchandise is much too serious a thing to be left to merchants," say I. Every good advertising person, I believe, should be concerned with merchandise. That concern may annoy the regular merchants in a store; but it's necessary all the same. I was not always popular with the merchants for this reason—but on the whole my merchandise record was good.

I'll admit I was no blazing genius in creating merchandise. Seldom is one person top-notch in many fields. In other words, you rarely get clean corners and light biscuits out of the same maid. That's why I am usually leery of an applicant who says, "I have so many talents I don't know what advertising field I should select" or "I would make an excellent stylist, because I have instinctive good taste and a rare feeling for good design. Of course my design flair should make me good in layout and art. But I am a wonderful writer, so maybe I should concentrate on writing."

God certainly doesn't give all talents to any one person. Let me illustrate by describing an advertising man who came into Macy's after Ken Collins had left to go to Gimbels.

This fellow was a jack-of-all-trades, master of none. We dubbed him "Master of the Murky." He was a high-powered guy who bristled in from a big advertising agency and claimed he could do anything and everything in advertising. He really wasn't good in any phase—layout, art, lettering, copy. But he did have a dramatic way of presenting things.

All the world's a stage, and there's definitely a part for drama in business. A good idea may seem a *better* idea if decked out in some theatrical finery.

Alas, if the theatrical finery is *very* fine, even a bad idea may seem good, but the success of this type of idea—and sometimes its sponsor—is fleeting. This advertising man usually put on such a show for the other important executives that every meeting he called was brilliantly attended. The president, all the vice-presidents, the general manager, the merchandise managers, and sometimes even the chairman of the board were usually there. When they had all gathered, my friend would announce humbly that he hadn't conceived a single idea for the most important event on the horizon, that he hadn't the faintest idea of how the ad should look or what it should say. Everybody would then sadly tell everybody else that he didn't have an idea either. After everyone had steeped an effective time in his own unproductiveness, my friend would give a shout (like Archimedes in his bath or Newton under the apple tree) and leap a Fred Astaire leap to the conference table, tap-dance down its length, dive off the end, pull an easel that happened to be standing nearby toward him and proceed to rough out headline, copy, art, and all. On the surface it usually seemed a fairly compelling creation. Everybody thought, invariably, that anyone who could suddenly pull from a barren brain such a roundly conceived idea must be among the geniuses of the age. What people didn't know—and what took them some time to catch on to—was that every movement, word, and pencil stroke had been carefully planned and painstakingly practiced many times before the meeting began, and every syllable had been methodically memorized. My friend's ads, you see, were never judged simply on their own merit but rather on their remarkable origin. Even the great are sometimes guilty—or I should say capable—of this kind of drama. Bernard Shaw once confessed, "I am the most spontaneous speaker in the world, because every word, every gesture, and every retort has been carefully rehearsed."

Before I list my merchandising triumphs, I'll tell you my merchandising blunders. And when I blunder, it's a beaut! When I am right, I am very very right, but when I am wrong, I am florid.

My face was never redder than after two pontifical prophecies I made years ago while I was at Macy's. Both prophecies were dead wrong, and the remembrance has helped keep me humble over the years. The first was made at a conclave of Macy's top-executive echelon, which had assembled to advise a manufacturer who had a problem. The problem was whether it would be a good idea to make radios to be installed in automobiles. Would the public buy them? One by one the top-executive boys rose to their feet to deliver enthusiastic opinions in favor of putting radios in cars. I arose. "I have never," said I, "heard anything so absurd. The purpose of driving is to get to the country and the purpose of getting to the country is to observe the ruminating animals and to hear the bees droning in the redtop clover—*not*, of all things, to listen to the radio." I also painted a gory picture of the accidents that would be the result of such a caprice: the collisions as Lou Gehrig hit a home run, the runnings-off-the-road as Wayne King lulled the motorists to sleep. I then predicted a dismal failure for the whole ridiculous scheme, appealed to the committee to vote no, and sat there and watched dourly while everybody voted yes.

A similar meeting occurred years later at which we were to consider the new fashion that Seventh Avenue had whipped up. This was the mother-and-daughter dress. It seemed to me at the time that the last thing a mother and daughter should want to look like was sisters. To me there was a kind of cosmic dignity and harmony in a mother's looking like a mother and a daughter's looking like a daughter. And why not try to sell mother and daughter different dresses? Again, I predicted gloom. Again I voted no. Again everybody else voted yes. I wish I had a ruminating cow or a droning bee for every mother-and-daughter dress combination I've heard advertised (here I *really* blush) on my car radio.

It may be that I am once again sticking out an about-to-be-guillotined neck. But out it goes! I declare that "in-flight movies" are for the birds. Who does the air traveling these days? Businessmen and businesswomen, vacationers, honeymooners, diplomats. Do any of these fare-paying passengers look forward to hopping aboard a pitch-black cavern and catching the last complete showing of *The Spy Who Came In from the Cold* or *Thunderball*? I doubt it. After a crucial day's business conference or an equally trying session of last-minute packing or struggling through "Here Comes the Bride" or an important military conference, the average passenger looks forward to a comfortable armchair, a good meal, and the delicious oblivion of being fifteen thousand feet above it all.

I can only smile smugly at the *New Yorker* cartoon showing a middle-aged couple buying a plane ticket and Mrs. Traveler protesting, "Let's not go on that one, I've already seen the picture."

So I've admitted that I'm no genius at merchandising. But dipping a tentative toe into merchandising is one of the fascinations of starting an advertising career in a retail store. I dipped in a tentative toe several times and came up with some fine results. Like the time I made a pillow more desirable by reducing the amount of its most desirable ingredient.

If it sounds like a contradiction, let me illustrate. Back in the middle of the Depression, Wanamaker's could not sell its down-filled bed pillows. People were sleeping either on feathers or on nothing. People just couldn't afford to pay $8 (which sounds like a tremendous bargain today) for a pillow that was filled with snow-white European goose down.

One day the bedding buyer was up in the advertising department, lamenting the good old days when one small ad would bring in hundreds of orders. He said, "If we could only lower the price. But we can't. There are just so many geese, and the geese have just so much down."

We said, "Let's cut the size of the pillow."

He answered, "We can cut it from twenty-one-by-twenty-seven inches to twenty-by-twenty-six—but no smaller, because people will want to be able to use their old pillowcases. And," he added disconsolately, "cutting off one inch won't save much down."

"But," we said, "let's cut down on the down, and make the pillow limp and soft and unplump."

He was horror-stricken. "You'd never sell a one. For the last century, people have been educated into wanting big fat, plump pillows, crammed and jammed and bursting with down."

We said, "You get us a twenty-by-twenty-six pillow with twelve ounces of down instead of seventeen ounces, cut the price, and we'll guarantee to sell it."

Naturally, when we sat down to write the ad, we stressed the logical advantages of the smaller pillow. Our headline was TO SAVE YOUR NECK! WANAMAKER'S DESIGNS A NEW, SMALLER PILLOW!! The ad began: "Are you sleeping on a pillow which twists your head at right angles to your body—a method sure to encourage that camel's back-of-the-neck effect, the Dowager's Hump? Much concerned to prevent a spread of Dowager's Hump, Wanamaker's has developed a new pillow just enough softer and smaller to keep your vertebrae and your cranium on happier sleeping terms."

We sold out. It took another shipment to fill the orders. And, to the buyer's consternation, some customers who had recently bought the larger pillows wanted to return them for the new non-dowager's-hump model.

Don't think for a minute that I made up this orthopedic advice on dowager's humps and pillows. I don't know any retail or agency writer who would make up medical advice out of whole cloth. Of course I had the written OK from a leading orthopedist. In my experience, advertising writers and merchants and manufacturers lean over backwards in matters like this.

Sometimes the smartest thing you can do is to turn a complete about-face and offer something in total opposition to a trend. Several years ago, doll manufacturers were breaking their necks to produce dolls that did everything but scrub the kitchen sink. In turn, we at Gimbels were breaking our necks to sell each new wonder as it came along.

One day, grown giddy with these attempts at verisimilitude, we stopped to reflect and were struck with an idea. We went instantly to Laura White, Sales and Promotion Manager of the Madame Alexander Doll Company.

Curiously enough (perhaps not so curiously, since it is a fact that the identical idea often pops up simultaneously in different minds), Laura and I were thinking along the same lines. She had already decided to bring out a simple old-fashioned doll.

So we put our ideas together, and the doll was advertised this way:

Meet Miss Flora McFlimsey who positively won't walk or talk or burp or coo or wet. Miss Flora McFlimsey is not the latest mechanical jerk in the doll business. She is, wonder of wonders, simply an exquisitely beautiful doll, meant simply to be loved. That is to say, she *does not* open her little yap or wail or say "mamma" or suck her thumb or sob real tears or dampen her didy or roller-skate or bat her eyes or upchuck. Her little heart doesn't tick-tock. She doesn't even go to sleep. She is merely a winsome model of old-fashioned Victorian decorum.

While all the manufacturers of automaton dolls watched in horror, we sold hundreds and hundreds of dolls from one eentsy ad, and even had some orders from the Union of South Africa, where the *New York Times* circulation cannot be very high.

And the squeak of the rocker is heard in the land

Although I had long noted that when a thing is very old and very much out of fashion it is likely to be on the verge of bounding back and of becoming very new and very much in fashion, still I had never applied this knowledge to the matter of a rocking chair until after I had dipped into a book on psychiatry. The rudest, jarringest jolt we ever experience in our lives, the book said, is getting ourselves born. Well, that makes sense, I thought. Surely being hurled headlong out of the soft, dark, rhythmic warmth of the prenatal state into the harsh, raucous, bright world must be terrifically hard on an infant. The least we can do for the baby is to keep on rocking him the way he was rocked before he was born. So I went to lunch with the furniture buyer.

"Look," I said, "let's bring back rocking chairs. Can you get a manufacturer to make some?"

"There are rockers around," the furniture buyer said, "they never really went completely out. Would a Boston rocker do?"

"No," I said, "this rocker ought to be smaller, lighter in a slim modern way, and have a more comfortable back than that long, sloping Boston back."

So the furniture buyer went to work and came back with a sleek, clean-lined, sophisticated triumph of modern design—completely different from the old overstuffed sausage or the spindly, thin booby trap. We called it "a lullaby in wrought-iron and wicker." And our copy went on to say, "Mommy can rest her back on *its* nice broad back. She can rest her arms on *its* sturdy arms. She can rest herself on *its* comfortable seat. And baby? Baby will be so well fed and well pleased and well adjusted that he'll never know Mommy is sound asleep too." The ad pulled, which probably meant that the time was ripe for the return of the rocker.

So if you long to create as well as describe and sell, get yourself into the advertising department of a retail store.

Where do ideas come from?

Where did you come from, ideas dear? Out of the everywhere into the here. Ideas pop out of books and the TV screen. They're tucked away in a childhood memory or in a play you saw sometime back. They spring from bird-watching or girl-watching. They burst forth from the mouths of little children or they sneak up on you in the middle of the night (always keep paper and pen at your bedside).

If you're lucky and smart, ideas can come through the mails. Such is the case with Les Pearl, the writer of the well-known Wallachs ads. Wallachs is a prominent chain of men's-wear stores. Les Pearl originated this famous campaign when he was with one of New York's top advertising agencies. So successful was the series that he was asked to continue it after he retired.

I hear that Mr. Pearl now sits on his own boat in his own harbor on an island off the Maine coast and tosses off each day's editorial between gobbling lobsters. Around New York, copywriters, green with envy, say that legmen in the New York Wallachs stores feed him facts. Mr. Pearl probably makes fistfuls of money, and nobody ever touches a comma of his copy.

The Wallachs ads—called rectangles—are 2 columns wide and 100 lines deep. They run almost every day up front in *The New York Times*. They are an exposition of the Wallachs philosophy of merchandising men's wear. They are wise and they are witty, and warm and friendly. They tell a man that Wallachs will sew on his button or fix his zipper even if he bought his suit elsewhere, that Wallachs will outfit a man who has only three hours before embarking on a ship, or Wallachs will get him dressed in his wedding suit on a moment's notice. Wallachs even provides a watering trough outside one of its Fifth Avenue stores so that a fellow can water his dog.

The aforementioned legmen are inspired digger-uppers, because the Wallachs-ana they forward to the writer on the island are fascinating bits of Wallachs history—men's wear fashion, hilarious anecdotes, brickbat and bouquet letters from customers, tidbits of world history, anything that will serve as a springboard from which to dive into a genial, soft-sell, topical dissertation on the wisdom of buying everything that goes on a man's back or feet or hands or head at the one store worth shopping in—Wallachs.

If you want to break into advertising or if you are now in advertising and want to better yourself, it would be worth your while to seek out these ads. Wherever you are, you should be able to find them in the file copies of *The New York Times* in your local library.

You could do worse with your time than to copy half a dozen of these Wallachs ads, word for word, in longhand. Ask yourself, Just what is the secret of this easygoing, completely convincing writing? Just why do you believe that every syllable is God's truth?

Then go ahead and write up other articles on men's wear, and see if one of your pieces could pass as one of the Wallachs series.

Try yours out, with a half dozen of the originals, on a critical friend. Think of the rewards. You too may someday be gobbling juicy lobsters as the salty spray cools you in July and August, the while you are making pots of money.

Speaking of Wallachs reminds me of a wonderful idea I had. One fine day almost five years ago, a handsome man from the William A. White & Sons real estate firm dropped into my office.

He said, "We like the way you write. Would you be interested in doing a small-space newspaper campaign—no artwork, just copy? We like the Wallachs ads. We like what they say. And we like the way they look. Our real estate firm is the oldest and finest in New York." After a quick survey of the real estate business, of White's past history and future plans, he left with this injunction: "Please give this some thought. We're ready to start a small-size, Wallachs-type campaign at any time."

I gave it thought. And the thought struck fire—because I had just finished reading a book that sparked a marvelous idea for a real estate company. What did I do with it? Nothing.

What these real estate people needed, of course, was not just a Wallachs-style campaign but a merchandising idea on which to hang a Wallachs-type campaign.

A book had caught my eye and piqued my curiosity: *African Genesis* by Robert Ardrey. On the flyleaf there is a subtitle: "A Personal Investigation into the Animal Origins and Nature of Man."

The author did some of his research in Africa—where, he believes, man originated. In the course of his investigations he read many scientists' studies of animal behavior, and these analyses help explain why people behave as they do.

What are the most basic natural drives of our forebears and, of course, of us? We must examine the fish, the birds, and the mammals. Until Ardrey's book was published, most people thought that survival came first and the sex drive second. But Ardrey's and others' investigations into the scientific literature on the subject revealed that the acquisition of real estate was the most important drive of all!

When the fish in the water swims round and round, he is not showing off to the female fish. At that point, he couldn't care less about courting or mating. What is he doing? He is staking out his real estate. He is saying, "Take note, all you big fish in the sea!

Everything in this circle belongs to me. Woe betide anyone who
sets a fin inside."

When the drake in the pond swims round and round, he is not
indulging in duck courtship; he is staking out his real estate.

When the robin in the top of the big maple tree flies round and
round, stopping between rounds to preen and switch his tail as he
prances and struts along the big maple branches, what's motivating
him? Sex? He couldn't be less interested. Survival? He doesn't
give it a thought. He's consumed with his most fundamental basic
natural drive, the acquisition of real estate. It's not till after he
triumphs as king of his domain that he turns his attention to woo-
ing a female, building a nest, and begetting a family.

Now back to that real estate campaign. Most of your 200 words,
Wallachs size, will be used driving home the point to the young
man on the way up the ladder that he should get busy acquiring
real estate. Your copy should stress the fact that more American
fortunes have been made through real estate than in any other
way! Which, of course, is a fact.

Tell all the young men that there'll be plenty of time, after
they've salted down their real estate fortune, to get saddled with
sex, a wife, offspring, and a house in Fairfield County. A little
case history, set off in italics at the bottom of each ad, would clinch
your argument. A case history like this:

*That's what Alfred K. H. did. He came to William A. White & Sons
just three years ago. We discovered three acres for him out in Douglas-
ton, Long Island. By now he has sextupled his money. What's he going
to do? Get married? Not on your life! Not now! He is selling the three
acres and putting the money in a hilltop we found for him out near
Princeton, or he may buy a marvelous old brownstone we found for
him in the East Seventies.*

Each ad will end up with a different case history. All case histories must be true, of course. A phony case history (like a phony

testimonial or a phony anything else) always betrays its phoniness! Honesty is the basic requirement of all good advertising. Of course the last sentence of these real estate ads must be a clincher showing why William A. White is best equipped to help a fellow roll up a fortune in real estate.

XXI

Instant honesty

If advertising is as noble as I have been insisting, why do I even take up the matter of honesty? Because of this incessant sniping at advertising which may make some people believe that where there's so much smoke there must be some fire. There really isn't any fire to speak of. Advertising's standards of integrity are as high as or higher than those in banking or medicine.

Why, then, all the attacks? Perhaps because advertising is less solemn and ponderous than other professions. Perhaps it's that persistent Calvinistic ethic that makes people frown on frivolity and makes them figure that anything as enjoyable as advertising can't be virtuous too.

I admit that there's room for some improvement.

There are little exaggerations and unfair implications that should be cleared up not, so help us, by Federal committees but by advertising itself.

First, let's not make up phony testimonials. If we quote pleased users of a product, let's use people's words . . . not pompous generalities we know were never said.

All that it would take to change advertising's image is clean

hands and a pure heart. Advertising's worst sin is preposterousness
—not deception. All the foolish whoop-de-do in TV and the wacky
unbelievability of most TV commercials hurt all advertising.

To achieve literal, bent-over-backward honesty in thirty days
requires the devoted personal support of three people: Mr. X, president of the industry that makes the product; Mr. Y, president of
the agency that advertises the product; Mr. Z, president of the store
or retailing chain that sells the product.

Long ago Plato wrote, "What is admired in a country will be
cultivated there."

Any head of a great retail chain can make his own advertising
white as snow instantly if he really wants to. Back in the middle
twenties when I went to Macy's, literal bent-over-backward honesty was achieved by Jesse Straus—because everybody knew that
he would be fired pronto if he altered the truth by a hair.

I have seen leading advertisers smile indulgently at the farfetched foolishness of their own TV commercials, not fully
realizing that every child-slanted exaggeration made their own advertising impossible to believe—and must eventually make all
advertising unbelievable.

People buy only when they believe. Farfetched foolishness
(housewives catapulted out of the kitchen because a powdered
cleanser cleans swiftly, or a white dove hovering over the kitchen
sink) hurts all advertising. The commercial for the detergent
Dash—"Makes your automatic clean like it's ten feet tall"—is as
illiterate as it is preposterous. And that hurts all advertising.

Bad as many commercials are, they are often better than the
programs they interrupt. For example, the one that says, "Mommy,
put a Curad on," to the tune of "Ach, du Lieber Augustin." The
whole thing rings true because it contains a charming childish
coined word, "ouchless."

Here's another example of a charming childish word-coinage.
Gretchen, my granddaughter, at her fourth birthday party said,
when I asked her, "How were the boys?" "Simply terrible. But

everybody knows that boys always *outbad* girls." For fresh direct expression Gretchen *outgoods* many writers I know.

And print ads, as well as radio and TV, should not present preposterous situations, and they should not quote users of a product as saying things that they never could have said. Illustration:

Take a silly little retail ad, like the one that shows a millinery saleswoman saying to an attractive prospective customer, "You will like this cloche, madam; it has been gladdened with flowers and veiling." That seems harmless enough. But even that mild misrepresentation is bad for all advertising. What's wrong with that? It never happened. No saleswoman ever told any customer that a hat was "gladdened with flowers and veiling." A customer would think such a saleswoman was cuckoo.

I once saw on TV a customer saying to her friend, as they were looking for the corset shop in a store, "I want a girdle that is laughter-light and gently pound-defying too." Kenneth Collins, Macy's advertising director, would have called the copywriter on the carpet: "Where were you when you heard that? Did you hear it with your own ears? Who said it? What did she look like?" Of course the copywriter would have to admit that she had never heard it. And that would be the end of that copywriter!

But not all the ads on radio and TV are bad. Some are natural —the way people talk. Like this one: "Wow! It sure doesn't taste like tomato juice!"

William James said something to the effect that every situation had its annoyers and satisfiers. One of advertising's most dreadful annoyers is, in my opinion, the singing commercial. I once created a singing commercial myself. It was very successful . . . and therefore maddening. That's the awful thing about singing commercials. The better they are, the worse they are. Mine was set to the tune of "Jingle Bells." Every fifteen minutes this beloved old American tune filled Greeley Square to announce Santa's going down the chimney in Gimbels' corner window. I described this Christmas feature earlier.

Gimbel bells!
Gimbel bells!
Gimbel all the way!
Oh! what fun it is to buy
And take six months to pay!

Besides the refrain I have quoted, there were dozens of verses. Several schoolteachers wrote in to say that Gimbels had ruined the old American classic and that no New York children could recall the original words, they sang only the Gimbel ones. Even now, *I* can't remember any of the original words—just the Gimbel parody.

Another "annoyer" commercial is that wailing, piercing "Sound your A for Ehler's." Ehler's coffee, of course. Now that isn't even good for Ehler's. Once, in a supermarket, a confused shopper was looking for Ehler's. I pointed it out. "Oh, that can't be it," she said, "because the commercials all stress the fact that the name begins with an 'A.' " The literalness of customers is no surprise to retail advertising people, who would have known enough to explain everything in the commercial. "You pronounce it 'A' but you spell it 'Ehler's.' Don't forget that Ehler's starts with a capital E." That's what a retail advertising person would have said.

People who have worked in retail stores know that the average person is literal-minded. To wit: Tourists in New York still try to go to Tiffany's for breakfast ever since the promotion of the movie *Breakfast at Tiffany's!*

It was at Wanamaker's that I learned how careful one must be. One day an irate woman came storming into the Corset Shop, brandishing a corset at the section manager. When that soothing gentleman murmured, "What's the matter, madam, doesn't the girdle fit?" she shouted, "Fit? How could it fit?" And she pointed to the label, "Made expressly for John Wanamaker." See how literal customers are?

Yes, all advertising needs to untarnish its present tarnished image is clean hands and a pure heart—on the part of everybody, the

art director as well as the writer. The situation in the print ad or
TV must be a believable situation.

Will this scrupulous honesty I am recommending throw out all
imaginative emotional copy? Not at all. National advertising has
been criticized for being too emotional. I disagree. I think that its
emotionalism complements the retail advertising. The big retail
stores need these emotional national ads. It's all right for the retailers to develop their own brands. But they must never drop the
famous brands made famous by the millions of dollars spent on
TV and in magazines. Some stores, I hear, are thinking seriously
of throwing out famous brands. That would be the maddest mad-
ness of all.

And now a word about national print ads and *their* preposterousness. I am sick and tired of seeing young women moved to tears by
the softness of a diaper or the softness of a roll of toilet paper. I
remember a four-color full-page ad of a few years ago. A chic
young woman is pictured wearing a Simonetta evening gown. She
is gazing out over a lagoon in Venice. The moon hangs in the sky.
She is gazing at the moon. And—so help me!—she is holding to
her cheek a roll of toilet paper, which trails across the page. And
her eyes are filled with tears. Why? Apparently because she is so
moved by the softness of the toilet paper and the dreaminess of the
moonlight, or maybe the other way around.

A similarly hilarious campaign is now running on Hudson's
rolls of kitchen paper toweling. The copy says that Hudson has
printed kitchen paper toweling. The three-line headline quotes the
young matron who is murmuring:

"PAPER TOWELS WITH
PRETTY PRINTED BORDERS
THAT FEED YOUR SOUL"

And then in small type: "They also dry, wipe, absorb, and polish."
Now, what's so bad about this? Is it dishonest? No. But it's not true,

because the young matron would never hug to her bosom a roll of kitchen toweling and say that its printed borders fed her soul. This was thought up, I am sure, in some advertising agency. My guess is that some elderly gentleman, in his kind elderly heart, really believed that today's young women actually feel and talk this way. I know where that male got his inspiration. He recalled the old Buddhist admonition: "If you have two loaves of bread, sell one and buy hyacinths for your soul." So he equated hyacinths with a roll of muddy-pink kitchen toweling.

That silly headline couldn't have been written by a woman; because every woman knows that another female is not moved to the point of tears by the softness of toilet paper or the softness and printed borders of a kitchen towel. She knows that a female would not caress her cheek with either. What poppycock!

I see quite a bit of today's young matrons. I have a daughter who is the mother of four. Like all young competent thirtyish-year-olds these days, she can do anything. She's family chauffeur, mechanic, lawn mower, and even snow-plow manipulator. She carries a screwdriver and pliers in her handbag. She never never stands gazing dreamily out of the window, caressing her cheek with a roll of kitchen toweling or a roll of toilet paper. And she never never cries because she is so moved by the softness of her kitchen paper products. If she ever explained to six-year-old Geoffrey that she was crying because of the softness of the toilet paper, he'd say, "Mommy, are you nuts?"

Let's be honest, in pictures and words, about everything—detergents, bleaches, tuna fish, everything! Literally honest. Recently a national ad ran showing a four-year-old child holding up a can of tuna fish and saying, "Mommy sees to it that at our house we never compromise with quality." Think a four-year-old ever said that? And, since you didn't believe *that* sentence in the ad, you didn't believe anything at all in the ad.

It's just this kind of preposterousness that has denigrated advertising. Anything absurd or unbelievable in copy or art rubs off on

the whole production. And helps make all advertising unbelievable. What would you do if your next-door neighbor came running
into your kitchen waving a box of water softener and crying, "It
kisses your clothes with softness"? You'd think she was crazy.

If I were a czar I could clean up and shine up the tarnished
image of advertising in less than thirty days.

Retail advertising is much easier to clean up than national advertising. I would start by putting into effect the rules that we had
at Macy's back in the middle twenties.

No advertising could have been more honest than the code that
Macy's lived by when I went there. If all retailers and national advertisers were to adopt these rules, then we'd get Instant Honesty.

No ad could be run with superlatives. Nowadays everything
has loosened up. When I go through the paper or listen to radio or
TV, I hear and see hundreds of violations of the old Macy code.

In every copywriter's office there hung a huge sign: "AVOID
SUPERLATIVES . . . they lead to exaggeration." Not a week
went by that Jesse Straus himself didn't take a look at the copywriters' walls to see if the signs were up.

I can't remember all the rules we had in Macy's then, but here
are a few:

No extreme statements.

No words ending in "est," no *best* or *finest* or *newest* anything.
We were never permitted to say that any article was the best of
its kind. No empty bragging statement—*choicest, greatest,* for example.

We were not permitted to use the words *ever, never, real* or
genuine.

We could never predict what prices would do in the future. I am
continually shocked by the wild statements made by even the most
circumspect radio and TV advertisers: "Go out to New Jersey and
look at these furs. All these prices will go up 20 per cent next
week," said a radio commentator.

If a copywriter ever made such a statement at Macy's in the

twenties, she would get a scathing phone call from the head of the store, asking how she happened to know what the price of furs would be in the future, because even Macy's merchandise managers didn't know the answer to that.

A good ad is a promise. The promise should be in the headline. But that's not enough. The promise should be beefed up and made believable in the body of the ad. And, as I have been saying all along, the only way to be believable is by being concrete—not dealing in generalities.

I saw two full-page ads on coffee in the same magazine. One was an empty brag. I was going to say that it was full of glittering generalities. But generalities have as little glitter or gleam as has the eye of a dead fish. The other page beefed up its headline promise by a concrete fact which made its promise completely believable.

Ad A was a page on Savarin coffee. "Coffee-er Coffee" is clever and catchy. It implies that the coffee is more full-bodied, that it has a deeper, more pronounced flavor—a good promise because everyone likes that kind of coffee. So I looked for the believable reason for this claim. There wasn't any. The ad said that the Waldorf-Astoria served Savarin. That's no reason.

Ad B was a page on Brown Gold coffee. It made the same promise—more full-bodied, with more pronounced flavor. This was beefed up by a completely reasonable reason.

Ad B explained not only that Brown Gold used 100 per cent Colombian beans, but that it used the two most expensive Colombian beans, "Medellin Excelso" and "Armenia Excelso." Brown Gold also admitted that its coffee cost 20 cents a pound more than other top-grade coffees. Which made everything even more believable. How do I happen to know that Medellin Excelso is so good? I don't—never heard of it before. But I believe it. From now on, I'll buy nothing but Brown Gold coffee.

Moral: In all your writing or talking learn to be concrete so that you will be believed.

Maybe the writer of Ad A thought he was giving a reason when he said that Savarin was served exclusively at the Waldorf-Astoria. But that is not causality—it is only correlation. Because two things coexist does not prove that one *causes* the other.

I have noted that men, more often than women, fall into this error in logic.

In one of my store jobs a merchandise manager kept making this plaint—to me privately, and to the whole board at our weekly meetings. "You know, Fitz, everybody everywhere (store experts as well as customers) says the same thing—that our advertising is the best store advertising in the nation. What bothers me is that no one ever mentions Store X's advertising. And yet we all know that Store X has a better profit showing than we have. How do you account for that?"

Fred Gimbel, the straight-thinking store president, tried to show him that Store X's good profit was not *because* its advertising was mediocre but because it was doing something *else* better than Gimbels was doing it. That "something else" was brilliant merchandising.

Complete literal honesty would solve everything. There should be no half truths. Today an airline features "We don't seat six across." This is not a straightforward honest claim, if what I *suspect* is true: that the airline does seat three across on one side of the aisle and two across on the other side of the aisle. In other words, the airline is implying that it seats four across when it is really seating five across. That's not honest. In other words, the people on one side are jammed together. Three across is barbarous. The poor person in the middle rides in anguish.

Tropicana orange juice claims it squeezes only the best Florida oranges. Is there a government stamp on orange excellence? Another airline says it has the best steaks. That is unbelievable. If it is really true, why doesn't the copy read not "We pay top prices for our steaks" but "Every steak we serve is cut from beef that bears the United States Government stamp PRIME"? Not only is a concrete statement more interesting than a generality; a concrete statement is more believable.

Retail copy doesn't make preposterous statements, but that doesn't mean that retail advertising is lily-white. Retail advertising has a lot of cleaning up to do too.

Comparatives are odious

In retailing parlance, "comparative" is a price quoted near the selling price stating that the article is worth more than the featured price. That's foolish. If it were worth more than the featured price it would be selling for more. At Macy's (I keep quoting the rules in the twenties, because I don't know each store's rules today) we were forbidden to say "Made to sell for X dollars." If we had an honest-to-God proof of all the facts, we would say "These were selling in Macy's own stocks last April for X dollars." The buyer of the department would have to produce proof that the shirts or whatever did sell for those prices at that time.

When retail copywriters, who are close to consumers every day in the store, put a quote in a consumer's mouth, it's probably a believable statement. A retail writer would never create the ridiculous emotional explosion of the young matron over her dishwasher detergent. The girl sobs as she discovers a speck on a glass and storms in hysterics, "Old Eagle Eyes will see this spot and I could just smash my dishwasher." She is in hysterics by the time the commercial comes on and explains that the sheeting action of Cascade's Chlorosheen will prevent spotting. What on earth does this unstable woman do when something really shattering happens in her life? Like mayhem, murder, fire, water shortage, transit strike? She'll have no pyrotechnics left. Incidentally, the sheeting action picture and explanation are convincing; but they are lost in the shuffle of all this phony overemotionalism.

Of course it is a simple thing to clean up retail advertising, compared with national advertising. I think the rule for both national and retail should be that *every fact* given in the ad must be gospel truth.

Why do I make such a point of the fact that little unimportant untruths in an ad hurt all advertising? Because when there is one slip or false quote the whole thing collapses and becomes unbelievable. As when the little girl says, "Mommy is a genius. She buys me Yoo-hoo syrup." If she stopped right there, I'd probably believe the stuff was delicious and might even buy a few bottles to worm my way into the affections of a grandniece. But when the little girl goes on to say, "My mommy buys me Yoo-hoo syrup —the chocolate energy drink that come in no-deposit, no-return bottles," she has lost me forever.

Like the small boy on TV who used to call out, "More Park sausages, Mom." If he had left out the brand name (it could have been flashed on the screen), I'd probably believe that the sausages were delectable. But he too lost me.

I am always amused when the top brass in industry or advertising agencies shake their heads in disapproval at weasel wording and dishonest insinuations. Of course, exaggeration and blatant misrepresentation are not the only things that have cast a slur on advertising. Tastelessness and foolishness also hurt advertising's image.

"Wonder Bread that builds strong bodies twelve ways" is an absurd slogan. The shrieking hysterical woman who runs away from the "white tornado" hurts the image of all advertising.

Does this mean that all advertising will have to give up its far-out promises to the user? Not at all. Instant honesty can be accomplished by the top brass in every organization. The president of the advertising agency or manufacturer should be held responsible for the contents of the ad. For instance: Bayer Aspirin had the ad: "The best aspirin the world has ever known." There is no such thing. All aspirin is aspirin.

When a charming matron in a 1966 Mercury ad is shown saying to her husband, "John, this is a new definition of driving pleasure," Mercury has lost me. Because I know she never said it. And if I disbelieve any of the ad, I disbelieve it all.

De Tocqueville, the Frenchman who visited America in the early eighteen-hundreds and then went home to write perceptively about us, said, "Americans have a curious trait. They rarely listen . . . and they practically never listen intently."

So learn to listen intently. Take out your pad and paper and write down whatever you hear people say.

If someone had been listening intently, I know of several toothpaste commercials that would never have been written. I can't believe any of them, because of all that chatter about brushing: "We know we ought to brush, but we can't always brush." Nobody ever said that. Just try it out yourself someday. Turn to your wife or your son and daughter and say, "Did you brush?" They'll gape aghast and mumble, "What do you mean, 'Did I brush?' Brush what?" That kind of talk simply is not English idiom. It isn't American idiom. It's just idiot idiom. Because nobody ever said it. And because nobody said it I just don't believe the ad—not even about the fluoride ingredient that prevents cavities. It's not deceptive—it is just preposterous.

Any head of an advertising agency or manufacturer should be personally responsible that no untruthful word goes to press from his shop, no matter what the article is: a tire, a cough drop, or a mattress. The president should see to it that not a word is hazy or misty or equivocal. So let the big shots in industry and advertising get to work on themselves instead of making speeches at 4A's conventions wishing that everybody else were more virtuous. Does this mean that advertising should lose its imagination and promise of great enjoyment? Not at all.

When it comes to cosmetics ads, the sky is the limit. It's perfectly all right to imply that the use of a product will make a female so irresistible that she is bound to win her man. But it's all wrong to make an untrue statement such as "The lanolin in this hair spray shoots right down the shaft of each hair and nourishes the scalp." Or one like this: "This moisturizer is absorbed and retained by the skin to give it a youthful dewy softness." That's bunkum, of course. And the president of the guilty agency should be phoned to that very day by all the presidents of agencies with other moisturizing creams, who would say, "Come, now, we all know the skin does not absorb and retain moisture from any cream. Shall we all get together and have an outside testing laboratory work out an honest permissible statement?" Don't you think that Messrs. Seymour and Brower and Burnett and Ogilvy (the heads of J. Walter Thompson, BBDO, Leo Burnett, and Ogilvy & Mather) could stop all that kind of hanky-panky? Of course they could.

Every cosmetics ad cheats a reader if it does not hold out hope. The ad says that if a girl uses a certain cream it will soften the skin and she will get a man. That's all right. But if the ad goes on to say that the skin absorbs the lanolin in the cream—that's all wrong. Every product statement must be literally true. A general statement that a cosmetic will make you look prettier or younger is honest. The chances are it will if you believe it will. Don't make the promise too big, because then it would be unbelievable. It is natural in this hard world to disbelieve a fantastic promise. A good ad, like a good essay or a good short story or a good sonnet or a good play, creates in the reader a "suspension of disbelief."

Let's pretend you are writing a Clairol ad on hair coloring. Your headline says DO BLONDES HAVE MORE FUN? Can that cause a suspension of disbelief in your reader? It certainly can. It tells the reader that for a ridiculously small amount of money a girl can suddenly have more fun, be more popular with the boys. Is it believable? Yes. It would not be if it came out blatantly with a guaranteed promise. "Blondes always have more fun" is not believable. The reader starts delving into her own experience and thinks of all the blondes she has known who have been social flops. But asking the question "Do blondes have more fun?" doesn't set up all this negation in the reader's mind. The reader thinks, "Well, it *could* happen to me." The ad doesn't make any wild extreme promises. Our girl keeps thinking, "Maybe this mild color rinse will bring out the natural highlights in my hair, and maybe my hair will look as it did years ago when everybody said that I had the prettiest hair in the Class Day procession. . . . Well, why not?" And she shells out her money on the counter.

You may be thinking, "Ah, but there must be repeat sales to make a profit. And of course, the hair color can't really deliver the promise. Sally, even with a Clairol blonde rinse, really won't have more fun."

How do you know she won't? The hair coloring *will* do something for her. Sally will look at her hair in the sunlight. She'll see glimmers and lights she never saw before. She'll be sure that it looks just as it did back ten years ago in the Class Day procession. She'll look at her hair and it will look prettier to her. And because she *thinks* she looks younger and prettier, the first person she meets will say, "You look wonderful, Sally. I can't put my finger on it—you just look different." That is repeated all day. And that night, on the big date, of course she has more fun. The ad *has* delivered. The promise in the headline has been kept.

Of course the Federal government should have strict rules on labeling and packaging of cosmetics and drugs and foods.

I was shocked and astonished when advertising agencies criticized Esther Peterson—President Johnson's adviser on consumer affairs—for saying that she believed in educating consumers, especially young ones, so that they could buy intelligently and get more for their money.

I am sure that Esther Peterson is the best friend advertising has ever had. She has been reported as saying that hair-coloring products are dishonest and that a woman shouldn't try to deceive anyone, especially her own husband and children, about whether she "does" or "doesn't."

I am certain Mrs. Peterson never said anything remotely resembling that! She couldn't be that humorless.

Should the Federal government scrutinize and police advertising? No. They have rules, but they cannot police. Policing must come from the advertisers themselves. Can the Better Business Bureau do it? No. I've heard that it took over twenty years for the Food and Drug Administration to get the word "liver" out of Carter's Little Liver Pills . . . although it had been proved decades earlier that said pills did nothing for the liver.

The job of policing all advertising is too big for any government agency. And it is far too big for media censors. There's only one way to do it. It must be done by the advertisers themselves: the president of the company that makes the product, the president of the agency that advertises it, and the president of the store that stocks and promotes it. They could do it, and do it quickly. All you would need is three Jesse Strauses. One each for the agency, the manufacturer, the store. Then all the people down the line would know that any dishonesty, any weasel words evading the straightforward truth, would result in the loss of one's job.

Should media censor advertising copy and refuse to run a statement that is weasel-y or flagrantly untrue? That job is too enormous for media. *The New Yorker* is one of the few magazines that have been able to make a dent in the mountain of preposterous and shady advertising brags. That's because *The New Yorker*, being the most sought-after and successful of all advertising media, can afford to be completely independent. In the newspaper field, the *Daily News* has been most successful in censoring copy.

Every advertising department should have a copy of the famous booklet put out by *The New Yorker:* "Don't Raise the Bridge, Boys, Lower the River." It contains statistics on unbelievable statements that were culled from *New Yorker* ads some years ago in a six-month period. Five years later the count was taken again and showed a reduction of 70 per cent. In a few years blatant untrue brags can become declassé, which again shows the importance of fashion in our mores. It's worse to be declassé than to be immoral.

Supposing advertising disappeared from our whole economy, what would happen? Quality would go down the drain. Prices would skyrocket. Take funerals, for instance. Jessica Mitford's exposé of American funerals—*The American Way of Death*—need never have been written if funerals had been advertised like those straight direct ads on sofas or lamps along with prices and merchandise descriptions.

Of course one does see a small institutional space run by an undertaking parlor. Such ads usually have a misty star shining down on a misty white rose, both floating on a pale wash ground. But that's not real advertising.

Now Mitford has told us the sales pitch. The undertaker not only talks customers into buying a more expensive coffin than they need; he may try to sell them special clothing for the corpse—such as footwear called Ko-Zee, described in the manufacturer's catalogue, according to Miss Mitford, as having "soft, cushioned soles and warm, luxurious slipper comfort, but true shoe smartness." Imagine that item in a direct ad! A funeral parlor advertising such an article would be laughed out of business. As it is, the distraught spouse or family pays many times the honest price for a funeral.

Supposing a housewife went to market not knowing anything about value—not knowing whether instant coffee should cost 79 cents or $5; a pound of mushrooms 49 cents or $6.50. That is the situation in America's funeral homes. If good honest advertising could get in there and clean up that shady business, it would be doing a wonderful service.

All heads of industries and stores in the nation must realize that even a small exaggeration and mild deception and preposterous TV commercials weaken the believability of all advertising. Then, and only then, will they also realize that advertising is the most important and least expensive tool in our whole economy; then, and only then, will advertising be made white as snow.

Want to go back to emptying the pan under the icebox?

Long ago Mother had an ice chest. It was oak. It was ugly. The top was lined with galvanized tin. This was where the ice went. Twice a week you put a sign in the window that said ICE. If you forgot, you got no ice. That was too bad. The buttermilk soured. Under the ice chest you put a pan. The ice melted and ran down into the pan. When you remembered, you emptied the pan. When you didn't remember, that was too bad. The water ran out onto the floor. In time, the flooring under the ice chest rotted away from the constant forgettings. Fortunately, before our whole back porch disintegrated, Mother saw an ad for a thing called a Frigidaire. She read the ad, believed the ad, bought what the ad had to sell. I was delighted. I didn't care if our buttermilk kept. I only cared that on Mondays and Wednesdays (those were my days) I didn't have to empty that darn ice-water pan.

We'd all be emptying ice-water pans if it weren't for advertising. It was all well and good for Paul Revere to jump on his horse and spread the news about the British. He did a good job overnight. But this person-to-person spreading of news isn't for us. Isn't word-of-mouth advertising good? It's very good but terribly limited. And about that better mousetrap? Without advertising, the manufacturer of the better mousetrap would be up to his ears in mousetraps. Ralph Waldo Emerson was dead wrong about the world's beating a path to the door of that better mousetrap company which was buried in the depth of the woods. You remember that Emerson said, "If a man can write a better book, preach a better sermon, or make a better mouse-trap than his neighbour, tho' he build his house in the woods, the world will make a beaten path to his door."

All this sounds lofty and noble; but I submit that it just isn't so. A middling good mousetrap (*not* buried in the woods), superbly marketed and superbly advertised, would far outsell the better one. Of course, if your mousetrap is functionally superior, a few people will traipse through the tangle to your cabin (one at a time); and you'll sell a better mousetrap or two (now and then). Eventually you might have a nice beaten track. But meanwhile you'd be up to your ears in unsold mousetraps, neatly stacked on the front stoop of your cabin.

Eventually, word-of-mouth praise might acquaint quite a few people with your better product—but you'd go broke while you waited. It gets mighty lonely out there in the woods—just you and your inventory and the intermittently beaten path.

Now, does this mean that a product is less important than promotion and advertising? Not at all. The product is of prime importance—more important than the advertising. People say, "Word-of-mouth advertising is best." Sure it is. But it's too slow. By the time Kate tells her sister-in-law two days later, who tells her cousin in Syracuse two weeks later, you're on your way out of business. Advertising is secondary . . . but absolutely indispensable. No product can live without it. No product can sell—and keep sold—without it. And it's the cheapest tool in the whole merchandising kit of tools.

What sort of economy would we have if the president of General Motors put a light in his window to announce a new Cadillac was ready? Who'd see the light anyhow? He's got a story he wants to tell a nation. And the only way to tell it is through advertising.

I don't believe advertising ever gets the credit it deserves. Sure, we make mistakes, blunders, booboos. But, believe me, if advertising stopped, this would be a ghost country with a ghost economy. We've been accused of creating wants. Why should we hang our heads? We *do* create wants. These wants are the pebbles dropped in the production pool, setting hundreds of little industrial waves in motion.

Take a towel—a plain white Turkish towel. Good enough for drying anybody's back, but what does it do for your soul? Who, in this world of crammed subway trains, littered highways, and automobile dumps, doesn't need—and I mean *need*—a little beauty in his surroundings even if it's only in his own bathroom? Good for Martex and Cannon and Fieldcrest for creating such luscious mopper-uppers as they have produced, and bully for advertising for spreading the news, through word and picture, that there was a more beautiful buy than an all-purpose, all-white, all-dreary towel around.

Now Junior can go down to his tub with ships on his towel; Father can blot himself with stripes of beige and cinnamon brown; Mother can wrap her damp size ten in the velvety folds of lavender and blue moonflowers. Certainly advertising created a want for beautiful towels. And think how towel sales zoomed. Think of the designers, the colorists, the weavers, the shippers, the clerks who were set to work. Certainly we could have stuck to plain towels. They'll dry anybody's back.

It is time for advertising to stop denying that it creates dissatisfaction and start *insisting* that of course it creates wants. Of course it pushes people into struggling to be able to afford more things and better things.

Man *needs* but little here below. Stew, as well as porterhouse, will sustain life. A frayed-at-the-cuffs coat will keep out the icy blasts as well as a new Brooks Brothers coat. A Lily cup or a fragile bit of Coalport English bone china will hold coffee.

Yet everyone wants (and almost everybody can have in our present soaring economy) the porterhouse, the Brooks Brothers coat, the Coalport.

Desire in America isn't out under the elms. It's instilled deep in the hearts of all of us because of the economy of abundance—the economy of luxury—in which we as a nation live.

Another absurd attack on advertising is the claim that it's unstable. The attackers say that advertising is an unstable business —unstable in its inability to hold products or to hold help. The products and the employees, the critics say, bob in and out as in a game of musical chairs. Not so. Advertising is a remarkably stable business. Most of the top agencies keep their clients longer than the leading internists keep their patients. Many products stay with the original agency from twenty to fifty years! How many doctors or lawyers or accountants can match that?

And advertising people themselves seem to like to build a wild picture of advertising. It's not a game. It's not a rat race. And don't *you* call it a rat race. As someone has pointed out, "Remember that even the winner of a rat race is a rat." And even the employee's situation is better and more stable than in other occupations. I once heard a young agency man say (he didn't really believe it; he was just trying to be funny), "We have meetings all the time, and everybody goes mainly to see who is still with the firm." Statistics disprove this completely.

Another accusation is that advertisers are in cahoots with industry to promote obsolescence, so that everything will fall to pieces quickly and have to be replaced. Nothing could be crazier. Even in fleeting fashion, it's become more and more upper-crust to build long life into things. America's foremost designers—people like Mainbocher and Vera Maxwell and Bonnie Cashin and B. H. Wragge—believe that their clothes should be worn for at least seven years. And Chanel clothes never go out of style. Whenever it is rumored that Ben Zuckerman, a septuagenarian, is about to retire, women rush out to buy a Zuckerman suit "to live in for the next ten years"!

And how about Maytag washing machines that serve several generations and usually have no more than a $4 repair bill in a couple of decades?

And then, to cap the climax, automobiles now have five-year warranties or 50,000-mile warranties. Chrysler's cheapest car, the Simca, has a five-year warranty. Think of the light bulbs that are now guaranteed for as long as you live! I could go on and on.

Why has the shining image of advertising become so tarnished? Why are the daily news columns full of bitter salvos fired at this noblest of all businesses? Advertising people themselves are to blame. They try to defend advertising with the wrong answers. When headlines say, "Advertising creates wants," or "Advertising makes the average housewife discontented with her lot," industry and advertising agencies' heads jump up with the wrong answers. They deny sharply that advertising creates wants or that advertising makes the housewife discontented. What should their answers be? Briefly this: "Of course advertising creates wants. Of course it makes people discontented, dissatisfied. Satisfaction with things as they are would defeat the American dream."

It's this dissatisfaction that has given America the highest standard of living the world has ever known.

Advertising prods people into wanting more and better things. Of course advertising makes people dissatisfied with what they have—makes them raise their sights. Mighty good thing it does. Nothing could be worse for the United States than 200,000,000 satisfied Americans. "Sad" and "satisfied" both stem from the same Latin root. It'll be a bad time and a sad time when Americans resign themselves to doing without. As Mother Fidelia said, "There are two kinds of discontent—devilish discontent and divine discontent." It's divine discontent that makes you reach up and try to get better things.

Years ago in a talk to the Rayon Institute, I gave some sound advice. I said, "Stop admitting you are rayon. Start *insisting* you are rayon."

Advertising's defenders should:

1. stop *denying* advertising creates wants,
2. stop *admitting* advertising creates wants,
3. start *insisting* advertising creates wants.

XXII

I got my jobs through The New York Times

Comes to everyone that moment of truth when she knows she's ready to set out on her own. It came to Dick Whittington. It came to Roger Williams. It came to Lindbergh.

It came to me in January 1954, after fourteen years at Gimbels. I had written advertising . . . taught advertising . . . budgeted advertising monies . . . bought advertising space . . . successfully advertised and sold millions of dollars' worth of merchandise for Messrs. Macy, Wanamaker, and Gimbel. Now I was ready and ripe for *soloing*.

Many a timid soul gathers up an associate or two (sometimes three or four) to join him in his venture. With a name like Fitz-Gibbon, I could hardly take the chance. Fitz-Gibbon, O'Flaherty, McSweeney . . . Fitz-Gibbon, Wertheimer, Finkelstein. No . . . for the sake of the cost of the gold lettering on the door I would go it alone. And don't think the cost of lettering on the door wasn't important what with the month's rent and stationery and all.

Had I had time to read all the trade papers, I should have known I couldn't open a real advertising agency on a shoestring.

Did I have clients? No. Did I have credit? Not that I knew of. Did I have agency recognition? No. What did I have? Fortitude, plain unadulterated fortitude, and the absolute conviction, supported by proof, that I could sell anything, but anything, through the printed word.

Print has always impressed me. That's why over the years I have always preferred print advertising to radio or TV. Of course, my common sense tells me that TV has the potential of being the greatest medium of all. But at this point I assure you that anything in print is more believable than in any other medium.

There is something so final, so irreversible, so clinching, about print. I once knew an old Scotsman who, when he wanted to prove that something was positively, absolutely, indubitably, without-a-shadow-of-a-doubt true, would crown his arguments with "And I myself saw it in print. Wad ye deny p-r-r-r-r-rint?" Nearly everybody feels the same way. I am not saying that something *is* true because it is printed. I am saying that *it's easy to believe that it's true*. There's a difference. It *seems* to be true. It's this finality, this clinchingness, that gives print its great believability. And it's what keeps frenzy and exaggeration and tastelessness, which we often find in TV, out of print advertising.

When you set out on your own in retail advertising, two choices lie before you. You can turn to the left and follow the road that says "Consultant Agency" or turn to the right to the primrose path marked "Advertising Agency." I chose the primroses. A consultant agency involves many things.

One of the best consultants in the business for many years was my friend Tobe. She had a service that advised clients where to buy, when to buy, what to buy, what to advertise. She had scouts on Seventh Avenue and Fifth Avenue, at the opera, at the races. She knew the second that white outsold pink and when sea-green bettered melon. I'd be no good at that sort of thing. I don't care whether women wear high necklines with low waistlines, or vice versa. I don't care whether they muffle themselves with mink or wear Battenberg to a barbecue.

All this comes under the intangible heading of "advice." I really had no advice for sale. I just had words to sell—words fitted and cunningly joined together in such a way they made a sweet siren song guaranteed to lure a customer upstream with his dollars in his hand.

Would people pay me for just writing ads? *Would* they beat a path to my mousetrap? They would, and they did.

It was lucky for me that I had spent three decades bathing in the beautiful glare of retail advertising. If a good ad of mine appeared in the Tuesday morning paper, by Tuesday evening everybody in town who mattered knew it was mine. I've always believed that a good retail advertising person (without blatant promotion of himself) does not remain long in obscurity.

Generally speaking, what's good for a store's advertising director is good for the store's business. If I'd spent three decades in the dark anonymity of a large advertising agency, I certainly would have been lost in the shuffle.

Did I feel that my retail background, which included no agency-type research, was adequate equipment for running my own small agency? Yes. I did.

Does one learn more about research and marketing in an agency than one could in a retail advertising department? If you want to get somebody's reaction to something—which is probably as good a definition of research as any—what better way to test your advertising judgment than the selling floor of a retail store?

You write an ad. You run it in the paper. If you are right, you don't need an expert interpreting inkblots to tell you so. The answers to your question come rorschaching through the doors at 9 A.M. on the button. No need to hand out questionnaires or con-

duct door-to-door surveys, or record group interviews on tape.
You'll get so you can tell by ear—by how big the crowd is—how
well your ad is pulling.

There's an old saying around retail stores that hangers speak
louder than words. (Well, there ought to be an old saying!) Anyway, that discordant scr-r-e-e-e-k of the clothes hanger as a dress is
taken from its rack sings a wild sweet song of success. As the
decibels go up, so go the sales. They used to say that Mr. Jesse
Straus could precisely estimate the day's business at Macy's by the
length of time it took him to walk from the Broadway entrance
through Macy's to Seventh Avenue.

In a retail store it doesn't take long to beat the egg whites of
uncertainty into the glorious meringue of truth. Just remember
what you have learned by experience. What research has to col-
lect, collate, evaluate, and conclude—you already know. It's a rich
feeling. But it does no harm to enhance your chances for success
with a little smart merchandising.

Another reason why you should start your advertising career in
a retail store is the firsthand understanding of merchandising that
you pick up.

A beginning writer's popularity and income depend on how his
ads pull. He wants desperately to see that they pull well. So he
gets his fingers right into the pie. Before the ad runs, he does all
kinds of promotion himself. He checks on the extra selling personnel that will be required, he'll see that the buyer of the department shepherds all the sales help, old and new, and instructs them
in the good points of the articles advertised; the copywriter and the
buyer will have nailed down a good window display and plenty of
interior displays.

Every retail writer quickly learns what most agency writers
never realize—display is more important than the ad. Display can
do almost anything that advertising can do—and do it better. You
are not cabin'd, cribb'd, confin'd by small space. You have color.
You have three dimensions. But above all, you have the *thing*

itself—not a vague picture of it. You can appeal to every sense—smell, touch, taste, hearing, as well as sight. The written ad has to depend upon a weak, faded far-removed description of a thing. You have the seeable, smellable, heftable, touchable, sittable-in article, right there before your eyes. *Everything* is so buyable. Seeing is most important, "Monkey see—monkey do." Nobody ever said anything about "Monkey read about—monkey do" or "Monkey hear about—monkey do."

Yes, I am sure that I learned more about moving goods from my experience in a store than I could possibly learn from the research and marketing memos that would come to my desk in an elegant agency.

Of course I might have learned in an agency about such things as depth motivation and how to spend hundreds of thousands of dollars on research. But it has always seemed to me if you don't know in your own bones the right answer you don't belong in the advertising business. Soul-searching thoughtfulness right at your own little desk should come up with the right answer—the same answer as the costliest survey would show.

I opened my own agency with a splash—two parties: one given at "21" by Bernard Gimbel, the other by me in my new Fifth Avenue office elegantly decorated by Eleanor Le Maire. Bernard Gimbel brought Gene Tunney and Jim Farley. Grover Whalen showed up with the usual fresh gardenia in his lapel. He explained, "I wear a fresh gardenia every day because for twenty-five cents it makes me feel important all day long—that's a bargain."

I think the Bernice Fitz-Gibbon agency was probably the most minuscule that ever existed. Just words on paper. No Art Department. No layout. No typography. No radio. No TV. As we explained to clients, this enabled us to go out and buy the best free-lance talent.

We did just fine. The business rolled in. What business? Three kinds:

1. Mostly retail institutional campaigns, anniversary celebra-

tions, openings of new stores; branches, shopping centers, and so on.

2. Working with huge advertising agencies where we provided the retail know-how. We were no threat to the agencies. (Stealing an account has always seemed to me to be unutterably low.)

3. A small amount of national advertising where our clients wanted to apply the 15 per cent kickback against our fee. That's the way most agencies are paid. No fee, just 15 per cent returned by the medium used.

How could we achieve agency recognition and the 15 per cent without a nice little nest egg of a million dollars or so? This is where *The New York Times* came in. And thank God for *The New York Times*. What did the *Times* do? It gave us unlimited credit. From then on we were assured of the same from the New York *Daily News*, and the New York *Herald Tribune* and *Women's Wear*. After we had run our Stroock woolen ads and Madame Alexander doll ads in *The New Yorker*, *Vogue*, and *Harper's Bazaar*, we were never turned down by any medium. Of course, if we had tried to buy color spreads in *Life* or a chunk of prime TV time, things might not have been so rosy.

Incidentally, when you start, as I did, on a very short shoestring, you must run a very frugal shop. We did. Our rent was high. Our equipment? Just brains, and typewriters, and paper (manila second sheets). Our decor—simple.

I don't cotton much to spending clients' money on collages and mobiles and maps of Alaska where your client is packing pemmican for distribution. I have heard of one arty agency that bought a Miro out of profits. Every day, legend hath it, the female copywriters go past it murmuring, "Miro, Miro on the wall, who is fairest of us all?"

How much to charge was our biggest problem. I asked Herb Mayes, former editor of *Good Housekeeping*, and for years the fabulous head of *McCall's*. He said, "Since you're not good at figures, Fitz, you'd better not have a scale of prices. You'd forget them. Better pick a round neat number, and stick to that for everything. Charge a thousand dollars for anything you do: an ad, an article, a speech, anything." Later Milton Biow offered the identical advice, and added, "If you're called out of Manhattan even for a few hours, charge a thousand dollars."

We followed the advice and did well. Of course, we were very chintzy in our expenditures. We didn't need to spend money trying to get business. And we didn't spend a penny entertaining clients. But it's not true that we'd take our smartest clients to Nedick's for a hot dog and an orange drink.

As a show-off gesture, we opened charge accounts at Chambord, "21," and others in that league. But we warned clients that while we'd love to have luncheon or dinner with them, they'd have to pick up the tab. They did.

Some time after I had opened my own agency the head of a fabulous store in Allentown, Pennsylvania, phoned and asked me to drop everything and to please come right over. It was the fabulous Max Hess, head of Hess Brothers.

Max wanted me to take a look at the Hess advertising. Hess's institutional pages were being done by Doyle Dane Bernbach—and, of course, were being done very well. But Max was troubled about his day-by-day pages.

I explained that it wouldn't be worth his while or worth my while for me to spend a part of the afternoon there since I charged a thousand dollars for even part of the day spent outside Manhattan. Max persisted. I went. We quickly went through his advertising books. I gave some off-the-top-of-my-head advice as to how the Hess store could improve its daily ads so they would be more in keeping with their superb institutional pages. A very elegant late lunch was served and as I was leaving—to get an early start home—Max handed me an envelope. When I got back to the office there was a check for a thousand dollars. A thousand dollars for an hour. I knew I hadn't earned it.

So I sat down, wrote Max a nice note and returned the thousand-dollar check.

Then what happened? Nothing. From that day to this, I never heard a word from Max.

I record this here because it throws light on the reason why women haven't done better in business. News stories today tell us that, although more women are working outside the home, their numbers in top-paying jobs are steadily dropping.

Women just can't think big. As I held the thousand-dollar check, I kept remembering that it would have taken me 150 days of district school teaching to earn a thousand dollars. That's no way to think. No man would. And no man would have returned the check.

The thousand-dollars-an-ad plan was lovely while it lasted. But soon our retailers (who were brought up, as I was, on the belief that a multiple sale meant a lowered price) began to ask, "If one ad costs a thousand dollars, how much will twenty ads cost?" So our prices eventually had to come down somewhat.

One factor that operated in our favor was the naïve belief on the part of the clients that I wrote every ad myself. They would say, "If I went to a larger agency, they'd probably give me a cub writer, but in a place as small as yours, I know you write it all yourself." I said I didn't, but they didn't believe me.

Of course I couldn't and didn't. I found free-lance talent among my former Gimbel and Wanamaker and Macy trainees.

I am a good teacher, and after years of solid experience, these trainees could usually write as well as I or much better.

When I started my own business, the biggest retailers in Holland (the Beehive in Amsterdam and Rotterdam) wanted me to do their institutional advertising. They told me that several articles about me had run in Holland and that Dutch people agreed with my ideas about thrift.

I had several other European offers (to promote endive for Belgium, to do institutional advertising for large chains in Great

Britain) because all retailers everywhere had been enchanted with the Wanamaker and Gimbel advertising.

I was not so smart. I turned them all down; because they didn't pay enough cash (not much cash could go out of European countries at that time). As I look back, I realize that I should have charged less money. I could have deducted traveling expenses from my income taxes.

Retail writing has been criticized for being shallow and superficial. That's partly true. A retail copywriter may turn out copy for a hat promotion, a sale of Pucci pants, an institutional page, and the annual hosiery sale all before lunch.

During the ten years I had my own agency, 1954–1964, we worked on as many diversified products as I had when I was in a retail store.

Our roster of clients sounded like the Who's Who of the retailing world. We worked with Saks Fifth Avenue, New York; Saks Fifth Avenue, St. Louis; Denver Dry Goods, Denver; Rich's, Atlanta; Stewart's, Baltimore; Gimbels, Milwaukee; Hengerer's, Buffalo; Pogue's, Cincinnati; Wanamaker's Cross County, Yonkers; Prange's chain in Wisconsin; Hathaway's furniture store, New York; Somer & Kaufman shoes in California; Roos Atkins in California.

We also took on Talbott knitwear, the Wool Council, Madame Alexander dolls, Black Angus electrical appliances, *Ladies Home Journal*, Studebaker, 20th Century-Fox, and for several years we were outside creative consultant for Chevrolet.

We had a supermarket chain in Canada, a florist's account in New England, Stroock Fabrics, American of Martindale furniture, General Foods Cook Book, Frigidaire (with the Kudner Agency Inc.), the New York *Journal-American*, *Good Housekeeping*, *Seventeen*, Coats & Clark threads and zippers, Northwestern Mutual Life Insurance Company, Baldwin pianos—and, it seemed to us, just about everything in the U.S.A. but U.S. Steel.

most children's shoes (like most children)

are good when they're asleep

Of course children don't go to bed with their shoes on. This picture is here to remind you that you, with the best intentions in the world, may have been putting your children in shoes that were designed for the static—not the moving—foot. No wonder poor Johnny was pedally retarded. He wanted to go. But his shoes said no. Maybe they were not properly designed to hold his heel nice and snug and cozy and keep his foot from slipping forward. Maybe they didn't let his toes dig in and push off the way toes ought to. Now you can give your child something your mother, for all her loving care, couldn't give you. You can give **Number 26** shoes—shoes designed for the moving foot. Shoes designed for normal, healthy, happy, hoppy, wiggly, twisty, wide-awake children. They look like any handsome shoes. But there the resemblance ends. **Number 26** shoes are designed to fit the moving foot all the time. And a small boy covers 15 miles a day. **Number 26** shoes are designed to grip the heel and guide the weight throughout every step, so that heels won't slosh around loosely – but will be gripped firmly. What improvements can you look for? In many cases, you'll notice that ankles will seem straighter and young egos will seem to bloom. Because the good life begins in good shoes—in **Number 26** shoes.

Boys, girls . . . infancy to 8 or 9 . . . $6.50 to $8.99.

your children's feet deserve fine fitting as well as fine shoes

1. **precision measuring** – child mounts low platform where length and width of feet are measured simultaneously.

2. **posture study** – during walking and in repose, the child's gait, posture, and foot development are studied by the fitter, and checked by supervisor.

3. **size recheck** – length, width, heel, arch and ankle fit are checked – each part of shoe must coincide with the exact shape of the moving foot.

4. **fitting register** – a case history is kept of each fitting and of each shoe you purchase for later comparison.

"Number 26" shoes now at **STORE NAME**

will you help this underprivileged child?

He's one of the youngest stockholders of AT&T. He's got a trust fund and a pony and a piano and a swimming pool. But chances are—80 out of 100—this pampered, well-bred, silverspoon-fed child will end up, like most adults, with poor feet. The little financial giant above is no better off than the piano-less, pony-less, pool-less mite with nothing but a wooden top and a kickable can to his name. They're both underprivileged when it comes to feet. Because they probably both are wearing shoes designed for the static foot. And children's feet are always moving. For 30 years a distinguished research team has been working on the development of a child's shoe designed to fit and move properly with every hop, skip, jump, turn, and tumble he takes. That shoe is here— **Number 26**—(there are 26 growing bones in the foot.) Every one of those bones moves. And **Number 26** is designed to move properly with them. **Number 26** is pure gold for 3 reasons: 1. The cup-shaped heel is designed to hug and hold the heel bone stable. 2. The inner edge is curved to match the contour of the moving foot. 3. The forefoot is level so toes can grasp and propel. Stop worrying about what you can't give your child. Start thinking about what you can give your child. You can't give him the world on a silver shoehorn. But, remember, the good life depends upon good feet. Bring your baby or girl or boy in today. The best of everything begins with **Number 26.**

Boys and girls . . . infancy to age 8 or 9 . . . $6.50 to $8.99

your children's feet deserve fine fitting as well as fine shoes

1. **precision measuring** — child mounts low platform where length and width of feet are measured simultaneously.

2. **posture study** — during walking and in repose, the child's gait, posture, and foot development are studied by the fitter, and checked by supervisor.

3. **size recheck** — length, width, heel, arch and ankle fit are checked — each part of shoe must coincide with the exact shape of the moving foot.

4. **fitting register** — a case history is kept of each fitting and of each shoe you purchase for later comparison.

"Number 26" shoes now at STORE NAME

Of course we never had all these accounts at one and the same time. Sometimes we parted company within an hour of being hired. Once we were asked to do some ads for Corning Ware, the hard-to-break stuff. The Corning man told us we *had* to use the phrase "with no breakage worry." We said we didn't like it. We said a woman would never call up her friend Susie and say, "I've just bought a whole Corning service and no longer have breakage worry." We said she'd go into her grave never having uttered that foolish phrase "no breakage worry." Of course we'd stress the same idea, but we'd put it into women's words. "No," said the Corning man. "It took a three-hour session to get that phrase OK'd, *and that's it!*"

So we didn't take Corning. It reminded me of years earlier when one of retailing's best art directors walked out of one of the best-paying art directorships in town even though he needed the money. But Harry Rodman, Lord & Taylor's art director for these many years, decided he had to go. Why? "Because," as he said disconsolately to his friends, "I can't stay here at Macy's any longer. Macy's likes Caslon." Harry is still at Lord & Taylor's—no Caslon.

You've got to care. You've got to be concerned. And you've got to stick to your guns when you know you're right.

Another time I encountered difficulty was when I worked on a slogan for a fashion accessory for a great magnate. I have found that the greatest business tycoons often have no "feel" for advertising, which is just another example of the fact that God never gives all of His gifts to any one person. This is true even within advertising itself. I have never known a great graphics man who was also a great copy man. This successful tycoon came into the office (we were working on various things for him). What he wanted this particular day was a slogan or theme for promoting one of his superb fashion accessories. It wasn't gloves; but I'll pretend it was since I don't want to identify the article here.

These gloves were of such excellence and worn by so many of

the socially elite that it would have been easy to launch a testimonial campaign with the slogan: "The most dazzling women in
the world wear Dizlafs."

But the brilliant genius-head of the business demurred at the
word *dazzling*. I wrote him this letter:

We have tried 83 words to replace "dazzling." You will remember we
had excellent reasons for selecting that adjective.

1. *Dazzling* and *Dizlafs* are lovely phonetically.

2. "*Dazzling* and *Dizlafs*" is easy to say, easy to remember.

3. *Dazzling* is a fresh fashion word—it's strong, has not been senti-
mentalized, and commands attention.

4. *Dazzling* is general enough to allow us to use all kinds of women
in all fields and of every age—women who are not, in the strict sense
of the word, beautiful.

Now any adjective we substitute must measure up to the original on
all four counts. Let's try some. *Sparkling?* Too coy and not great
enough. (Sequins sparkle, but they don't dazzle—it takes a diamond to
dazzle.) *Enchanting?* Too sweet. And "enchanting" has become en-
feebled by overuse. As has *charming*. In fact, *charming* has been used
so much and so insincerely that it has become civilization's last-ditch
word for homely women. *Ravishing, stunning, radiant, exquisite?* These
are limiting words—they refer mainly to physical assets. Then there are
*captivating, delectable, prepossessing, dashing, bewitching, tantalizing,
breathtaking, devastating*—not one so good as *dazzling*. Or harmless
words like *gracious* and *entrancing*—inoffensive except for the fact that
they might become nauseating by the third week. With all there is to
say for our original choice, there is only one thing to say against it . . .
the point you brought up, the possibility that *dazzling* may be a little
theatrical. Well, there isn't a woman in the world who would object
to being called *dazzling*—from Judy O'Grady to the First Lady. However, it would be insulting to tag some fabulous much-heralded beauty
like the Vicomtesse ——— de ——— with a washed-out word like "en-
gaging." Actually, the faint nuance of theatricalism about the word
dazzling is another point in its favor. The whole basis of women's dress
is theatricalism. And what is the word most used in fashion copy and

fashion selling—from couture on down? *Dramatic.* If women weren't dressing to be noticed, if they weren't trying to upstage their female competitors, they wouldn't be buying 12-button Dizlafs . . . they'd be buying rough leather mittens with bunny fur inside and an elastic at the wrist.

Back came our client's suggestion that we use the word "knowledgeable."

Our letter to him:

Knowledgeable means *informed, intelligent, shrewd, cunning, wide-awake, discerning, perceptive, conscious, sensible, cognitive,* and *wise.* Now maybe women ought to be flattered at being called "discerning, informed, aware, sensible, cognitive, conscious." But you and I know they won't be. Men—yes. Women—no. But flattered women must be. You need something as romantic and dramatic as "dazzling" . . .

But *dazzling* died on the stem. It must be that the genius to run a behemoth of an industry successfully is enough of a gift. We didn't get the glove job—and we didn't get his other job.

Trifles make perfection . . .
but perfection is no trifle

People write me (both in and out of advertising) saying, "You put too much emphasis on words and how they are placed. How possibly can the exactly proper adjective sell more than a carelessly chosen approximate adjective? If the bare lean recital of the salient facts runs as an ad, they will or will not sell the article depending on whether the public wants these facts in an article."

Father always laid great stress on the importance of searching and searching for the exact word. He said there really wasn't any such thing as a synonym; every word carried its own distinct difference.

About once every month he'd read us the same few pages from James Barrie about sentimental Tommy and his search for the exact word. Here's the anecdote: Try it on your own family round-the-dinner-table English students:

Tommy, in an essay competition for a scholarship, found himself after the first hour at a loss for a word, searched his brain for it until the allotted time was up, and lost the prize.

He had wanted a Scotch word that would signify how many people were in church, and it was on the tip of his tongue but would come no farther. Puckle was nearly the word, but it did not mean so many as he meant. The hour had gone by just like winking; he had forgotten all about time while searching his mind for the word.

When Mr. Ogilvy heard this he seemed to be much impressed, repeatedly he nodded his head as some beat time to music, and he muttered to himself, "The right word—yes, that's everything," and " 'the time went by like winking'—exactly, precisely." . . .

"You little tattie doolie," Cathro roared, "were there not a dozen words to wile from if you had an ill-will to puckle? What ailed you at manzy, or—"

"I thought of manzy," replied Tommy, woefully, for he was ashamed of himself, "but—but a manzy's a swarm. It would mean that the folk in the kirk were buzzing thegither like bees, instead of sitting still."

"Even if it does mean that," said Mr. Duthie, with impatience, "what was the need of being so particular? Surely the art of essay-writing consists in using the first word that comes and hurrying on." . . .

"I thought of mask," whimpered Tommy, "but that would mean the kirk was crammed, and I just meant it to be middling full."

"Flow would have done," suggested Mr. Lorrimer.

"Flow's but a handful," said Tommy.

"Curran, then, you jackanapes!"

"Curran's no enough. . . . I wanted something between curran and mask," said Tommy, dogged, but almost at the crying.

Mr. Ogilvy . . . spread a net for him. "You said you wanted a word that meant middling full. Well, why did you not say middling full—or fell mask?" . . .

"I wanted one word," replied Tommy, unconsciously avoiding it.

"You jewel!" muttered Mr. Ogilvy under his breath, but Mr. Cathro would have banged the boy's head had not the ministers interfered.

"It is so easy, too, to find the right word," said Mr. Gloag.

"It's no; it's as difficult as to hit a squirrel," cried Tommy. . . .

And then an odd thing happened. As they were preparing to leave the school . . . there appeared . . . the face of Tommy, tear-stained but excited. "I ken the word now," he cried, "it came to me a' at once; it is hantle!" . . .

Mr. Ogilvy . . . said in an ecstasy to himself, "He *had* to think of it till he got it—and he got it. The laddie is a genius!"

Many people think that I exaggerate the importance of one word over another. They say, "How can one little adjective, whether carelessly or carefully chosen, change the response to an ad—just as long as you make the product seem attractive?"

A couple of adjectives make all the difference in the world. All the difference between a mediocre description of an article and a description so irresistible that it makes money tumble out of wallets *fast*.

I can illustrate the power of carefully chosen adjectives by directing your attention to a brilliant advertising campaign for the KLM Airlines. Up to the time this campaign started, I was unconscious of the existence of KLM. But now I couldn't buy an overseas flight ticket on any other airline without a nagging suspicion that I really ought to take the trip with the "careful" and "punctual" Dutch. Those are the two adjectives—"careful" and "punctual." Of course, no airline can advertise that it is safer than any other airline, but every word has connotations beyond its literal meaning—overtones that impress the reader mightily. Those two words "careful" and "punctual" run through the whole body copy of the ad and make one feel that everybody in KLM bends over backward in being careful. And what could be more irresistibly appealing when you fly than carefulness? Nothing.

Before I leave this subject of the importance of the *mots justes* in writing, let me answer a protest that is typical of a sort I often receive.

"If you think that vivid powerful placing of words is so important, how can you explain the terrific response to an item in a Sears Roebuck catalogue where there is no room for writing—just a lean skeleton listing of specifications?" Here is my answer: A store or an industry pulls business partly because of listing attractive specifications of an item and partly because of the reputation of the advertiser. A Sears item sells because it is wanted, well-timed, and because of what Sears has been all along. All along Sears has been terrific!

"I'd do the same things—only with different people."

I have often been asked, "If you had to do it all over again, would you do the same things?" And my answer is the one a Hungarian beauty gave to that question: "Yes, I'd do exactly the same things —only with different people." What different people?

Oh, I wouldn't change the stores. Macy's taught me the pursuit of excellence. And it was a lesson that proved valuable to me in a personal way.

Later, when I was going to build a house on the Wisconsin farm, people said, "Don't spend thousands of dollars on an architect. Mike Peterson is a good builder and he won't charge anything for a plan."

But I thought of Macy's, and got the best architect in the Middle West. Maybe the second-best—because Frank Lloyd Wright lived at Spring Green, only twenty miles from the farm. But his own place, Taliesin, wasn't pretty enough—no grass, all weeds right to the front door. I was looking for something prettier in an agreeable Georgian way.

And of course long before the house, we had to put in a big waterworks system. Again I thought of Macy's and asked the University to come out to find if the farm had enough water.

We had a couple of wells and windmills. We had always called in Mike, a water-witch neighbor, to learn where to dig a well. Mike never failed. He walked around with his hazel wand, which would suddenly spin and Mike would point to the ground and say, "Dig here." We always found water.

The University experts said, "Mike couldn't fail. Your whole farm happens to be on the Duluth water table. You'll have plenty of water as long as we have the Great Lakes."

Another reason I wouldn't change the stores is, of course, that Wanamaker's and Gimbels were perfect showcases in which I could shine. Because both stores had had such dreary monotonous advertising, anything interesting that I did shone out as dazzlingly brilliant. Then what do I mean when I say I'd do it again with different people? I mean that I should have learned how to run a huge national advertising account. My background is lopsided: all retail. Yet I had one such chance—and muffed it.

The head of a big advertising agency kept a dossier on me. Whenever he came across a good Macy ad, he pasted it in a book on the assumption that I had written it. Sometimes I had. Around 1927 he invited me to join his agency—to try it out for six months.

I pulled a boner the first week I was there. The brilliant Oswald Knauth—one of the "brain trusters" who had left Princeton for Macy's—had just taught me that advertising can sell only things that can sell well without advertising. The agency's biggest client came to town. I was invited to the meeting. The client's problem was that six of his twelve designs weren't selling. What should he do? The head of the agency and the account executives all looked sympathetically worried and thoughtful. Fresh from Macy's, which I felt knew everything, I spoke up: "That's easy. Throw out the designs that are not selling well. Macy's has proved that trying to sell something that's hard to sell is never worth the effort." And I even quoted Knauth's doggerel:

> *They told him, by golly,*
> *It couldn't be done.*
> *With a smile he went right to it.*
> *He tackled the job*
> *That couldn't be done,*
> *And—couldn't do it.*

The silence was horrendous.

Leaving that agency without having learned the vast amount it could have taught me was one of the biggest errors of my career. But if I had stayed in an agency I would have missed the dazzling decade from 1927 on—when a plain, old, homely discount store soared so high that it became—almost while nobody was looking—the General Motors of all department stores!

Like a homing pigeon I flew right back to Macy's and to Kenneth Collins, who was waiting for me. (Collins always gallantly insisted that he had to work tooth and nail to get me back.) Eddie Marks was glad to see me back too. Wild horses couldn't have kept me from going back.

I probably would not have been a success in national advertising anyway. With all my solid retailing experience, how could I have ever fitted into the crazy theatrics of thinking up white knights on armored horses chasing dirt, or white doves flying in kitchen windows, or white tornadoes skittering around the kitchen sinks, and young housewives having to put on dark glasses because of the blinding whiteness of their laundry?

No, perhaps six weeks was enough agency experience for me. But maybe eventually I could have taken agency work in my stride.

The motto on the Fitz-Gibbon coat of arms would indicate that I could. After one of my many trips to Ireland, where the Dublin papers always gave me reams of publicity, one friendly Dubliner sent me a framed painting of the Fitz-Gibbon coat of arms in crimson and gold. It consisted of a wild-eyed rampant boar with the motto *Nihil admirari*—"to be astonished at nothing." Being astonished at nothing has been a help in advertising.

XXIII

Would I wither on the vine?

After I had opened my own advertising business, I was shaken by
the realization that I might curl up my toes in total obscurity, fade
out of the advertising world, because, in leaving a big store with
its four-million-dollar yearly newspaper budget, I would no longer
have a steady showcase for my work. At Gimbels, I had the world's
best—the back page of every Sunday's *New York Times*, and similarly spectacular positions in the New York *Herald Tribune*, the
New York *World-Telegram*, and the New York *Journal-American*,
and one of the largest papers in the world—the New York *Daily
News*. Never again would people say, "Did you see Fitz's ad last
night?" or "I wonder if Fitz has left Gimbels."

I suddenly appreciated the astuteness of Bernard Gimbel, who,
decades earlier, had sewed up these wonderful positions for Gimbel
advertising.

I decided that the only way I could keep myself in the limelight
was through making speeches. It would also bring me in a little
income.

For several years I had received each year over two hundred
requests to speak in the United States and Europe.

My $1,000 fee (expenses extra)—that neat round figure suggested to me by Herb Mayes and Milton Biow—didn't mean so much when I was on salary. Now it loomed large. Besides, one difficulty in getting that much money had resolved itself. When advertising clubs had explained that they didn't have that much to spend on a speaker, some of the more enterprising ones got in touch with local industries and found that big steel or electric companies would be delighted to pick up the tab. That happened repeatedly.

Because I did not want to fade into obscurity, I worked hard on the speeches, which brought me loads of publicity and headlines coast to coast.

The reason for the spectacular success of the speeches was my putting into practice the admonitions of my father around the farm dinner table decades earlier.

My father was eternally after us to be specific and never to generalize. He told us to write or speak in sentences that would evoke pictures. "When you do," he said, "people will listen and believe what you say."

My aunt remembers the day when I ran into the house screaming, "I have just been stung by a wasp." Before he put wet mud on my sting, my father stopped to say, "That wasn't a wasp—that was a yellow jacket. I saw it buzzing around the Indian mound where you were playing." Be specific, and be accurately specific, and then you will be interesting.

Another time my older brother Wayne got butted by a sheep. When I ran to the house to report it, I knew that the word *sheep* was probably inaccurate, so I said carefully, "Wayne is being rolled over the ground by a big black-and-white woolly ewe."

I thought the animal must have some kind of gender, and at the moment that was the only gender I could think of. Later my father told me that it was not a ewe but a ram—a battering ram. Seems there's no such thing as a "battering ewe."

I knew that my speeches would have to follow the rules that I had learned in writing ads. The title of a speech (like the headline of an ad) would have to create a disturbance in order to get attention. The speeches would have to be startling and shocking. They would have to be attacks—justified attacks on something that had hitherto been regarded with exaggerated reverence.

My first talk was an attack on the tastelessness of church articles. I placed the blame on the hierarchy of the Church, not on the manufacturers. With this subject I caused a commotion that rumbled from 50th Street and Madison Avenue right down to Barclay Street—which is the church-goods capital of the Catholic world.

"Why must we have spaghetti Madonnas on our altars?" "Why all this whoopee *in excelsis?*" I didn't generalize. I started out saying that the average church altar was an architectural monstrosity of Connemara green marble with bloated cherubs in pink and gold tossing about garlands of Gothic flowers; and I averred as how it must be an abomination in the eyes of the Lord. I took up the statues of the saints one by one. I quote:

"I think you'll agree that nobody could achieve sainthood that wasn't a robust tough character. Yet the saints are almost always portrayed as insipid, sappy, and simpering. Certainly John the Baptist should look like a towering oak (as he does in Malderelli's modern sculpture), not like an old moss-beard with a mawkishly sentimental expression. And please observe the statues of the Little Flower—she is spilling roses all over the south side of 32nd Street; and I'll wager she rues the day she ever mentioned roses. And, speaking of roses, have you seen a photograph of the magnificent modern sculpture of St. Elizabeth of Hungary by Henry Kreis? He gives her a lapful of roses—but the difference! Even roses needn't simper."

Needless to say, everything I said had the blessing of the finest minds in the liturgical art field. They had been saying the same things for years in their highbrow journals. But they were writing in generalizations—not in particulars. Advertising writing had taught me always to be concrete.

I went on to criticize the monstrance that Dublin had just presented to Our Lady of Fatima's shrine in Spain. I quote:

"The only adjective for that monstrance is 'monstrous'! The Dublin goldsmith who made it is a man of fine character and integrity. He slaved over this piece, in deep piety and devotion. It was his own idea; he contributed all of the labor and much of the gold. He broadcast an appeal for contributions; and dowagers and humble souls alike sent in a mountain of jewels—old rings and brooches with priceless rubies, sapphires, emeralds, diamonds, and old gold. Well, the pious Dubliner slaved over it, gave his heart's blood, and came up with a violent piece of curlicues, gingerbread, and jimcrackery. Piety isn't enough. Impeccable taste is necessary. Just think what a masterpiece could have been turned out if those materials had been put in the hands of an Arthur Novill Kirk."

I proved my contention that the priests and nuns who were ordering religious art were not qualified to do so. They had neither the training nor the background. I got hold of an actual order sent by a parish priest ordering a painting of the Sacred Heart for his church. Here is the order:

DEAR MANUFACTURER OF RELIGIOUS ART:

I would like to order the Sacred Heart with the following instructions: . . . from feet to top of head 5½ feet. Put feet on mound 12 inches high. Put cross in background 14 inches above head. Lilies in foreground and snakes in background. Width of earth should be 5 feet wide. See layout for positions of pigeons, lilies, angels, etc. Angels should be 5 feet in height from head to feet, with wing-spread extending at least 4 feet. Make angels' heads nice in proportion to bodies. Your last angel heads were too small. Shade wings of angels in very loud colors. Make garments of angels ivory, and shade in the folds with a little green. Make lamb white and shadow with a little green. Make halos around Sacred

Heart's head yellow with maroon inner cross. Make big cross oak color. Outer garment of Sacred Heart a beautiful soft red. Tone down—nothing loud. Inner garments white shaded. Make seat of throne in loud colors. Make snakes appear ferocious as if they are going to bite you. Make them loud. Make lilies beautiful and shade strong. I can pay only $125 for the Sacred Heart, angels, snakes, lilies, lamb, and clouds.

With best wishes,

This was followed by the signature of the parish priest in a small town in northern Wisconsin.

People hooted in disbelief. But every word was literally true. This attack on hierarchical bad taste got big publicity. Yes, speeches that could stop, stir and startle would keep my name out in front. And being out in front would bring me business.

Yes, that $1,000 fee (plus expenses) was very high as speakers' fees go, especially as my talks were always brief. A psychologist once told me never to talk for more than thirty minutes: "Stop before the half hour is over or you'll start telling lies."

I was delighted to keep my talk under thirty minutes. I have never held with that old idea, "I am writing you a long letter because I don't have time enough to write a short one." It has always taken me longer to write a long anything than to write a short anything.

By the way, those requests to speak have never stopped coming in—they still crop up in every mail. I think I know why. I always get banner headlines in the local press plus interviews on radio and TV. Every important talk I have made has had national (and sometimes international) syndicate coverage, because I saw to it that every speech title created a disturbance.

Five years after I had been out on my own, I was still getting more publicity than at any other time in my entire career. *Fortune* named me as one of the seven leading businesswomen in the United States. *Time* magazine and *The Saturday Evening Post* wrote me up. And the requests for speeches increased more than ever before.

When I was elected to the board of directors of Montgomery Ward, I was written up in practically every newspaper and magazine from coast to coast.

I was given the Man of the Year award by the University of Wisconsin Alumni Association, the first time the award was given to an alumna. I was in fine company. Grayson Kirk, president of Columbia, won the award the year before I did. Dr. Edward L. Tatum of the Rockefeller Institute, winner of a Nobel Prize for his work in genetics, won the year after me.

Now, it doesn't take any brilliant originality to speak in concrete picture-making words. But it does take work. You have to look, remember what you see, and put it down on paper.

Years earlier, when I was at Wanamaker's and was trying to interest millions of New Yorkers who had become disenchanted with Wanamaker's and never wanted to darken its doors again, I learned the power of specific information. I ran a Corset Shop ad that worried the merchandise manager who feared that women would be offended. I ran it anyway. Women weren't offended. Here was the headline:

MADAM, DO YOU HAVE A
ROLL-TOP TORSO?

We were advertising a one-piece corselette that was fairly expensive for those Depression days. Dozens and dozens of orders poured in and almost all of them referred to the headline saying something like this: "You must have been thinking of me in your ad this morning, because I've always known I had a figure like my grandfather's roll-top desk. Your vivid description makes me feel that I'm safe in ordering your $12.98 corselette which I think will better distribute my weight and make me look slimmer up on top as well as below."

Another equally successful Corset Shop ad was headed:

MADAM, ARE YOU
PEAR-SHAPED?

Another ad which brought in a ton of mail was on stockings. It was written at the height of the summer heat when most women wore no stockings at all. The headline was:

MADAM, *WHERE* ARE YOUR STOCKINGS?
BARE LEGS LOOK LIKE THE BOTTOM
OF AN OLD TEAKETTLE!

The headline jolted the reader into a realization that she must wear stockings every day whether the temperature was up or down.

This style of simple down-to-earth words, filled with vivid descriptive pictures, when carried over into my speeches, made me a sensational success.

I followed up the attack on ecclesiastical taste with an attack on the taste of the average American homemaker. I believe it was Samuel Butler who pointed out that people will forgive you for attacks on their virtue, their honesty, their integrity, but they never forgive an attack on taste. My title for the talk on taste in home decorating was: "The Lady Is a Tramp." Here are some excerpts:

"What do I mean by 'The Lady Is a Tramp'? I mean that when it comes to taste, the average American woman is really a hobo. She doesn't know what's good, what's bad. The female customer of today has plenty of luxury, plenty of husbands, plenty of security, plenty of dough. She has also plenty of time on her hands. But she is really a hobo when it comes to taste.

"She's always out tramping up and down the avenues, up and down the escalators, up and down the elevators. She tramps from continent to continent, from hemisphere to hemisphere, hunting, searching, wishing, delving for culture.

"She is well aware of the fact that the quickest way for her to 'up the image' of her family is by creating a home interior that will make people believe that her folks are upper-crust. She picks up Corinthian bric-a-brac in Athens for her home in Toledo, and Mexican masks for her Westport rumpus room.

"Women today tramp their whole lives through with limp little swatches clutched in their hot hands—trying to discover *what* they really like . . . if anything. What they're searching for is *you*—ladies and gentlemen of the home furnishings fields. Yes, 'the lady is a tramp.' But she's a lovely one—with good negotiable money tucked inside her bra.

"Every designer, decorator, furniture manufacturer, furniture buyer, store head, advertising executive, and so on should be made to work for one week in real estate. Then you'd find out about the average woman's taste. Never mind being a Fuller Brush man and catching the housewife with her hair down (or, more likely, her hair *up* in rollers). The real estate agent sees America *the way America wants to be seen*—oak woodwork gleaming, cupids beaming, sunlight streaming through the stained glass!

"There are women, of course, who've been told they have a 'flair' and will want to devastate their own interiors. But they're easily scared, if you'll just talk like the professional you are. It's time you put aside your bedspread-side manners and threw them off balance with professional mumbo-jumbo about form, scale, rhythm, flow, color, pattern, and texture. After all, how long do you think M.D.'s would last if they came straight out and told the patient she had housemaid's knee instead of burbling on about the bursa and patella? Not long.

"Tell a woman how *technical* decorating is, how difficult, how mysterious are the problems of lighting and spacing. Tell her that she is no more equipped to be her own decorator than she is to be her own lawyer or theologian or dentist. And her home proves it.

"Just how bad is it? Much worse than those in the furnishing and decorating businesses think it is. They have good taste, and chances are they visit friends whose taste is similar to their own. They write and read beautiful articles in elegant monthlies that are devoted to art and design and architecture—articles about the exquisite beauty and dramatic simplicity of understatement in decoration. The persuaded are always persuading the already persuaded!

"Interior designers and home-furnishings manufacturers and store advertising managers should try to get through to the *unpersuaded*. And by unpersuaded, I don't mean unwashed. Income has little to do with taste. It's often the well-heeled citizen who lives in this House Horrible.

"Did you ever drive through towns at night and peek in the windows? Next time you go driving, get lost, and stop at a dozen houses at random and ask directions; then you'll get inside the average American home—and what you will see will leave you shaken!

"You'll see a chandelier that looks like a hand of yellow bananas hanging from the ceiling of a little boxy dining alcove. You'll see cellophane-covered lamp shades. And ivy-papered breakfast nooks. And funny lawn signs like THE O'TOOLES LIVE HERE. And nursery cutouts. And nasty little half-vases of pottery made to hold rosebuds on walls. And Paisley scarves on pianos. And shirred curtains on French doors. And dotted-swiss scarves on bureaus. And clever signs on the walls of the rumpus room. And paper-pleated boudoir lamp shades with ruchings and roses. And heavy maroon draperies on swing-out arms with rosette fasteners. And poodles all over the powder room. And plastic protectors on the three-piece 'suite' and on the 'sexual' sofas. And orange lanterns in vases. And—holy cow —what you'll see on the lawn! A beat-up old wagon wheel leaning against a tree, and deers and elves, and flamingos, and mirrored balls on pedestals.

"Money is not the answer! Just as many hideous lamps sit kerplunk in the middle of the picture window in fifty-thousand-dollar houses as in the picture window of ten-thousand-dollar houses. And over the lawns of the well-to-do (like white iron doilies) are sprinkled curlicued white Victorian settees.

"Then there are the pictures. *End of the Trail* in the living room. *Boy Removing Thorn from Foot* in the dining room.

"Women not only *need* help in deciding what to buy for their houses, but in how much they should spend.

"Now to get back to our tramp. I have written some stanzas that might be sung to music from the Rodgers and Hart song, 'The Lady Is a Tramp':

> *She likes Monaco, she's chummy with Grace,*
> *She calls Liz Arden to fix up her face,*
> *But bogus glads are all over the place.*
> *That's why The Lady Is a Tramp.*
>
> *She carries swatches from Magnin's to May's,*
> *She walks through stores in a deep purple haze,*
> *She wants new sofas 'cause Bill got a raise.*
> *That's why The Lady Is a Tramp.*
>
> *Over her sink there's an Edgar Guest verse,*
> *Her bathroom surely needs Ben Casey's nurse,*
> *Her bedroom looks like the rear of a hearse.*
> *That's why The Lady Is a Tramp.*
>
> *Although her laundry is late IBM,*
> *Her taste in decor is dese, dose, and dem,*
> *All her slipcovers are down at the hem.*
> *That's why The Lady Is a Tramp.*
>
> *She swims at Nassau, she skis up at Stowe,*
> *She has a checkbook that's loaded with dough,*
> *Her ship's come in, but her rug ought to go.*
> *That's why The Lady Is a Tramp.*

She's from the home of the bean and the cod,
Two generations away from the sod,
She has no brains, but she's richer than God.
That's why The Lady Is a Tramp.

She's trimmed with diamonds and dripping with furs,
Her Thunderbird has two different chauffeurs,
Still all her towels are marked His and Hers
That's why The Lady Is a Tramp.

"Yes, women need furnishing help desperately. They'd spend *ten times* as much on their homes if they were properly stimulated and guided.

"And finally, members of the decorating field, learn the way the fashion industry promotes. It doesn't *ask* women what they want to wear next season. It *tells* them in no uncertain terms. And the girls love it—and they buy what they're told to buy.

"Tell 'em—and you'll *sell* 'em. Tell them with audacity. Winston Churchill was once asked how he accomplished so much in so many varied fields—from painting to politics. His answer was 'Audacity is the only ticket.'

"There's nothing like a dash of audacity in a sea of servility. Stop reassuring women that they have the talent and taste to choose for themselves. Tell them that their unique individuality can be better interpreted and presented by an outsider than by themselves.

"Remind them that a beautiful home is *the* most important of all status symbols—far more than the purchase of a third car, or the building of an expensive record library.

"And remind women that they'd better hurry—that they'd better do over the house than buy that new sheared kangaroo coat. Did you know that beaded evening dresses are now selling for five thousand dollars? Mink babushkas! Chinchilla pullovers! Talk about audacity! Hairdressers have it. The fashion people have it. Home furnishings people haven't had it.

"But most of all, remind women that life is slipping away. Tell them to hurry and not miss this golden opportunity, to 'up' the image of the whole family.

"The burden of the sales message to your consumer would be this:

"Have it now. Do it now. Buy that breakfront today. Splash on that new bedspread today. Call in a professional to work out your storage pattern. Your traffic pattern. And call him in *today*. Don't wait for tomorrow.

"What you put off till tomorrow may turn into a lost daydream. Enjoyment and serenity and all the good things you get out of living in a beautiful environment are like Vitamin C in that you can't store them up. They have to be had every day. This day. Now. And *don't* do it yourself."

These speeches were typical of dozens of other talks I made after I started my own business. Were my ideas original? Not at all. The same things had been stated in articles and speeches by famous designers and decorators all over the United States, but they talked in generalities. I was concrete; my listeners could actually see the bad in their minds' eyes. So it became believable. Other speakers, better qualified than I in the field of decorating, got little press coverage. Why? No picture—no rememberability. No sale. And that is what advertising is all about.

XXIV

Flying is for the birds

I said I wanted to take it easy. How easy? I'd like to keep my headquarters in New York City, but be free to go darting off in various directions. In cold weather I like to spend my time in the Caribbean (which I adore) and in Greece and Mexico (where I've never been). Of course, I'll always go back to the farm briefly for a Currier and Ives Christmas and New Year's. Christmas on the farm always looks like one of those old paperweights filled with flurrying snowflakes.

The rest of the time I'd like to write articles and books on careers in advertising and how to streak up the ladder of success. Despite everything I've said about big agencies, I'd still like to help one on an airline account. Why an airline?

I know why women hate flying. After thirty years in department stores, I know women as well as I know the back of my hand. Women aren't scared of flying because of possible crashes. They don't like airplanes because planes are so wretchedly uncomfortable. What do you do in an airplane? You eat, and you sit. And the eating and sitting are dreadful. The food is bad. True, it's no worse than you'll find anywhere as you drive across the U.S.A. stopping off at random roadside eateries. All airplane salads are bad; because no airline knows how to make a decent French or Italian dressing. A little plastic container holds a thickish orange-colored goo called French dressing. It's Middle West cuisine at its worst. Why can't some airline use a catering service that know how to make the simple dressing that is common to all decent New York restaurants and all restaurants on the Continent—oil, vinegar, and garlic? The main dish, in its tightly sealed plastic container, should be a perfect lamb stew or beef Strogonoff—or any meat dish that is supposed to be moist or liquid. If it is roast or broiled chop or steak (any of which would be very welcome if served properly), it's inedible because the container creates wetness inside. The best taste in meat is a crispness achieved by flame-searing. How about preparing a steak or chop in the plane in that new charcoal-taste quartz broiler? Let the hostesses do that instead of flashing their relentless smiles as they tuck pillows under one's head and push magazines into one's hands. The airlines can't afford top-grade prime meats? Nonsense. They could, if they stopped slopping around with second-rate free champagne and poisonous little moist canapés. And hostesses could learn to make coffee. They should copy "21" or Caravelle or the St. Regis, where a cup of coffee sells for 75 cents and is well worth it. With a superb salad, a fine porterhouse, and a good cup of coffee, women would be happy to fly.

What else do you do on an airplane? You sit. And the seating is terrible. All the airlines are so greedy that they have ripped out the footrests. Women want to arrive at their destination with normal, not swollen, ankles. Put the footrests back—nice high roomy ones. And then more space, please—horizontally. Make it two seats on each side. It is positively barbarous to expect anyone to sit in the middle of a three-across setup. Above all, make more leg room, so that, when a person lets down the back of his chair, he won't squash the person behind him. I've seen people flattened into their seats in physical anguish. And, of course, have the best orthopedic talent redesign the seats. The medical profession has proved that the most healthful restful bed is a hard one. (If you can't find a hard firm mattress, sleep on a bed board.) If the medical profession can redesign beds, why can't it redesign seats? The orthopedically designed beds are firmer and harder, and therefore better and more restful to the spine. Airplane seats should be more erect. Probably the most healthful chair should have a back-board hardness similar to the bed-board hardness. The Mercedes car people are on the right track with their wonderful new copy on their new erect seats into which you do not collapse as into a nest of squishy marshmallows. (Only David Ogilvy could write that superb Mercedes copy.)

Then, airline advertising should say to the public: "We're not greedy. We seat only four across. We give you lots of leg room, and a high footrest, so your legs will look prettier and you'll feel better when you reach your destination. And we give you top-notch food." Wouldn't people rather have this than a stewardess hovering over and blinking at them through false eyelashes?

Did I research this? Yes, the way I have always researched everything. You don't need a Ph.D. in psychology.

One day you're a ninny . . .
Next day you're a genius

The exigencies of retail advertising keep one from getting a swelled head. The awareness of my many errors in judgment kept me humble. I told you earlier of several of my wrong guesses. Here's another. Fred Gimbel decided that the only justification for running heavy advertising in the expensive Sunday papers was to feature items that had great telephone-order appeal. So he decided to open the Gimbel telephone board on Sunday—so that people would pick up the phone and order while they were reading the Sunday paper. I objected because I felt that our churchgoing customers would equate an open Sunday telephone board with an open Sunday store. Fred won. We had far fewer protests than I had anticipated. And phone business zoomed.

Another innovation which I would have vetoed in recent years if I had had an airline account is in-flight movies, which still seem daffy to me but which I hear have been very successful.

And I still believe that the Braniff appeal, "Fly with Braniff because our stewardesses change their uniforms four times during a single flight," is unsound. I would have tried that out on myself. I would have said to me, "Can I imagine a woman saying to her sister-in-law, 'Let's fly Braniff, because I understand that the hostesses change their uniforms *four* times on the trip'?"

The frequent changing of uniforms could interest only a Seventh Avenue manufacturer of uniforms and there are not enough of them to bother with. Of course if the hostesses modeled a complete line of Pucci originals, that might well interest women, but not uniform changes.

I know why wives don't want new cars

I'd also like to work on an automobile account. Because I know why women always vote against the acquisition of a new car. They are for new carpeting, a new playroom, a pool, a vacation house, in fact anything but a new car. But every home needs at least two cars. A woman doesn't know how desperately she needs a car of her own. If I made or advertised cars, I'd tell her. If I made automobiles, I'd lickety-split advertise to women.

How come *I* think *I* know so much about women and their buying habits? You can't spend thirty years in Marshall Field's, Macy's, Wanamaker's, and Gimbels without learning something about women. Since 90 per cent of the buying in department stores is done by women, I *have* learned something about how to catch a *woman* quick and hold *her* fast. Finding out what makes women tick has been made a hair easier because I'm one too.

I've discovered that women—and I'm not being facetious—are different from men. They look different, act differently, think differently. They are more like each other than men are like each other. That fact makes it easier, more economical, for advertisers.

A picture story in *Life* once showed the fundamental difference between the girls and the boys, even when they're *little* girls and *little* boys. Subject of the piece: recess. The lead photograph was a shot of the boys bursting through the school doors onto the playground, their faces contorted with erupting energy. Other photographs showed the *boys* engaged in the following violent activities: wrestling, tug-of-war, "firing squad," playing "horse"—in which riders, astride human mounts, attempt to "unhorse" one another— all of this done with furious, passionate activity.

And the girls? Alongside all this unhorsing and wrestling is a photograph of little girls sitting placidly on a grassy slope *braiding grass* and making cat's cradles of string, as little girls have sat on grassy slopes and braided grass since the days of Babylonia. Even at this early stage girls are utterly *feminine,* and reveal the inherent characteristics which separate the girls from the boys all through life.

Automobile makers and their advertisers can learn a valuable lesson by opening their eyes and looking. Just let them be around a school when the bell rings for recess. They'll see serene little girls sauntering out to their grass-braiding and jacks-playing and rope-jumping. They'll see that females don't like violence. Automobile advertising is still full of violence.

Perhaps there is recently a little less emphasis on speed and horsepower. That's good, because a woman does not want a snorting, charging, cavorting steed beneath her, flame streaming from its nostrils, its tail flicking as it vanishes across the horizon with her and the kids in it. She pales at the thought of a car's ability to roar vertically to the pinnacle of Pike's Peak. She quails at the prospect of taking off like a galloping gazelle with the least depression of the accelerator. The average woman is scared out of her wits at something that responds with hair-trigger instantaneity. Men must love it; because a good portion of every car ad is devoted to this split-second response.

All right—a woman's a poke. She potters. She dawdles. She never worries about whether a car can go fast enough. She does not long for hot, hotter, hottest performance. She does not want a baby that can "flick its tail at everybody else" and "won't take sass from any other car." She doesn't want to sit on top of an engine named Fury. In other words, a car is not an instrument of aggression for her—as it often is for a man. She's not mad at anybody. She's *not* out in the car to get even. She's out in a car just to get somewhere. This may explain why women's safety records are so much better than men's. Even teen-age girls have lower insurance rates than teen-age boys. Also a woman does not respond to all the technical nuts-and-bolts stuff; ball-joint front suspension, canted blades, twin traction, power-punch pistons, automatic variable-rate rear suspension, and turbo and torque. She would be horrified at a headline that read "If you hear a thump, it's only your heart." A woman would be sure it was a broken connecting rod, whatever that is. And there's another difference between men and women drivers: A car is not a love object to a woman as it often is to a man. She doesn't want a panting passionate lover. She just wants a brother to take her places. A man wants a car so that he can be transported emotionally. A woman wants only physical transportation.

It's all right to keep on playing up the length of cars in ads directed to the boys. Nothing builds a man's ego faster than a long car. But when you're talking to the girls, devote that space to talking about easy handling. Because, although women are better *drivers* than men, men are better *parkers*.

Some years ago there was an anecdote in the "Talk of the Town" department of *The New Yorker*, in which one woman said to another, "The thing I hate most about parking is that awful crash." You see, women *are* different.

But, while all of this talking about women's liking to live mildly and men's liking to live wildly is sound, it doesn't mean that a car is any more necessary for a man than it is for a woman. It's just that many a woman doesn't seem to realize what a car of her own can really mean to her. For example, she seldom asks herself, "Am I a *no-car* wife in a *one-car* family?"

Mayhem in the A.M.

Automobile ads should remind women that without their own cars they are menials. If the husband is off all day with the family car, the wife's status is even lower: She's a prisoner in the home. But I'm thinking chiefly of the young mother who has to drive her husband to the commuting train in the morning and meet him every night, so that she can have the use of the family car during the day—for necessary trips to the supermarket, the drugstore, the hairdresser, for chauffeuring the children to Cub Scout meetings, dentist appointments, piano lessons. (Peter De Vries has written: "Any suburban mother can state her role sardonically enough in one sentence: it is to deliver children—obstetrically *once* and by car *forever after*.")

Yes, there are enough road miles that she *must* cover every day. Why on earth should she also be called upon to serve as unliveried chauffeur for Papa? And the driving isn't the worst of it; it's the mayhem in the A.M.: the storm and stress of Getting Papa to the Train. This operation can be fraught with frenzy when it involves her hauling several tots out of bed (after all, they can't be left alone at home) while simultaneously serving Papa his breakfast. And all this before the glaze of sleep has left her eyes. Start the coffee—change the diaper—put the bread in the toaster—zip up the snowsuit—fry the eggs—throw on an old coat and warm up the car for a quick getaway. What a way to begin a day!

Only one and seven-eighths families out of ten who own cars have a second car. You can see the other families every morning at any suburban railroad station—Mama blowzy and frazzled from her untimely exertions, while Papa steps on the train looking immaculate and serene. (He only *looks* serene. That bland expression signifies relief: He's glad to get away from the commotion.) You can also see them in the evening—and what an underprivileged lot they seem when the train is an hour late: Mama worrying about the overdone pot roast while the hungry tots, penned in the car, get out of hand from sheer frustration. And what a waste of Mama's time! Think of all the interesting things she could be doing at home while she's sitting out that hour, losing patience with the children. And that's exactly what *she's* thinking. She's in danger of creeping neurosis because:

> *We die of what we eat and drink*
> *But most we die of what we* THINK.

Plainly, a second car would not only add hours to her day; it would add years to her life.

If the industry sold a new car to each woman who doesn't have a safe new car of her own, it would sell many millions more cars. Automobile ads should keep *pounding* on the right every woman has to meet the day on her own terms, the right *not* to have to focus her waking moments on the mad dash for the 7:43.

Yes, a car of her own is one of woman's Most Important Possessions. First her husband, then her children, then the home, then *her own car,* far more important than other big-ticket items—wall-to-wall carpeting, a mink coat, a new recreation room. Automobile ads must persuade a woman that a car of her own is the one thing that can help lift her own level of living. Automobile ads must show a family that not wanting a car because it *has* a car is like not wanting a book because it *has* a book.

Discontent already seethes in Mama, who should be made the protagonist in the drama of getting a second car. Advertising should appeal not only to her selfish interest (pretty appealing) but to her interest in being a more capable and relaxed mother (very appealing). A second car makes a woman a better wife and mother, and there is no reason why the advertising shouldn't come out honestly and say so.

A car manufacturer is like the manufacturer of vaccine. He is *unlike* a manufacturer of foolish frills like the paper panties you put on the ends of lamb chops. He is noble. He is necessary. It's wonderful to sell millions more cars and also realize you are noble too.

Through the entire insidious advertising campaign would run the thread—the *true* thread—that a second automobile is the family's Most Urgent Need.

Now I am going to tell you about someone a woman ought to be interested in but isn't—the automobile dealer. If a woman could be lured into liking to browse around her dealer's showroom when the new models are launched, a car manufacturer would be made! One browses only among friends, and, at this point, dealers aren't women's friends.

When a woman goes to her beauty parlor, she asks for Antoine. She has similar friendly relationships with her milkman, who puts the milk into her refrigerator, and with her butcher, who knows the cuts she likes. She feels she's a match for even the burliest plumber; but she shies away from an automobile dealer as the devil does from holy water.

Most dealers, of course, are eager to build good will; it is not their fault that women picture them as wolves in Grandma's nightie. This distrust of the dealer is what keeps many women out of showrooms and service departments (wives simply leave all automobile negotiations to their husbands).

Advertising that promotes a dealer's service department, even to the extent of *offering discount coupons* for specific services like oil change or wheel alignment, will eventually help improve the dealer image. Look how trading stamps captured the affection and the business of American women.

Let's see how automobile advertisers can sprinkle a little retail stardust over ads to make them more enticing to women:

1. Get urgency into the message.
2. Be specific—don't generalize.
3. Be easy, relaxed, informal; cultivate what-the-hell abandon.
4. Be *friendly*—one can't be friendly and polysyllabic at the same time.

While I admire greatly the dignity of national advertising, still I often wish there were a little more immediacy to it. Understatedness can be carried to the point of inaudibility. And women can't stand stuffy talk or polysyllabic pomposity. Let me quote from one of the recent automobile ads: "The spacious new interior is what you will judge first—and we invite that judgment."

Imagine Mrs. Thistlehopper of Rockville Center calling her sister in Hempstead and saying, "Let's go in and see car X—they are inviting our judgment."

Another car ad says that it permits perfect ease of entry and exit instead of saying it's easy to get in and out of. Can you imagine a woman in her right mind saying to her husband, "Aren't you glad that our new car permits perfect ease of entry?"

Somerset Maugham once gave some good advice to writers. He said, "If you want to say it's raining, for God's sake say it's raining." The department store ad comes right out and says it's raining.

Women like immediate facts more than abstract ideas. Women like neat, clear, straightforward facts which make it easy to compare one store's merchandise with another's. For instance: In an ad for a carving board, a woman wants to know, besides the fact that it costs $4.95, that it's solid maple, that it is 12″ x 18″, that it is hand-rubbed with steel wool and then with wax, that it has rubber feet to prevent slipping and scratching, that it won't warp or split, that the roast holder is chrome, adjustable and removable, that there's a well-and-tree to catch juices. If you omitted these facts and merely offered a woman a board "for her carving pleasure," she'd be confused.

Now obviously it would be absurd to list the specifications and to catalogue every part and dimension of an automobile. But since a woman is used to specifics she is suspicious of generalities. She wouldn't know what Macy's meant if Macy's ran a mixing-machine ad which said "for your mixing pleasure" and she doesn't know what an automobile ad means when it says "for your driving pleasure."

I'm not suggesting, of course, that national advertising give the gauge of the steel in the fender. But I do think that a more convincing impression can be formed of a product in a woman's mind if generalities are avoided.

In one recent automobile ad appeared the following generalities: top performance, years ahead in styling, big car ride, big in durability, that fine car feeling. With women, generalities like these simply don't earn their keep.

Just to prove my point, I have written an ad on electric fans as the automobile people might write it—in fact using phrases lifted directly from automobile advertising. (Art: woman standing in front of fan in Simonetta evening gown. Palm Beach is visible through open window.)

GIANT 20″ FAN FOR YOUR COOLING PLEASURE $38.98

Here is one of the wisest purchases in all fandom. Nudge the switch and you're bossing 110 volts of surging power. No other fan gives you quite the same easy confidence, winged by the spectacular smoothness and performance of the most modern motor yet brought to the American scene. It literally seems that *magic* has come to fanning. Full length drop center torque tube drive, with swept back ball-joint front suspension. Long low lines are clean and right as the conformation of a race horse. Big fan blow at small fan price. Between you and our trademark— a synonym for integrity of product—has come a wonderful bond of mutual faith and understanding—along with the great promise which it implies for the future. Why settle for secondhand cooling? Gimbels eighth floor.

All I've been saying is that in a day and age when women will settle for nothing less than the newest, the biggest, the best of everything, the car industry has let them become satisfied with second-rate transportation—or worse, no transportation at all.

Getting women to want something better is primarily a problem of making them dissatisfied with things as they are. Whether it's simply a new family car or a second family car, somebody has to stir up a woman's dissatisfaction and channel it to the proper place —the dealer. Advertising to women is the only way it can be done.

If one says the right things to women, they will think and respond in a fairly predictable fashion. If one doesn't talk to them directly in words they understand, you might as well be winking in the dark.

Letters addressed to both Mr. and Mrs. X are often ignored by Mrs. X. Only when a letter or a magazine is addressed exclusively to Mrs. America, with "hers" stitched on it as on a bath towel, is she at full attention.

As for the woman who has never learned to drive, she knows

in her heart she's a schmo. Here's a slogan: Get the schmo on the road.

When an advertiser urges a woman to learn how to drive and to demand her own car, he is helping her yield to a temptation to do what she unconsciously wanted to do all along. Show her how a car *unjangles* the nerves—psychiatrists tell us that driving through heavy traffic is soothing. Show her why a car is good for what ails her.

It may be slow going at first—like walking in a bucket of yogurt. Why won't the women respond quickly to something that is so obviously for their own good? Because it's like slavery: the worst thing about slavery is that slaves too often get used to their condition and get to like it.

Advertising will have to remind such women that they are worse off than women who lived centuries ago. They had their vehicles—though they didn't have many places to go. Cleopatra had her barge. Europa her white bull. Mother Goose her gander. Lady Godiva her horse. What does the woman without a car have? Shank's mare.

What is it that a devoted husband always says to his wife? "Darling, nothing is too good for you." That's right—and nothing's what she's got.

The ads should say to her: "You think you are modern, emancipated, free, and airy? Don't be too sure, my girl. Just because you get a mink stole once every seventeen years and get taken to '21' every five years, that doesn't mean that you have not been left in the lurch. Get a car. Live a little. Live a lot—up, down, and sideways."

I don't have the space to go into that most important of all considerations—safety. If women had had their own cars all these years, cars would be safe today. Women have sharper imaginations. They can't bear the thought of their chests being pierced by steering wheels or an eye being gouged out by a metal drawer handle. They would have demanded interiors that were marsh-mallow-safe. There I go picking up those double-jointed agency adjectives!

If I don't get a chance to help a big agency on an airline or automobile account, what'll I do in between my travels, here in my high-in-the-sky New York apartment?

Will I try to write fiction? No. I'd be scared stiff. I'm not that good. As I told you before, advertising writing calls for a lesser talent than does sustained writing.

The best composition course I ever had was Professor R. E. N. Dodge's Daily Theme course back at the University of Wisconsin. Daily meant daily. Although the class met only twice a week, one had to drop a piece of writing into Mr. Dodge's mailbox every day except Sunday. There were only ten in the class. Was I the star? Far from it. The shining star was Marjorie Kinnan Rawlings, who later wrote *Cross Creek* and *The Yearling*. Was I runner-up? No. That was Esther Forbes, author of *Paul Revere* and *O Genteel Lady*, and several other New England-based biographies and novels.

I know my place. It's anybody's, but anybody's, place—the field of advertising.

In fiction you have to conjure up your plot and your characters. In advertising you just look at a thing and describe it in irresistibly winning words. Anybody can look. A cat can look at a *king*. Anybody can look at a *thing*.

XXV

I like to live high . . .
in the sky

One of the big reasons for my not retiring to the Wisconsin farm—now that I have reached retirement age—is my long-time love affair with New York City. I agree with whoever said, "After you cross the Hudson, everything is Hoboken." I'm not ready for Hoboken.

New York is still the Big Town where everything starts. New York, in advertising as well as in everything else, sets the pace for the rest of the world. See? I'm hooked.

I am writing this in my apartment on New York's upper East Side—looking out over the snarling, churning waters of the East River. Why, after all these years in the hurly-burly of New York, don't I call it a day and retire to the old family farm near Waunakee, Wisconsin, which my husband and I bought from my mother thirty years ago, and which I still own? There are several reasons. Is it because I would miss the theater? Quite the contrary. Last time I was on the farm everybody had seen *Hello, Dolly!* I haven't seen it yet.

I like living high in the sky and looking down on wild water. My grandfather, who emigrated from County Limerick to southern Wisconsin around 1840, had a motto: "Buy on a hill overlooking water—wild water." So he bought—from the state or from the Indians; I forget which—some land on a high plateau eight miles north of Madison, overlooking Lake Mendota. (The original 1,000-acre tract has now dwindled to 250 acres.) Mendota is an anomaly. In the middle of the placid rolling hills and peaceful meadows lies Mendota, a turbulent tempestuous mountain lake. But there are no mountains around anywhere. Madison is built on four lakes. My grandfather turned thumbs down on the other three—Monona, Waubesa, and Kegonsa—because they weren't wild and raging. Why wild water? "Wild water," he said, "stills the nerves." So when I opened my own business in 1954, on the corner of Fifth Avenue and 56th Street, I chose a high floor with a view of the Hudson River. But I found the Hudson was calm.

So when I closed my office in 1964, I settled down in this apartment high in the sky looking down on the East River. I can watch the light play on the river's treacherous little eddies and twisting currents and savage whirlpools—all of which, I am sure, "stills the nerves."

Why did I close my Fifth Avenue office? Because I figured I'd take things a little easier. Since I wanted to cut down on jobs and clients, I didn't need to be down in the heart of things. With a few irons in the fire, I could just as well work out of my apartment and therefore pay only one monthly rent bill. My apartment, like all New York apartments, is too expensive, but it's a lot cheaper than my $12-a-square-foot office was. I pay $350 for a four-room apartment in which I live alone. (My husband died fifteen years ago.)

Now that I have admitted that I have reached retirement age and want to take things easier, why don't I call it a day and stop writing ads and articles and books on advertising? Because it's more fun to be *in* advertising than out of it. Of course I have never tried settling down on an island in the blue Aegean. That might be nice too. Another reason for my staying in advertising is that I have a particular passion for pushing people up. It is an odd quirk. My friends say that I am like the little boy scout who helped the old lady across the street even if she didn't want to cross the street. I have always been possessed with this passion for pushing people up—even if the pushees are unenthusiastic and the results inconvenient for me. Perhaps I am still doing it with this book. Generally people who have been successful try to discourage others from entering their fields. But look at me! Do I tell you, "Be a broker, or a bricklayer, or a bookkeeper, but keep away from that impossible job of advertising"? Never, but never! You've already taken the first step (as the Chinese say, a journey of ten thousand miles *starts* with the first step), by reading this book. I imagine that you have clothes to iron, babies to burp, or a whodunit to finish, or a college final to study for—and wouldn't be reading this unless you *were* interested.

To be a success in advertising takes work—that's probably the most important thing you have to realize if you are going to jump into advertising—tough work, sweaty work, irritating work, and lots of it. But believe a person who made it: In my field there are still lots of elegantly appointed rooms at the top, as well as more sparsely furnished ones at the bottom. Yes, you start at the bottom and work your way up, but that can go faster than you think. If you have the wit to have come this far with me, and the wisdom to profit by it, you too can make it. Take it from someone who did —who simply said, "Neither discouragement, nor doldrums, nor dollar deficiency, nor gloom nor fright will stay this not-so-swift courier from her appointed rounds."

While I was going on my appointed rounds, how did I manage one husband and two children and a household and a full-time job? It was not easy. And it was not inexpensive. But I think it was successful. Because the children, even when they were very young, were self-reliant and independent. Elizabeth, from the age of six, used to make frequent trips to the Wisconsin farm all by herself, aided by tips to the people on the Twentieth Century and notes to Traveler's Aid in Chicago, where she had to change trains for Madison. And Peter must be well adjusted. He apparently didn't inherit my claustrophobia or he couldn't be skipper on a submarine —which job he has had for the past two years: the submarine *Ronquil* out of San Diego.

But the most important thing of all for a career woman is to be married to a man who is a signal success himself. There must be no husband-wife rivalry. Probably it's best for the husband to be in his own business or profession where he is his own boss. And he should be very successful in his own firm. My husband had no real interest in retailing or advertising. But he was interested in writing. And some of my best headlines came from him and from my children.

Yes, my husband helped me with advertising copy. Was I of any help to him? Yes—although obviously I didn't know anything about law. He always said that I was a good person to try out cases on; because I had an instinctive sense of rustic justice. Although I am sure rustic justice doesn't always prevail in court, still it must mean something.

Maybe having a sense of rustic justice without any knowledge of law is like having good horse sense in advertising—without knowing much about psychology or research.

As I've told you, I have always believed that if one couldn't analyze a problem himself and come up with pretty much the same answer that a lot of costly research would divulge, one probably didn't belong in advertising. Sounds awfully unscientific. Of course I've been influenced by the flyer we took into research back in the Macy days. Kenneth Collins hired a research organization to question a vast number of housewives on their preferences in New York daily newspapers. A majority declared they were readers of the

New York *Herald Tribune.* Very few admitted to reading the tabloids. But the tabloids had all the circulation, and the elegant tasteful *Herald Tribune* had hardly any.

Then several years ago there was that research into "Who reads what magazines?" A majority of women claimed they read Collier's faithfully—week after week. Only trouble . . . Collier's had been out of existence for seven years!

The help problem at my suburban house was difficult, especially at first. Like many career mothers, I thought no baby could survive without a starched registered nurse in charge who ran the house, the housekeeper, the children—all of us. Her salary, over $400 a month, would be a bargain now; but it seemed high back in Depression days. But it was the registered nurse's bossiness, rather than her salary, that made us change after the first three years. We changed to a wonderful Scotch nurse and then to an English nanny. Our live-in housekeeper was always a girl in her twenties from a farm near ours in Wisconsin. These girls were delighted to be able to get to New York; because they knew that I'd eventually work them into some phase of fashion work in the city.

After we dropped the bossy registered nurse, our nurse expense dropped from $400 a month to $350. The farm girls were delighted to work for $150 a month with a chance to see New England and Washington, D.C., for example, with expenses paid. We also hired an outside couple one day a week for heavy cleaning. They took the laundry home to do.

Myrtle, our first farm-girl housekeeper, was a pretty blonde of Norwegian extraction who had a talent for sewing. She was a home-economics graduate of the University of Wisconsin. I persuaded the Singer Sewing Machine Company to take her—and she eventually became Singer's fashion director. Then I had to hunt for her successor. I found Millie, who weighed 200 elegantly stacked pounds . . . she had a lovely face. Soon Millie, also a Wisconsin graduate, became Wanamaker's widely publicized 200-pound fashion model. We advertised her far and wide, and Millie always got the most applause at the Wanamaker fashion shows. When Millie returned to her Wisconsin farm on vacation, she showed her boy friend the ecstatic clippings in her publicity book. He promptly married her. So I had to start hunting again. Millie now is a farm wife and mother of several children. So on and on and on.

The only thing that gave the household some semblance of stability was the fact that the Scotch and English nurses stayed on for years and years. *They* didn't want other careers. What they liked, and also what the university-graduate housekeepers liked, was a flexible time schedule. When the nurse was away the housekeeper ran things. When the housekeeper was off to Washington for a weekend, the nurse managed without her. Each knew that she could always go to a matinee, meet a friend in the city, see somebody off on a boat. Neither was tied to the house by a rigid time schedule. So what was good for the Scotch nurse appealed to the farm-girl housekeeper. This same elasticity in hours kept my creative writers happy too.

It was this elasticity of *daily* hours, rather than the long vacations, that kept most of my Gimbel Phi Beta Kappas from succumbing to Madison Avenue agency enticements.

And the same policy kept my university-graduate housekeepers from succumbing to the enticements of suburban neighbors.

Myrtle, my university housekeeper, once reported this interview with a suburban neighbor who tried to lure her away: "Mrs. X presented a pretty picture of how little I'd have to do if I worked for her. Then Mrs. X said, 'Now for your time off—that would be the usual Thursday.' " Said Myrtle, "That Thursday stuff made me feel like a maid." After that Myrtle wouldn't even listen to any wheedling overtures.

I decided then and there that I would never let any demeaning word discourage my household staff . . . or my office staff.

They were all free as air to come and go. And, like all very intelligent people, they never took advantage of this freedom. I never had to hire an hour's extra work to make up for some writer's being away from his desk. Everybody was delighted to double up and take over extra work when someone else was away.

What gave the household complete freedom was the fact that if the housekeeper and nurse both wanted to be away on the same weekend, I took over for both of them. Like the average career woman, I was not fed up with the children. And the children were not fed up with me. It's not only the quantity of time a career woman spends with her children—it's the quality of that time.

What I learned in running an office helped me in running a household. And vice versa.

So if you think the job (in the home or in the office) is important, remove the little nagging annoyances and the petty provocations. They upset the help more than an occasional overtaxing high-pressure job ever does. To quote from an old issue of *Punch*, "It ain't the 'unting as 'urts 'un, it's the 'ammer, 'ammer, 'ammer along the 'ard 'igh road."

But what if your Personnel Department won't let you play fast and loose with organization rules? Then do it covertly, *sub rosa*. By the time the busybody biddies (male and female) in the Management Division catch up with you, your smooth-as-cream operation will have received the admiration of the whole business.

Be a pragmatic academician—like Fred Gimbel. If it works, it's good. And, take my word for it, this elastic hour arrangement for employees works.

The farm orchard and Burnham and Dunsinane

You may be thinking that I am really a Big Brain—otherwise I couldn't have written and directed the writing of ads which sold millions and millions of dollars' worth of goods. That's not so. I like to think it was because I had two fairly smart grandfathers. But I am sure they were no geniuses.

I didn't know Grandfather Fitz-Gibbon—he was much older than Grandfather Bowles. They had both grown up in that lovely dairy country—"the Golden Vale"—which lies between Limerick and Cork. But they had never met in Ireland.

Why am I so impressed with my Grandfather Fitz-Gibbon? He moved the orchard! He built his first house, a large rambling log cabin, down in the pasture near the creek, so that he would be near freshwater springs. He planted an enormous orchard of hundreds of trees. Thirty years later, after he had prospered considerably, he decided to build a stone house about three quarters of a mile away on the highest point on the farm. He couldn't bear to leave his full-grown, thirty-year-old trees—no dwarf fruit trees; these were giants. So he decided to move the whole orchard and place it on the northern slope running down from the crest of the high hill. Every good orchard is on a northern slope. The neighbors thought he was batty: "You can't move enormous old trees." But he said, "I have it all worked out in my head. In the summer while the earth is soft, I'll dig a circle around the base of each tree. The ball of earth will be so big that there will be no shock to the root when it's moved. Then," he went on, "that same summer I'll dig holes of the same circumference and the proper depth up in the new location. After Thanksgiving when the ground freezes, I'll move each tree on a stoneboat and drop it into the waiting hole." He did. He didn't lose a tree.

Later when I lived in Manhasset, a suburb about twenty-five miles out on the North Shore of Long Island, we were negotiating with Lewis and Valentine, the leading tree movers on the Eastern seaboard, about the moving of a huge dogwood tree. "We can do it," they crowed, and they went on to describe, to the letter, the method that James Alexander Fitz-Gibbon had thought up by himself many years earlier.

That was smart. Also it was smart to be the first southern Wisconsin farmer to take carloads of hogs and cattle into Chicago. For years Dane County farmers had taken carloads of livestock to Milwaukee, 100 miles away. But it had never occurred to them that Chicago, 175 miles from the farm, was a bigger and better market.

Grandfather Fitz-Gibbon worked this out without benefit of a marketing or research department.

I am not too impressed with the marketing and research going on in advertising agencies today. One reason I am so suspicious of research is that Macy experience in tabloid versus standard newspaper readership I just told you about.

The back of my hand to research!

If you detect a faint anti-agency note in these pages you are detecting right. Remember, this charmed life and those golden rewards I am promising you are in the field of retail (not national) advertising. Retail advertising is my only specialty.

But what I admired most in Grandfather Fitz-Gibbon (from what I heard of him—he died before I was born) and my father (from what I knew of him) was their irreverence toward tradition. They didn't think a thing had to be so because a lot of people had believed it for a long time. They ridiculed the old copybook maxim: "Plough deep while sluggards sleep." My father said, "Every old saw ain't so. The sleeping sluggards are smart; because the guys out doing the deep plowing are ruining the land." Our German farmer-neighbors in Wisconsin set their plowshares deep and were out in the fields before daybreak. My grandfather told them that that was cockeyed—that one shouldn't mine the land. He said that the ideal way to plant a seed was to scratch the soil a little, stick the seed in, and step on it, then scrunch it and grind it under your heel. If you must plow, plow shallow, not deep. He also told them not to plow up to the very fence lines, and not to clear out the brush and weeds and tangled undergrowth in the fence lines. He said that a luxurious wild untidy tangle on every fence was good for the land because it would hold the moisture. They didn't agree. They thought his way wasteful and untidy. Their crops faltered. And my grandfather's crops flourished mightily. They were especially lush as they neared the fence lines with their sumac, hazelnut bushes, and tangle of wild roses and weeds, which attracted an abundance of small wild life: rabbits, badgers, woodchucks, partridges. And wild choke-cherry trees which were filled with the gabbling and gobbling of brown thrashers and orioles and blue jays.

"Nature doesn't like a tightwad," said Grandfather Fitz-Gibbon. "You must not try to squeeze every inch out of the land." He was dead right, as the agricultural schools in our great universities found out many decades later.

Grandfather Bowles wasn't any slouch either. He predicted that insecticides would result in a great increase in insects, because the insects would soon get inured to them.

Along this line, my father, who must have inherited a skeptical "Oh, yeah?" outlook, delighted us when he rewrote "The Hare and the Tortoise." He said, "That ending was cooked up just to please some poky old plodder. Of course the hare won the race."

He also destroyed the myth about the thrifty, farsighted squirrel. He said that the squirrel was a dope and always forgot where he had stored the hickory nuts and acorns. The fact that I come from a long line of non-gullible balloon prickers has helped keep my advertising copy honest.

Both grandfathers worried about soil erosion, and did contour plowing on our terraced hillsides. And they wouldn't let anyone drain a marsh. They said, "A marsh is good for a farm." Rachel Carson would have loved them.

Both grandfathers also warned against wasting water—"Remember, North America now has all the water it will ever have. What'll we do when the population increases?"

Anent the population increase: Each of them sired ten children!

XXVI

Advertising needs you!

Did I decide in college that I wanted to write advertising? No. Back in 1918, I didn't know that advertising existed. It scarcely did.

My ambition at that time was to get to New York, and to live in a high airy apartment in Greenwich Village. There I would write articles for the *Atlantic Monthly*—subjective essays with a wry, sardonic twist, similar to pieces then appearing in the *Atlantic* by Agnes Repplier.

I didn't know at that time that Greenwich Village apartments were low and non-airy. I realized, of course, that I'd have to start my writing career in a job which I was certain I'd get quickly through the letters of recommendation which my University of Wisconsin professors had written to Houghton Mifflin and Mac-millan, their own publishers. I never used those letters. I still have them.

The nearest I ever got to literary writing was being asked a few years ago to submit pieces to the *Saturday Review*. I never did, not even one, in my past forty years in New York. I was smitten by advertising. I am still smitten, and probably always will be.

Advertising is like typing and driving. Once you learn, you never forget. You carry your copywriting competence right along with you down through the years.

Perhaps my case histories have featured young people too much. They shouldn't have. Among the more than a thousand whom I have helped to become successful advertising writers, probably a fourth were older people.

I am not using the phrase "older people" as the government uses it, meaning females thirty-five or over. The older people I hired or sponsored were in their forties and fifties.

You *can* teach an old dog new tricks—and sometimes faster. A course in Russian was once given to a class ranging in age from fourteen to the middle forties. The students over forty learned faster than the high-school students. And, remember, women don't age so fast as men. They stay younger longer. They go on and on like Tennyson's brook. Women are seldom too old to learn a new craft. Clara Barton learned to type when she was eighty-nine. Even Benjamin Franklin, a mere man, learned to speak French when he was past seventy.

Grandma Moses started to paint when she was about eighty. And think what an advertising writer Winston Churchill would have made in his decade between eighty and ninety!

I have an aunt, Win Bowles, now in her late seventies, who retired a few years ago from her Schuster, Milwaukee, job of writing all the institutional ads. She was probably the best institutional advertising writer in the Middle West. Was? Is.

If I were the head of a small store and wanted to raise the image of my establishment at not too great cost, I'd hire some semiretired oldster on a free-lance basis—maybe a former newspaper writer or a high-school or college English teacher, or just maybe anyone who had learned to look and listen and put things down on paper.

Why are old people more likely to be fresh, frisky, and flexible? Now you'd *think* that it would be the *young* that would do the jolting and shocking—that they would be the ones who would come up with the wild untrammeled original approaches to problems in retailing and industry. But do they? You can bet your last slide rule that they don't. The young aren't kicking over any traces. They are conforming. They are too respectful, subdued, tractable, docile, mild. The young have the *mild* ideas. The old have the *wild* ideas.

It has never been true that what has been for a long time must necessarily be right. Youth often has a kind of curator complex— an urge to preserve the mores, superstitions, and foibles of the past without a glance of appraising doubt. No museum has a more zeal- ous staff of curators than that monument to the nineteenth century, the so-called department store. That's fine—if you're in competi- tion with the Smithsonian. It's terrible if you're in business to make money. How about your store? Are you stuck in the status quo? Are you rule-ridden? More important, are you even capable of taking a good hard analytical *look* at yourself? It's hard to look at one's self—because one is too close.

The older copywriters have learned to look at a thing freshly with no preconceived ideas about how it ought to look. They have had to learn this in order to be good advertising writers. They know that nothing on earth is uninteresting; there are just disinterested people, who have never learned to look. They know that a spear of grass is interesting . . . that the very whorls on one's thumb can be interesting.

I once heard my copywriter aunt say, as she listened to peepers (young frogs) in the spring, "They sound like faint faraway sleigh bells." And they do! And another time, looking at a walnut meat, she said, "Why, it looks just like a little old wrinkled heart." And so it does!

So jump into advertising so that you'll never be bored in your old age. Old copywriters don't grow old: because their sharpened sense of observation gives them that precious old-age security that is the very foundation of a young optimistic outlook on life. They never lose their sense of excited appreciation of the beauties of this earth.

As I said earlier, there must be no husband-wife rivalry in a home. My children were fascinated with my advertising problems, and they worked hard on headlines. But not for a moment did they believe that Mommy's advertising work was so important as Daddy's law. It probably wasn't. Neither did they think Mommy was so bright as Daddy. She wasn't.

The children did realize that the income from advertising provided many an extravagance that might have been difficult on one income—such as buying the farm, building the fascinating barns, the silos, the beautiful house, and for the many many trips between Long Island and Wisconsin. One of the biggest expenses was the planting of avenues of wine-glass elms—frankly copied from the avenues of elms on the estates of Long Island's North Shore. I figure that when my grandchildren's grandchildren spend their vacations on the farm, the elm tops will meet in Gothic arches. Daddy, of course, paid all expenses of running the household, food, clothing, and so on. But the children knew that it was advertising income that paid for the beautiful hilltops (all overlooking wild water) which I started to accumulate.

I have toyed with the idea of building me a house for my retirement days. Perhaps on one of the high hilltops or near the highest Indian mound on the farm. Or maybe I'd take an apartment in Madison—less than ten miles from the farm and only eight miles from most of the hilltops. Then I get to thinking, "Could I ever leave Madison Avenue? I don't mean just Madison Avenue advertising. I mean Madison Avenue-Madison Avenue. When I want a fascinating walk, I walk down Madison, down through the eighties, the seventies, the sixties and the fifties and see in the shopwindows some of the most beautiful things in the world. I can drop into art galleries, or attend an auction at Parke-Bernet. What could I see in a walk around the Capital Square in Madison, Wisconsin? Nothing. I am not denigrating Madison. A few years ago, *Life* magazine ran a feature story headed: "Is it true that Madison, Wisconsin, is the loveliest city in all the U.S.A.?" Ever since then, Madisonians have been taking as many bows as if they were picking a bushel of peas off the floor (simile by Bugs Baer).

Advertising has made me thing-minded. And New York—the largest city in the United States and the second largest in the world —has more beautiful *things* than any other place I have ever been.

New York and New York advertising have made it possible for me to own a few of those things—for instance, an eighteenth-century Philadelphia walnut highboy. It now stands in an upstairs bedroom of the big house on the farm. I have the bill of sale with which William Randolph Hearst acquired it. He paid around $4,000 for it. I paid much much less. On its bottom is glued a sticker label saying that the next possessor will be my granddaughter Betsy. Am I making Betsy *thing-minded*? Every time she passes it she caresses the lovely shimmering, winy-brown walnut wood. And every time Victoria, Betsy's two-year-old sister, passes it, she puts a stubby forefinger on it and murmurs "Betsy's." And if Betsy and Victoria both became thing-minded? That's all right too.

Of course advertising creates wants, and nudges and nags people to get a hustle on and satisfy those wants. Which is fitting and proper. "The world is so full of a number of things, I'm sure we should all be as happy as kings."

Seems to me if I were the Maker of the Universe, the people who would vex me most would be the ones who went unseeing and unwanting through this fascinating world.

ABOUT THE AUTHOR

Bernice Fitz-Gibbon was born and educated in Wisconsin. She grew up on a farm in Waunakee and attended the Sacred Heart Convent in Madison. To help pay for her tuition at the University of Wisconsin, she taught in a one-room district school for a year. After graduating from the university, she taught high school English for one year in Chippewa Falls, and one year in Hudson, Wisconsin. She worked briefly as a reporter on the Rockford (Illinois) Register Gazette *and then turned to selling space and writing copy for the paper's advertisers. Her first department store job was with Marshall Field's in Chicago; her second with Wanamaker's in New York.*

In the mid-twenties, when she went to Macy's, where she stayed until 1935, Miss Fitz-Gibbon's advertising career moved into high gear. The following year she returned to Wanamaker's as Advertising Director. In 1940, she became Advertising Director of Gimbels. She established her own agency, Bernice Fitz-Gibbon, Inc., in 1954 and subsequently became a member of the Board of Directors of Montgomery Ward & Company. The Women's Editors of the Associated Press named her the Business Woman of the Year and Fortune *magazine cited her as one of the seven top business women in the United States. She has also written many articles which have appeared in* McCall's, Good Housekeeping, The New York Times Magazine *and* Glamour.

Bernice Fitz-Gibbon has a daughter, a son and six grandchildren.